ANTHRAX
TO ZODIAC

A SNARKY PI DELVES INTO THE
MOST NOTORIOUS UNSOLVED MYSTERIES
OF THE PAST 150 YEARS

D1600168

DENISE DIANA HUDDLE

Copyright © 2024 by Crimes & Passion, LLC.

All rights reserved.

Editing & Proofreading by Beth Attwood

Cover design by Damonza.com

Contact email: denise@denisedianahuddle.com

ISBN: 979-8-9858912-6-3 – Ebook

ISBN: 979-8-9858912-7-0 – Audiobook

ISBN: 979-8-9858912-8-7 – Paperback

All rights reserved. This book or parts thereof may not be reproduced in any form, stored in any retrieval system, or transmitted in any form by any means—including but not limited to electronic, mechanical, photocopy, recording, or otherwise—without prior written permission of the publisher. For permission requests, contact the publisher at denise@denisedianahuddle.com.

In honor of Lynn Wilson Hamby

CONTENTS

PART 1

WHO MAILED THE ANTHRAX LETTERS?

CHAPTER 1

BACKGROUND

September 11, 2001, is forever etched in the history of America. Americans watched in disbelief as jumbo jets crashed into the World Trade Center, the Pentagon, and a field in Pennsylvania. The country was under attack. President Bush was whisked into Air Force One and hidden away as the members of the presidential line of succession were secreted in bunkers. United States airspace was cleared by order of the president. Families huddled around their televisions, waiting to see if other hijacked planes were still in the sky, ignoring the emergency grounding.

In the weeks following the attacks, American air travel came to a virtual standstill, leaving the skies eerily empty. Devastated New Yorkers with thousand-yard stares posted photos of their missing relatives on makeshift shrines. Footage of an army of rescue and recovery workers sifting through the rubble of the Twin Towers flooded the twenty-four-hour newsfeeds. Images of the flag raised at the World Trade Center filled Americans with a frantic patriotism reminiscent of the day six United States Marines hoisted the flag on Mount Suribachi. In a state of collective shock, America anxiously waited for the next shoe to fall.

Then the anthrax letters came.

What Is Anthrax?

Anthrax is a disease caused by the bacteria *Bacillus anthracis*. Anthrax primarily affects livestock, but humans can contract anthrax by coming in contact with infected animals. In normal times, the disease in humans is the province of farm workers and others who are employed in veterinary work or the processing of livestock. The bacteria enters the body through either ingestion, inhalation, or touch. The gastrointestinal type affects the GI tract and results generally from eating the meat of infected animals. The inhaled type affects the lungs and is more serious than the cutaneous type contracted through touch, which causes skin infections.

The disease is very serious in humans. Untreated, it is frequently fatal. According to the FDA, about 20 percent of people with untreated cutaneous anthrax die. Somewhere between 25 and 75 percent of patients with gastrointestinal anthrax don't survive, and the mortality rate for inhalation anthrax is a whopping 80 percent.

The scariest aspect of *Bacillus anthracis* is that the bacteria forms spores, which are extremely resilient to harsh conditions, making cleanup of a contaminated area extraordinarily difficult. The spores can lie dormant for months or years then find their way into the body and "wake up," multiplying and releasing their dangerous anthrax toxin into the body of their victim. It was this spore aspect of *Bacillus anthracis* combined with its high mortality factors that made it so attractive as a bioweapon—and what brought it into the US government labs, which were the source for the material used in the attacks.

Denise Diana Huddle

WHAT HAPPENED?

In September and October 2001, in the immediate aftermath of the 9/11 terrorist attacks, at least five envelopes containing significant quantities of *Bacillus anthracis* were mailed to media organizations located in Boca Raton, Florida, and New York City, and to United States Senators Thomas Daschle and Patrick Leahy at the US Capitol. The opening line of the poison-laced letters sent to Tom Brokaw and the editor of the *New York Post* answered the question that had been fueling the country's anxiety since the morning of September 11: "This is next."

Letter sent to Tom Brokaw and the *New York Post* and envelopes. (FBI.gov)

According to the Justice Department's investigative summary of what the DOJ called the Amerithrax case, the letters addressed to Tom Brokaw and the *New York Post* did not have a return address, and they both contained the same photocopied letter.

Letter sent to Senators Daschle and Leahy and envelopes. (FBI.gov)

The two envelopes addressed to Senators Daschle and Leahy bore the same fictitious return address. The mail purported to have been sent by the "4TH GRADE, GREENDALE SCHOOL, FRANKLIN PARK NJ 08852." They, too, contained the same letter, but the text of the Senate letters was not the same as those mailed to the media.

Like a German U-boat sneaking up on an unsuspecting Allied freighter, the terrible anthrax plot was well underway before the country had the slightest idea anything was wrong. The first inkling of a bioweapons attack came when Robert Stevens, a photo editor employed by the publisher of the *National Inquirer*, American Media, Inc. in Boca Raton, was admitted to a Florida hospital for pneumonia-like symptoms and was subsequently diagnosed with inhalation anthrax.

The individual events involved in the attacks transpired in the context of post-9/11 chaos, fear, and confusion. Law enforcement and intelligence resources were laser-focused on the events of September 11, probably providing some working room for the anthrax attacks to proceed more effectively than what might have been the case in calmer times. Government agencies hurried to downplay the events, possibly in an effort to calm an already-on-edge public. Were they the victims of their own wishful thinking? Were they confused by fragmented and incomplete information? Were they lying through their teeth? We'll probably never know, but in any case, the government bungled the early days of the investigation and woefully misinformed the public about the status of national security.

Timeline of Events

In order to understand what actually happened, it's helpful to put the critical events of the crime in a timeline. I found a very well-done chronology at the website of the UCLA School of Epidemiology (www.ph.ucla.edu/epi/bioter/detect/antdetect_sept01.html). Working from that and the timeline the FBI included in its investigative summary of the Amerithrax investigation, we can get a fairly clear picture of the muddled series of events that sputtered into the light during and immediately following the attacks.

It Begins

Unlike the other sites, no anthrax envelope or letter was ever recovered from American Media, Inc., so it was not possible to determine when the weaponized mail was sent or from where. But we do know that just a week after the 9/11 attacks, the letters to Tom Brokaw and the *New York Post* entered the mail stream sometime between 5:00 p.m. on September 17 and noon on September 18. On September 18, the media letters were postmarked in Trenton, New Jersey.

Flying under the Radar

In the chaotic time following 9/11, Johanna Huden, an editorial page assistant at the *New York Post*, was a very busy woman—way too busy to open what she took to be a crank letter to the editor that arrived in her daily mail. She stuck the letter in a box by her desk where it stayed—unopened. On September 21, Huden became ill with a sore on the middle finger of her right hand. She sought medical attention and was given antibiotics.

Meanwhile, on September 18, at the NBC offices at Rockefeller Center, an intern named Casey Chamberlain opened the envelope addressed to Tom Brokaw. Perplexed by the odd letter, Chamberlain brought the strange correspondence and the powdery substance that came with it to the attention of Brokaw's assistant, Erin O'Connor. On September 22, Chamberlain noticed a blister on her finger. O'Connor noticed a skin lesion on September 28. While both women became ill, the connection between their illnesses was not recognized, and the cause of their maladies was not known. The same day O'Connor noticed her rash, a producer at ABC brought her seven-month-old baby to work with her at the network's New York headquarters at 147 Columbus Avenue in Manhattan.

The Plot Thickens

On September 30, AMI photojournalist and editor Robert Stevens of Boca Raton, Florida, started coming down with something.

On October 1, the terrible effects of the attacks in New York and Florida bubbled closer to the surface. Erin O'Connor of NBC started feeling ill. She went to her doctor with a fever and a rash and was prescribed Cipro, a broad spectrum antibiotic. The baby who went with its mother to her office at ABC became ill with a rash and was admitted to the hospital with a mysterious ailment originally thought to be a bite from a brown recluse spider. And AMI mail-room employee Ernesto Blanco was hospitalized with pneumonia.

The next day, the second of October, Robert Stevens was admitted to the hospital with a fever, vomiting, and confusion. On October 3, Stevens's doctors determined that anthrax infection was the cause of his illness. His condition deteriorated, and he was placed on a ventilator.

Trust Us, We're from the Government

Here's one of my favorite parts: On October 4, while their mail-room employee was in the hospital with pneumonia and their photo editor was on a ventilator with anthrax, AMI did the responsible and appropriate thing and called the CDC to ask if their offices should be evaluated as a possible source of the illnesses. The CDC told AMI that no evaluation was appropriate, and, acting on their advice, the entire AMI staff continued to work in the offices.

Here's a quote from the CDC website:

> Most people who get sick from anthrax are exposed while working with infected animals or animal products such as wool, hides, or hair.
>
> Inhalation anthrax can occur when a person inhales spores that are in the air (aerosolized) during the industrial process-ing of contaminated materials, such as wool, hides, or hair.
>
> Cutaneous anthrax can occur when workers who handle contaminated animal products get spores in a cut or scrape on their skin.

The CDC seems pretty clear on their position that folks nat-urally contract anthrax from working with or around infected animals. Mr. Stevens was a photo editor for a tabloid in urban

Florida, not a sheep shearer wrestling animals to the ground in the filthy feedlots of remote West Texas. Yet, this apparently didn't ring any alarm bells with the CDC, enlightening them with the idea that Stevens's office might offer clues to the source of his infection.

The First Horseman

On October 5, sadly, Mr. Stevens succumbed to the inhalation type of the bacteria in the hospital in Boca Raton and became the first fatality associated with the attacks—and the first person in the US to die of anthrax since 1976.

Better Late than Never

After Mr. Stevens died, the CDC decided then would be a dandy time to take a look at where an office worker who had no contact with livestock might have gotten a fatal dose of anthrax. The public health folks raced to his home and the AMI offices on October 5.

The Second Horseman

While the CDC was chasing its tail around the AMI building and the infections from the letters to Brokaw and the *New York Post* hadn't been properly diagnosed yet, the killer was launching the second wave of attacks. The letters to Senators Daschle and Leahy were mailed sometime between 3:00 p.m. on October 6 and noon on October 9.

Shutting the Stable Door after the Horse Has Bolted

After finding anthrax spores on Stevens's computer keyboard, the CDC got hip to the gag, and at 7:00 p.m. on October 7, over three days after AMI management called asking if the building was a potential risk to workers, the CDC decided to seal off the AMI offices.

Worse, in the course of their investigation, the CDC also found anthrax spores in mailroom worker Ernesto Blanco's nasal passages. On October 8, Mr. Blanco was officially diagnosed with anthrax exposure. While he was battling pneumonia in the hospital, the rest of his coworkers at AMI were lined up down the block to get their supply of Cipro. The UCLA Department of Epidemiology reports that 1,132 AMI workers were subsequently placed on prophylactic antibiotics between October 8 and 10 due to their potential exposure to anthrax spores while working in the AMI offices. Thank you, CDC.

Meanwhile, evidence of the other attacks was still rising undetected beneath the surface like Mount Saint Helens quietly preparing to blow. On October 9, Ms. Chamberlain at NBC was having trouble with the rash on her finger. She went back to the doctor, who was concerned about what appeared to be a very serious infection and took a biopsy.

The Third Horseman

While Ms. Chamberlain was visiting her doctor in New York City, those second-wave letters to Daschle and Leahy were creeping through the postal service like ninja assassins. Both were postmarked on October 9, again in Trenton, New Jersey.

Denial Ain't Just a River in Egypt

On October 9, the FBI still insisted that the events at the AMI offices in Boca Raton constituted an isolated incident, and President George Bush echoed their finding, telling the American people that there was no cause for national alarm.

On October 10, the FBI announced that the anthrax poisonings at AMI were the subject of a criminal investigation. Between October 10 and 11, two more AMI employees tested positive for exposure to anthrax, and the FBI found more spores in the AMI mailroom.

More Shutting the Stable Door after the Horse Has Bolted

On October 12, the infection on NBC staffer Chamberlain's finger was diagnosed as cutaneous anthrax. While President Bush was busy telling Americans the Boca Raton infections were a one-off, Ms. Chamberlain had struggled through her undiagnosed disease alone. Once her doctors figured out on their own that she had cutaneous anthrax, the FBI hustled right on over to the NBC offices, shut the place down for testing, and retrieved the letter along with the powdery substance in the envelope, the same letter that had been in the NBC offices since Ms. Chamberlain opened it on September 18—almost a month before.

On October 15, Mr. Blanco was officially diagnosed with inhalation anthrax. (Previously, it was only certain he had been exposed, not infected.) Senate aide Grant Leslie, working in the Hart Senate Office Building, opened the anthrax letter addressed to Senator Daschle. The Senate office building was then closed for testing, and authorities announced that the anthrax mailed to Senator Daschle was a pure and highly potent version of the bacteria. Because nothing gets past the G-men, considering the handwriting and the postmarks, the FBI determined that the letter to Senator Daschle was linked to the letter sent to Tom Brokaw. To round out the October 15 triple-header, postal inspectors in Boca Raton announced that anthrax spores were found Boca Raton's main post office.

On October 16, the baby of the ABC producer who had been hospitalized with a rash thought to be a spider bite was diagnosed with anthrax.

On October 17, investigators announced that preliminary tests indicated that the anthrax in Boca Raton was the same strain as the anthrax in New York. Even absent an envelope in the Boca Raton attack, it was then clear that the two events were linked. (So much for those "isolated incident" comments from the feds on October 9.)

On October 18, CBS anchor Dan Rather's assistant was diagnosed with cutaneous anthrax, as was a New Jersey postal worker.

In light of the multiple diagnoses in New York and New Jersey, Ms. Huden of the *New York Post* was tested for the bacteria and shown to be positive. When Ms. Huden was diagnosed with cutaneous anthrax on October 19, investigators found the unopened envelope containing a powdery substance by her desk at the *Post*. The substance was later determined to be anthrax. However, the FBI was not certain that the anthrax that infected Ms. Huden came from the unopened envelope they confiscated, implying there could have been other contaminated correspondence that was not detected at the *Post*, as was the case at AMI.

On October 20, anthrax spores previously thought to be restricted to Senate offices were found in the Ford House Office Building where the mail stream for members of the House of Representatives was processed.

The Fourth Horseman

Sadly, on October 21, Thomas Morris, an employee of the Brentwood Postal Facility in Washington, DC, where the Senate letters had been processed, died of anthrax poisoning. He had made multiple attempts to convince his superiors at the postal service that he had anthrax, but no one believed him.

The next day, on October 22, another employee of the Brentwood facility, Joseph Curseen Jr., went to the ER. He was admitted to the hospital, but died of anthrax poisoning the next day. Two more postal workers were hospitalized and another nine were sick. The postal service finally began testing employees—seventeen days after Robert Stevens died in Boca Raton, nine days after the Brokaw letter tested positive for anthrax, and seven days after anthrax spores were found in Boca Raton's main post office.

The Genie Is Out of the Bottle

On October 23, anthrax spores were found on a mail sorting machine used to sort mail for the White House. On October 25, a mailroom employee at the State Department was hospitalized with anthrax.

The Lake of Fire

On October 29, Kathy Nguyen, a stockroom worker at the Manhattan Eye, Ear & Throat Hospital, tested positive for anthrax and was placed on a ventilator.

On October 31, Ms. Nguyen died of inhalation anthrax, but the source of her infection has never been determined.

Between November 10 and 12, anthrax spores were detected in the Hart building offices of seven more senators.

After the Daschle letter was found, authorities sequestered 250 barrels of congressional mail that were waiting to be delivered. On November 16, hazardous materials specialists sifting through that mail found the letter to Senator Leahy. Mercifully, it had never been delivered or opened.

On November 20, anthrax was also found in the mailrooms of two more US senators.

On November 21, ninety-four-year-old Ottilie Lundgren died in Connecticut of inhalation anthrax.

Denise Diana Huddle

The Toll of the Apocalypse

Again, according to the Amerithrax investigative summary, all told, at least twenty-two innocent victims were infected with anthrax as a result of the mailings. Eleven folks got sick from inhaling the spores, and eleven more got the infection by touching the powder and absorbing it through their skin. The five victims who died from their infections all got sick by inhaling the spores, not by touching them. Thirty-one more people tested positive for exposure to anthrax spores, and as many as 32,000 people who were deemed "at risk" from possible exposure were treated with prophylactic antibiotics.

The fact that the AMI anthrax letters were not identified as suspicious when they arrived at the AMI offices, or even when the victims handled them, gave the attackers a head start, allowing them to operate undetected until the actual anthrax diagnoses were made. The attackers gained even more of a lead while law enforcement processed that information and eventually made the connections between the AMI offices in Florida and the ABC, NBC, CBS, and *New York Post* offices in New York City.

It was only after anthrax was positively identified in Mr. Stevens and Mr. Blanco that it was clear a bioweapons attack was taking place. By that time, the spores had contaminated all of the AMI offices, multiple postal facilities, and the ABC, NBC, CBS, and *New York Post* locations in Manhattan. Eighty-five million pieces of mail processed in the affected facilities after the attack letters were sent and before the facilities were closed were potentially contaminated. Contaminated mail leaving those postal facilities undetected carried the spores, spreading it throughout the country like a odorless, invisible poison gas seeping out of a leaking tank. While not a certainty, it is most likely that cross-contaminated mail was responsible for the deaths of Ms. Nguyen and Ms. Lundgren.

While the connection between Mr. Stevens and his colleague, Ernesto Blanco, had been made and linked to their common employment, since there was no letter or envelope found at AMI, it was not immediately clear how the AMI staffers got infected. Investigators eventually determined that the anthrax spores traveled into the building through at least two different pieces of mail, because the two different post offices that served the location were both contaminated with anthrax. Investigators later surmised that copy paper stored in the AMI mailroom likely became contaminated with the spores. When the paper was loaded into photocopy machines, the fans inside the copiers disbursed the spores throughout the office space. Tests later showed that every single copier in the AMI offices was contaminated.

CHAPTER 2

THE MAILINGS

Pandora's Box

The four envelopes recovered from Capitol Hill, the *New York Post*, and NBC each contained a Trenton, New Jersey postmark. Unfortunately, 48 postal offices and 625 street mail collection boxes fed into the Trenton mail processing facility where that postmark was applied. FBI personnel swabbed 621 mailboxes in search of the entry point of the letters into the postal service. (I don't know why they ignored four street collection boxes or which four they skipped.) In any case, analysis of those swabs led investigators to identify a heavily contaminated blue box located across the street from the main entrance to Princeton University. The address of the box was 10 Nassau Street, Princeton, New Jersey 08542. Investigators concluded in August of 2002 that this was the box from which all of the attack letters were mailed. The box is now in the Smithsonian's National Postal Museum.

The mailbox where the anthrax letters were mailed.
(National Postal Museum, Smithsonian)

The Poison Pens

Analysis of ink samples from the handwritten addresses on the front of the envelopes showed that the same type of pen was used for the envelopes mailed to Brokaw and the *New York Post*. A different writing instrument was used for the envelopes mailed to Senators Daschle and Leahy, which also matched each other. None of the envelopes exhibited indented writing, watermarks, hair, or latent fingerprints. All envelopes were sealed by moistening the glue on their flaps, and all four were reinforced with strips of transparent tape, along both the closure strip and the folds of the envelopes. Five to nine pieces of tape were affixed to each of the four envelopes.

The Eagle Has Landed

The envelopes used in the anthrax attacks were produced by the US Postal Service and sold with the postage already printed on them. They were called "federal eagles." Investigators identified printing defects in the federal eagles used in the anthrax mailings. After an extensive study of the distribution chain for envelopes with those particular defects, the FBI determined that the envelopes used in the attacks were supplied by the Dulles Stamp Distribution Office (SDO), located in Dulles, Virginia. The Dulles SDO distributed these envelopes to post offices throughout Maryland and Virginia, where they were then sold to the public.

Is It Real or Is It Xerox?

Three "trash marks," or copy imperfections, of forensic value were identified on the Senate letters. No such marks were found on the letters to Brokaw and the *New York Post*. These trash marks were compared to letters maintained in the FBI's Anonymous Threat Letter File, but no matches were found. A clue to the sheer scope of the FBI Amerithrax investigation is demonstrated by the revelation in the investigative summary that the FBI collected exemplars from every copy machine they could find in or near any lab that possessed the strain of anthrax used in the letters for a grand total of 1,014 samples. No matches were found in these exemplars, either.

THE CONTAMINATION & CLEANUP

Thirty-five postal facilities and commercial mailrooms were contaminated. The presence of *Bacillus anthracis* was detected in seven buildings tested on Capitol Hill. The US Postal Service closed two heavily contaminated processing and distribution centers. Trenton P&DC, located in Hamilton, New Jersey, was closed from October 18, 2001, to March 14, 2005, and Brentwood P&DC, located in Washington, DC, was closed from October 21, 2001, to December 22, 2003.

More than 1.8 million letters, packages, magazines, catalogs, and other mailed items were quarantined at these two facilities. The Environmental Protection Agency used $27 million from its Superfund program to pay twenty-seven contractors and three federal and state agencies for the cleanup of the Capitol Hill facilities. In their article "Total Decontamination Cost of the Anthrax Letter Attacks," the authors, Schmitt and Zacchia, described their exhaustive study of the cleanup effort and estimated that the total cost of the decontamination from the attacks was $320 million (the equivalent of $528.4 million in 2022 dollars).

THE INVESTIGATION

General Investigative Strategies

In addition to specific suspects Hatfill and Ivins discussed below, the task force focused on several different possible suspect pools. While these approaches were intriguing, none bore fruit. They do, however, provide an interesting insight into the methods and reasoning behind the task force's investigative plan.

Colonel Mustard in the Post Office with Anthrax
Who Had a Profit Motive?

Task force agents analyzed interviews, obtained business records, and examined publicly available cor porate information to identify any business that might have been motivated to commit the anthrax attacks for financial gain. At the time of the anthrax mailings in 2001, a biopharmaceutical company, BioPort (later called Emergent BioSolutions), headquartered in Lansing, Michigan, was the sole provider of the only anthrax vaccine licensed by the US Food and Drug Administration for human use in the United States. Production of the vaccine had previously been suspended for the company's violation of Good Manufacturing Practices. In the aftermath of the 2001 anthrax mailings, the FDA granted BioPort's long-sought approval to continue manufacturing, positioning the company to reap substantial profits from the increased demand for its vaccine generated by the anthrax attacks. The FBI investigated this company, its employees, officers, and shareholders to identify any indications of their involvement in the anthrax mailings—and apparently did so with negative results as the government continued to purchase the anthrax vaccine from BioPort.

Barnyard Bad Guys

More than 200 entities in the agricultural and veterinary communities were investigated to determine if any strains of *Bacillus anthracis* had been collected at the facility, and, if so, who at that facility had access to those strains. No results.

Check the Legal Drug Dealers

Commercial entities with the technical personnel and necessary equipment to produce the type of refined spore powder recovered from the anthrax mailings were investigated, with particular emphasis on those companies located in the greater New Jersey area and those using level 3 biosafety (BSL-3) laboratory containment facilities that would be necessary to work safely with the anthrax. Zippo.

Agent Orange, Anyone?

Theorizing that the same skill sets, manufacturing equipment, and production facilities used to make certain pesticides could also be used to produce an anthrax spore powder like the one present in the mailings, investigators identified and investigated the companies that produced those pesticides and the individuals there with appropriate expertise. No dice.

You Can't Cook This Stuff in a Bathtub

Assuming that the perpetrator must have used some type of containment device to produce the anthrax powder and load the envelopes, investigators collected environmental samples from biological "glove boxes," or containment devices, located near Trenton, New Jersey. They also canvassed companies that serviced and maintained glove boxes, and they visited a resupplier of used and surplus laboratory equipment. One hundred and twenty-five glove boxes were swabbed at twenty-four facilities in a five-state area encompassing New York, New Jersey, Maryland, Pennsylvania, and Washington, DC. Nada.

Haters Gonna Hate

Investigators interviewed Senators Daschle and Leahy, their staff members, and interns regarding any previous threats or suspicious contacts made to either senator. They reviewed the files of the US Capitol Police, the US Secret Service, and other pertinent records for instances of threats made against either senator. Investigators determined that none of these had any ostensible connection to the anthrax mailings. Back to the drawing board.

The Fourth Grade Class Did It

Investigators pulled student records dating back several decades from the Greenbrook elementary school and cross-referenced those records to the Amerithrax investigation databases. Greenbrook Elementary was located near the contaminated mail collection box in Princeton, New Jersey, similar in name to the fictitious "Greendale Elementary School," and situated not far from the town of Franklin

Park and the 08852 zip code mentioned in the return addresses of the DC letters. No deal, Lucille.

While I think the Greenbrook angle is interesting, it's a little too needle-in-a-haystack for my investigative taste. A quick Google search shows a village in Wisconsin, a town in Missouri, a city in Indiana, a golf course in Virginia, a school in Milwaukee, several businesses in central Massachusetts, a 2003 movie, Neil Young's twenty-fifth studio album, and the neighboring town to Riverdale in the Archie and Jughead comics with Greendale in the name. I think I would have spent my investigative time elsewhere.

Big Brother Really Is Watching

Task force agents collected logs for all internet traffic accessing the contact or mailing address pages of NBC.com, NYPost.com, PageSix.com, Congress.org, Senate.gov, MSNBC.com, CBSNews.com, and all websites maintained by AMI, focusing on the ninety-day time period prior to October 15, 2001. The collected logs were consolidated into a database of 10.4 million records from which 234,827 distinct IP addresses were identified. The database was then searched for IP addresses that viewed the contact pages at all of the relevant websites prior to the postmark date on the envelopes. While the database search did eventually yield two statically assigned IP addresses that met the criteria, both were found to be web crawlers. Net investigative benefit was zero.

Karmic Boomerang and Suspicious Deaths

Working on the theory that the person who deposited the anthrax letters in the mailbox in Princeton may have become infected and died in a manner that escaped the attention of authorities, investigators conducted a review of suspicious deaths and deaths from unknown causes that occurred in Mercer County, New Jersey, during the period of October 2001 through February 2002. The names and identifiers of these individuals were checked against a series of databases. Of the seventy-seven suspicious deaths studied, none was found to have a significant connection to any facet of the investigation.

From an investigative point of view, I have some questions about this methodology. This plan would have been perfectly legitimate as long as the bad guy died in Mercer County and was also already in the database. If he died in another county or had never before hit the database radar, the methodology would have failed. While I like the theory, I think the parameters were faulty.

Al Qaeda, the King of Evil

The organization had just attacked the US weeks before on 9/11, and the notes referred to Allah and hating Israel. Task force investigators claim to have exhaustively explored the possibility that al Qaeda or another international terrorist organization might have been responsible for the anthrax attacks. Their summary report states that they conducted witness interviews and evidence collection efforts on six continents. While the task force admitted it was undoubtedly true that al Qaeda was trying to build a bioweapons program in 2001, agents were unable to find any connection between al Qaeda and the anthrax attacks in the US.

EXTENT OF THE INVESTIGATION

In the seven years following the attacks, the Amerithrax task force expended over 600,000 investigator work hours involving in excess of 10,000 witness interviews conducted on six continents, the execution of 80 searches, and the recovery of over 6,000 items of potential evidence. The case involved the issuance of over 5,750 federal grand jury subpoenas. Investigators collected 5,730 environmental samples from 60 different locations.

This investigation did not result in a single indictment or arrest (let alone a conviction) associated with the actual attacks. Bupkis. Zippity doo dah.

THE AMES STRAIN

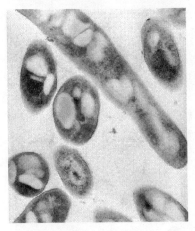

Electron microscopic image of *Bacillus anthracis*. (CDC.gov)

The anthrax spores found in the mailings were derived from what was identified early on as the Ames strain of *Bacillus anthracis*. The Ames strain was a common strain of anthrax originally isolated from a diseased fourteen-month-old Beefmaster heifer that died in the town of Sarita in Kenedy County, Texas, in 1981. After the first research was done on the strain at the United States Army Medical Research Institute of Infectious Diseases (USAMRIID) at Fort Detrick, Maryland, the Ames strain was then distributed to sixteen different American bioresearch labs and three foreign locations—one in Canada, one in Sweden, and one in the United Kingdom.

DNA sequencing of the anthrax taken from the first fatality of the attacks, Robert Stevens, was conducted at the Institute for Genomic Research beginning in December of 2001. The Lawrence Livermore National Laboratory used radiocarbon dating in June 2002 to determine that the anthrax used in the attacks was cultured no more than two years before the mailings were sent.

The technical aspects of the science associated with the research on the genetics of the anthrax spores used in the attacks is extremely complex, and the interpretation of the results is highly controversial. The gist is that the FBI originally based their investigation on suspects with access to the Ames strain in general. Later on in the investigation, in 2007, the task force adopted the position that the spores in the letters were derived from a single spore batch of Ames strain anthrax called "RMR-1029."

At that point, the government eliminated suspects who did not have access to RMR-1029, even if those individuals had access to other mutations of the Ames strain. This development is the basis of the task force's switch from accusing Steven Hatfill to accusing Bruce Ivins of conducting the attacks.

CHAPTER 3

THE SUSPECTS

Dr. Steven Hatfill—Sorry We Ruined Your Life...Our Bad

Steven Hatfill was the first primary target of the task force's investigation into the anthrax attacks. Dr. Hatfill had been employed from 1997 to 1999 at USAMRIID, the Department of Defense's go-to lab for biological warfare research. Accusers indicated that Dr. Hatfill had in the past boasted to coworkers that he knew how to weaponize anthrax, quizzed colleagues on their knowledge of the topic, and repeatedly stopped people in the hallways to warn them about the dangers of anthrax as a biological weapon. (So now, I guess having your professional scientific opinions vindicated by real-world events makes you a bioterrorist.) While later in his career Dr. Hatfill was involved in bioterrorism research and training, the core of his work was virology—the study of viruses. Oops...anthrax is a bacteria.

In the first four months of the investigation, eight individuals allegedly brought Dr. Hatfill's name to the attention of the FBI as someone they suspected of being involved in the attacks.

One of these individuals was Don Foster, a professor of English at Vassar College and a self-styled literary detective who had identified Joe Klein as the author of the anonymously written novel *Primary Colors*. Dr. Foster identified Mr. Klein by examining punctuation and other linguistic fingerprints in the book. Foster had since consulted with the FBI on investigations of the Unabomber and Atlanta's Centennial Olympic Park bombing, among other cases, and he was asked to analyze the anthrax letters for insights as to who may have mailed them.

According to an article in *The Atlantic*, Foster found an interview Dr. Hatfill had given while working at the National Institutes of Health in which he described how the bubonic plague could be made and used in a bioterror attack. (Never mind it was Dr. Hatfill's job to know such things.) Foster also learned that Hatfill had written an unpublished novel about a fictional bioterror attack on the nation's capital. (What else would a government bioterrorism researcher write a novel about?) Add in Foster's discovery that Hatfill had been in Rhodesia (now Zimbabwe) during an anthrax outbreak there in the late 1970s and that he'd attended medical school near a Rhodesian suburb called Greendale—the same name as the fictional school in the return address of the anthrax letters—and Foster formed the opinion that Hatfill was a viable suspect in the attacks. (All this from an English professor at a liberal arts college.)

Simultaneously, Dr. Barbara Hatch Rosenberg, a molecular biologist and expert on biological weapons, published at least two articles on the internet describing her opinion about the perpetrator of the anthrax attacks. Dr. Rosenberg maintains that she never mentioned any individual by name in her posts. I haven't read them, so I can't say. But in any case, she believed that Dr. Hatfill was possibly the perpetrator.

Foster and Rosenberg met and compared notes in April 2002 when neither had been able to interest the FBI in their theories about Dr. Hatfill. Two months later, according to Foster's account reported in *The Atlantic*, Rosenberg met on Capitol Hill with Senate staff members and described the theories she and Foster had developed. Special Agent Van Harp, the senior FBI agent on the Amerithrax investigation, reportedly attended the meeting, along with other FBI officials. It is unclear from sworn deposition testimony if Dr. Hatfill's name was mentioned specifically by Rosenberg during this meeting.

"Did she mention Dr. Hatfill's name in her presentation?" Hatfill's attorney, former federal prosecutor Thomas G. Connolly, asked Harp during a sworn deposition.

"That's who she was talking about," Harp testified.

In a June 2002 search of Dr. Hatfill's apartment in Frederick, Maryland, investigators discovered detailed anthrax production protocols, some of which matched techniques used by the United States Army to produce anthrax for the now-defunct US Offensive Weapons Program. Also recovered from Dr. Hatfill's apartment was an anthrax simulant powder.

Dr. Hatfill also appeared to know the specific steps for using the mail to disseminate anthrax, having commissioned, through his job, a risk assessment report from a renowned bioweaponeer, which described in detail the tactical effectiveness of an anthrax letter sent through the US mail, including the specific quantity of anthrax that could be packed into an envelope without arousing suspicion. In 1999, after going to work for SAIC (according to Wikipedia, Science Applications International Corporation, Inc. is an American company headquartered in Reston, Virginia, that provides government services), Hatfill (again, in the scope of his job) had a hand in developing a brochure for emergency responders on how to handle anthrax hoax letters.

Multiple PowerPoint presentations used by Dr. Hatfill prior to the attacks specifically depicted an anthrax letter attack scenario, one of which contained a slide entitled "Multiple Hoax Mailing Trends" that referenced: "Single letter containing WMD threat sent to multiple targets. Letters similar in content and point of origin. Letters delivered to...Government Agencies...News Agencies."

Dr. Hatfill also aroused suspicion early in the case because pharmacy records from Frederick, Maryland, revealed that he filled multiple prescriptions for the antibiotic Cipro, the only drug approved by the Food and Drug Administration for the treatment of inhalational anthrax. He filled those prescriptions in January, July, September, October, and November of 2001, including refills of the antibiotic two days before each of the anthrax mailings. It was later determined that Dr. Hatfill had undergone sinus surgery and required the antibiotics.

I couldn't find numbers for Cipro use in 2001. The earliest year I could find statistics for was 2013. According to ClinCalc.com, in 2013 alone, 7,189,976 prescriptions for Cipro were filled in the US for 4,976,306 patients. So, I think it's fair to say that Dr. Hatfill was not the only person taking Cipro in the summer and fall of 2001.

Early in the investigation, agents determined that isolates of the Ames strain were accessible to any individual at USAMRIID with access to the biocontainment or "hot" side of Building 1412, including but not limited to Dr. Hatfill.

Later in the investigation, RMR-1029 was identified as the original material from which the anthrax powder used in the mailings was derived. Because Dr. Hatfill—who left USAMRIID two years before the anthrax attacks—never had access to the area in which RMR-1029 was stored, he was ultimately eliminated as a suspect on June 27, 2008.

The Five-Million-Dollar Screwup

Hatfill sued the government for damages associated with inappropriately leaking his name to the press as a person of interest in the investigation in violation of the Privacy Act. The suit was settled by the US Department of Justice for $2.825 million in cash plus a twenty-year annuity paying $150,000—for a total of $4.6 million along with an unequivocal public exoneration of Dr. Hatfill of any involvement in the anthrax attacks. The settlement was essentially a multimillion-dollar consolation prize for the years of personal hell and career decimation Dr. Hatfill had endured at the hands of the relentless FBI and media machines.

Dr. Bruce Ivins

Next up in the batter's box of evil government scientists accused by the Amerithrax task force of perpetrating the attacks was Dr. Bruce Ivins.

Dr. Anthrax

Dr. Bruce Edwards Ivins was a senior microbiologist in the Bacteriology Division of USAMRIID. Dr. Ivins began his work with *Bacillus anthracis* at USAMRIID in 1980. At the time of his suicide, he had been employed there for the preceding twenty-seven years. He was considered one of the nation's leading experts in the growth, sporulation, and purification of *Bacillus anthracis*. This assessment was confirmed by his more than fifty professional publications regarding anthrax.

Once the task force concluded that RMR-1029 was the source of the spores used in the attack, their overarching position was clear: whoever mailed the letters had access at some point to RMR-1029. That person must have either had direct access to the source flask, which was created and controlled by Dr. Ivins and maintained in the walk-in refrigerator in his lab, or to a sample of RMR-1029 provided by Dr. Ivins.

It's Your Baby, You Mail It

Dr. Ivins created RMR-1029 in his lab, B-313 in Building 1425 of USAMRIID at Fort Detrick. He also stored flasks of RMR-1029 in the walk-in cold room there. By all accounts, Dr. Ivins was the sole custodian of this material. Investigators allegedly interviewed every coworker of Dr. Ivins and every researcher at USAMRIID with access to the cold room in which RMR-1029 was stored, and everyone reportedly agreed that no one at USAMRIID legitimately used RMR-1029 without the authorization and knowledge of Dr. Ivins. According to the investigative summary published by the task force, they effectively investigated and cleared everyone with access to RMR-1029—everyone besides Dr. Ivins.

Blaming Their Own Expert

Dr. Ivins had the skills to execute the attack. Dr. Ivins's own comments upon examining the evidence supported the conclusion that the anthrax spores used in the attack letters were created in a high-tech lab by someone with knowledge and experience. These comments came in a report Dr. Ivins made to the task force after they asked him to inspect the Daschle letter. (Yes, you got that right...the task force was asking Dr. Ivins to consult on the anthrax case because he was the leading expert in the field.) Dr. Ivins wrote, "If this is a preparation of bacterial spores, it is an extremely pure preparation, and an extremely high concentration. These are not 'garage' spores. The nature of the spore preparation suggests very highly that professional manufacturing techniques were used in the production and purification of the spores, as well as in converting the spores into a very fine powder."

Drying anthrax spores requires either a sophisticated drying machine called a speed-vac concentrator, or a whole lot of time and space to let the spores air-dry in a lab. Because drying anthrax is a major violation of a truckload of international treaties, using any of these methods out in the open at a facility like USAMRIID where everyone knows the rules would have immediately sounded alarm bells.

The Lonely Speed-Vac Dryer Repairman

The record is rife with considerable contradiction about whether or not Dr. Ivins knew how to use a sophisticated drying machine that may have been employed to dry the spores sent in the mailings. Evidence purportedly exists showing he purchased a drying machine for USAMRIID, attended at least one class on how to use the machine, and agreed to instruct a colleague on its operation. However, in other correspondence, Dr. Ivins flatly denied knowing how to use the equipment.

Workin' after 9 to 5

Investigators found that Dr. Ivins worked late unsupervised around the time of the attacks. A detailed review was conducted of off-hours access by USAMRIID researchers to B-313 (Dr. Ivins's lab) during the time frame leading up to the mailings—August through October 2001—and then generally over the preceding two years and again for the year that followed. It was clear that, from time to time, Dr. Ivins would enter the lab during evening and weekend off-hours. These entries were typically supported by his lab notebooks and those of the other researchers he was assisting, which detailed the experiments he was working on that would require this off-hour lab time.

However, beginning in the middle of August 2001, there was a noticeable spike in his evening and weekend access to B-313, which continued in spurts through October 2001, and then trailed off to his typical pattern. There was no big experiment or project going on in September and October of 2001 that would justify all of the additional off-hour time Dr. Ivins spent in the hot suites. Even Dr. Ivins could not explain this change in his work schedule.

Dr. Ivins's Professional Future Was in Jeopardy

The investigative summary claims that Dr. Ivins's life's work in anthrax appeared destined for failure, absent an unexpected event. Primary among these damning conditions, the report lists the production issues at the BioPort labs discussed above. Dr. Ivins and other scientists were working with BioPort to overcome the manufacturing difficulties.

After the anthrax attacks, BioPort was allowed to recommence manufacturing operations despite the cited issues. The theory appeared to be that by launching an anthrax attack on America, Dr. Ivins spurred the FDA to allow BioPort's production of the anthrax vaccine to resume despite any unresolved difficulties at the plant. While this may have been the case, I am not clear why problems at a vaccine manufacturing site would ruin the career of the government research scientist who developed the vaccine.

The report implies that Dr. Ivins was at personal risk of losing his job in September 2001 when the last remaining supplies of the anthrax vaccine were dwindling during the BioPort shutdown, noting that he feared he would not be able to continue his work if he was not able to obtain an anthrax vaccine. However, I do not see any evidence in the report that Dr. Ivins was immediately due for his next vaccine nor that he lacked a reasonable expectation that some of the remaining vaccine would be allocated to him and his team. Moreover, I'm not sure how a PhD-level scientist with twenty-seven years' service to the federal government would be terminated because a required vaccine to be supplied by the government was not available—particularly because the shortage was a result of the governmental shutdown of the manufacturing operation that produced it.

Additionally, the report refers to manufacturing problems with Ivins's new anthrax vaccine. The report does not describe in detail exactly how these problems could have damaged or ended Dr. Ivins's career.

The report discusses possible plans by USAMRIID to phase out work on anthrax and transfer Dr. Ivins to work on *Burkholderia mallei*, also known as glanders. Reportedly, Dr. Ivins did not welcome this potential transfer. However, not liking your job assignment seems like a pretty flimsy motivation for a lifetime DOD employee to commit a bioterrorist attack on his own country.

In a joint investigation between *ProPublica*, PBS *Frontline*, and *McClatchey* published in *ProPublica* on October 10, 2011, and aired on PBS *Frontline* on October 11, 2011, the investigators questioned if Dr. Ivins's job or career was ever in peril. The article states,

> "In the summer of 2001, Ivins shouldn't have had any worries about his future," said Gerard Andrews, who was then his boss as the head of USAMRIID's Bacteriology Division. "I believe the timeline has been distorted by the FBI," Andrews said. "It's not accurate." Months earlier, Andrews said, the Pentagon had approved a full year's funding for research on the new vaccine and was mapping out a five-year plan to invest well over $15 million.

Other Hands in the Bacterial Cookie Jar

The summary report of the Amerithrax investigation provides general descriptions of the agents' efforts that supposedly successfully eliminated other possible suspects besides Dr. Ivins who potentially had access to RMR-1029.

Building 1425: There were apparently fourteen people who had access to the hot suites where RMR-1029 was created and stored in September and October 2001—the relevant time period leading up to the mailings. Except for Dr. Ivins, all of these individuals visited the lab only during standard work hours, with a few limited exceptions. The investigators determined that theft of the material during work hours was not likely, and the times when these individuals besides Dr. Ivins were in the lab during off-hours were not suspicious. The FBI cleared these subjects of involvement.

Tests in Building 1412: Dr. Ivins kept a record of the times that he sent RMR-1029 over to Building 1412 for tests called "aerosol challenges." Agents investigated each of these transfers and confirmed that the material was used in experiments and any residual material was autoclaved. There were times, however, that Dr. Ivins sent the tubes of RMR-1029 over to Building 1412 the night before the experiment, so there were a handful of occasions when an isolate of RMR-1029 was left in the hot suites of Building 1412 overnight. Thus, another scientist could theoretically have stolen a tiny amount from the tube. Since these original samples were small, the investigators surmised that any missing product would have been noticed, and no such reports of missing product were made.

A commercial laboratory in the Midwest: In May and June of 2001, Dr. Ivins sent some RMR-1029 spores to a commercial laboratory located in the Midwest. Allegedly, only forty-two people physically accessed the lab where RMR-1029 was stored from the time the first shipment arrived on May 9, 2001, until after the second anthrax mailing had occurred. During standard lab hours, no researcher was ever alone in the lab, and detailed records were kept of lab activities for billing purposes. However, during a consecutive four-night period from June 13 to 16, 2001, after-hours work took place in the lab. But, there were always two employees in the suite where RMR-1029 was stored, and each night it was a different set of employees who worked late. Background investigations were conducted on all forty-two people with access to RMR-1029 at this facility with what the report terms "unremarkable" results.

A university in the Southwest: In March of 2001, Dr. Ivins sent a sample of what may have been RMR-1029 to a microbiologist at a university in the Southwest. However, this sample did not have the mutations that appear in the material used in the attacks. The report lists two possible explanations for this apparent discrepancy: one, the anthrax that Dr. Ivins sent was not RMR-1029 at all, or two, the RMR-1029 that was sent to this facility was so diluted that it could not be adequately matched to the material used in the attacks.

Teetering on the Edge

Much has been made of the fact that Dr. Ivins had been obsessed with the Kappa Kappa Gamma sorority all of his adult life. The task force emphasized that Ivins freely admitted to investigators that he had been obsessed with the sorority since the 1960s when his romantic advances were rebuffed by a member of the organization.

Yet, it is unclear to me why Dr. Ivins's obsession with the KKG sorority was germane to his alleged role as a suspect in the anthrax attacks. While Dr. Ivins's issues with the sorority demonstrate his propensity for petty criminal behavior and his significant, longstanding psychological instability and history of obsessive-compulsive behavior, I fail to see any direct link to the anthrax mailings.

Ivins admitted to driving hours out of his way to visit KKG sorority houses on a variety of college campuses over a span of decades. He also admitted to breaking into at least two of the sorority houses and, each time, stealing the club's ritual book and the cipher used to decode it. The postbox from which the letters were mailed was reportedly very close to the Princeton University KKG sorority house (and to many other buildings on the campus).

Ivins also admitted to maintaining a post office box for a number of years under the name Carla Sander from which he answered responses to ads he ran in *Mother Jones* and *Rolling Stone* magazines offering free copies of the KKG ritual book, thus revealing the organization's internal secrets. He supplied the copied books only after determining that the responses were not from individuals associated with KKG by using a master list of sorority house addresses he had amassed from telephone books at the Library of Congress.

Nearer to the time of the anthrax attacks, Dr. Ivins was obviously suffering from severe mental illness. He had a long-standing history of these issues, which eventually overcame him. He developed unhealthy and inappropriate obsessions with female colleagues and wrote them disturbing, and often unwanted email messages that became progressively more desperate.

Shortly after an unsuccessful suicide attempt, at a group therapy session on July 9, 2008, Dr. Ivins revealed to the group that he was a suspect in the anthrax investigation and that he was angry at the investigators, the government, and the system in general. He said rather than facing the death penalty, he had a plan to "take out" coworkers and other individuals at Fort Detrick. He claimed to have a bulletproof vest and said he had made a list of coworkers who had wronged him. He reportedly went on to say he was going to get a Glock from his son the next day, claiming he couldn't get a gun on his own because he was under surveillance by federal agents. He added that he was going to "go out in a blaze of glory."

Based on these statements and advice from Ivins's treating psychiatrist, the social worker associated with the group therapy session reported the details of Dr. Ivins's comments to the Frederick, Maryland police department the next morning, and the police took custody of Dr. Ivins that afternoon. He was subsequently transferred from Frederick Memorial Hospital to Sheppard Pratt Health Systems in Towson, Maryland, for further forensic evaluation. Over objections from the counselor who first reported the group therapy session threats, the hospital released Dr. Ivins from its care on Thursday, July 24, 2008, finding that he was not a danger to himself or others. He overdosed forty-eight hours later.

CHAPTER 4

INVESTIGATOR'S COMMENTS

The Amerithrax task force has unequivocally declared Dr. Ivins to have been the perpetrator of the anthrax attacks. They then formally closed the case on February 19, 2010. Dr. Ivins was never indicted, tried, or convicted of the crimes because, unfortunately, Dr. Ivins took an overdose of over-the-counter medications on or about July 26, 2008, and died on July 29, 2008. He took his own life before he was ever even charged. Personally, I've never been fond of the blaming-it-on-the-dead-guy resolution to unsolved cases.

According to a report on NPR, the possible impending indictment of Dr. Ivins was still a ways off in the future. While the grand jury had been approving subpoenas all through their investigation, the grand jurors had yet to hear the evidence about the case in its entirety, and they had not yet been asked to vote on whether or not they were actually going to bring an indictment. That could've taken weeks, and the outcome was by no means certain.

I haven't read the thousands of pages of investigative notes, witness statements, etc. that resulted from the 600,000 hours of investigative work on this case. All I have to go on is the investigative summary that describes why the FBI is so certain that Dr. Ivins committed the attacks. So, it is with some trepidation that I make these comments about the Amerithrax task force's investigation. But, I just can't help myself, so here goes.

First, while the task force was locked on Steven Hatfill, surveilling him around the clock, monitoring his every written and spoken word, leaking his name and their suspicions about him to the press, where was the uber-evil, it's-him-for-sure mad scientist Bruce Ivins—besides working for the feds and consulting for the task force about the source of the anthrax? If Ivins was such a slam dunk obvious choice as a perpetrator, then why did the task force lock on to a virologist like Hatfill before concentrating on one of the country's leading experts in anthrax bacteria? In the beginning, it seems that an English professor pointed them in Hatfill's direction. That sounds about as logical as cooking spaghetti in a toaster.

As the task force was so anxious to point out in their report, Dr. Ivins had obviously been emotionally disturbed for decades and was severely mentally ill for at least several months before successfully completing his second attempt at suicide, so what in the hell was he doing with access to—let alone sole supervisory custody of—anthrax in the first place?

How is it that no one in the government noticed that a senior bioweapons researcher working in a high-security military facility was sneaking around the country, breaking into sorority houses, stealing secret ritual books, then advertising them in national magazines? While they were focused on Dr. Hatfill, the task force went out of its way to paint him as an unstable eccentric. Dr. Hatfill had been on the government payroll, as well, with access to anthrax. It's like the government's background checks for those working in the field of weapons of mass destruction were being done by Huey, Dewey, and Louie.

As I understand the information publicly available in the Ivins Did It scenario, the anthrax attacks were carried out with anthrax spores developed by a USAMRIID scientist, stored in a secure US Army facility, held in the custody of a United States government employee, packaged in envelopes purchased from a United States post office, and delivered to their targets by the United States Postal Service, an independent agency of the United States government.

After the attacks, the United States government essentially spent 600,000 hours of investigative work trying to figure out who among their own ranks did it, only to end up paying almost five million taxpayer dollars in damages for illegally leaking information and blaming the wrong guy, and then eventually closing the investigation only after "conclusively" blaming it on a deceased mental patient the government had placed in control of the alleged source spores.

Yikes.

INVESTIGATOR'S TIPS

Here's a handy list of danger signs alerting you to suspicious mail brought to you by the Department of Homeland Security:

Characteristics of a Suspicious Package

Always remain aware!
Look for the anomalies:

- Rigid or bulky
- Lopsided or uneven
- Wrapped in string
- Badly written or misspelled labels
- Generic or incorrect titles
- Excessive postage
- No postage
- Foreign writing, postage, or return address
- Missing, nonsensical, or unknown return address
- Leaks, stains, powders, or protruding materials
- Ticking, vibration, or other sound

QUIZ

Take this quiz from the University of Rochester Medical Center to see how much you know about anthrax.

Anthrax Quiz

https://www.urmc.rochester.edu/encyclopedia/content.aspx?ContentTypeID=40&ContentID=AnthraxQuiz

SNARKY HUMOR

I like the postal service just fine. But, this supposedly real screenshot made me laugh so hard, I cried. I'd credit the source, but I have never found one. I got it from Cheezburger.com

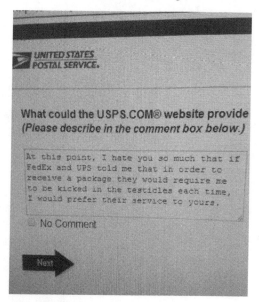

REFERENCES & COOL SITES

Ciprofloxacin - Drug Usage Statistics, ClinCalc DrugStats Database
https://clincalc.com/DrugStats/Drugs/Ciprofloxacin

Irradiating the Mail: The Anthrax Attacks of 2001 | IEEE Spectrum
https://spectrum.ieee.org/
irradiating-the-mail-the-anthrax-attacks-of-2001

FBI — The Search for Anthrax
https://archives.fbi.gov/archives/about-us/history/famous-cases/
anthrax-amerithrax/the-search-for-anthrax

FBI conclusions in anthrax probe meet skepticism | CIDRAP
https://www.cidrap.umn.edu/anthrax/
fbi-conclusions-anthrax-probe-meet-skepticism

FBI — Linguistic/Behavorial Analysis of the Anthrax Letters
https://archives.fbi.gov/archives/about-us/history/famous-cases/
anthrax-amerithrax/linguistic-behavorial-analysis-of-the-anthrax-letters

Remarks Prepared for Delivery by U.S. Attorney Jeffrey Taylor at
Amerithrax Investigation Press Conference (2008-08-06)
https://www.justice.gov/archives/opa/remarks-prepared-delivery-us-
attorney-jeffrey-taylor-amerithrax-investigation-press-conference

Head of the FBI's Anthrax Investigation | LewRockwell LewRock-
well.com
https://www.lewrockwell.com/2015/04/no_author/
head-of-the-fbis-anthrax-investigation/

New Report Casts Doubt on FBI Anthrax Investigation | The Anthrax Files | FRONTLINE | PBS | Official Site
https://www.pbs.org/wgbh/frontline/article/
new-report-casts-doubt-on-fbi-anthrax-investigation/

New Evidence Adds Doubt to FBI's Case Against Anthrax Suspect | ProPublica
https://www.propublica.org/article/
new-evidence-disputes-case-against-bruce-e-ivins

Chronology of anthrax events
https://www.ph.ucla.edu/epi/bioter/chronologyanthraxevents.html

Oxford Woman, 94, An Unlikely Victim Of Anthrax Attacks | Hartford Courant
https://www.courant.com/2014/04/14/
oxford-woman-94-an-unlikely-victim-of-anthrax-attacks-2/

What Really Happened During The 2001 Anthrax Attacks?
https://www.grunge.com/600255/
what-really-happened-during-the-2001-anthrax-attacks/

Cipro Recipients Developing Side Effects
https://www.ph.ucla.edu/epi/bioter/ciprosideeffects.html

Anthrax and the FBI
https://nypost.com/2011/10/23/anthrax-and-the-fbi-2/

The United States Department of Justice
https://www.justice.gov/archive/amerithrax/docs/amx-investigative-summary.pdf

Total decontamination cost of the anthrax letter attacks | PubMed
https://pubmed.ncbi.nlm.nih.gov/22313022/

PART 2

WHO KILLED JONBENÉT RAMSEY?

CHAPTER 5

BACKGROUND

Beauty Is Only Wallet Deep

Child beauty pageants are big business. Estimates vary, but the consensus is that pageants comprise a five-billion-dollar industry that sees about 250,000 girls participate in roughly 5,000 pageants held in the US annually. Some estimates are as high as 290,000 participants in 16,000 pageants per year. The industry took a hit in 1997, after the tragic death of its most famous participant, six-year-old JonBenét Ramsey, but participation has come roaring back—and the cash registers are ringing as the tiny tots strut their stuff on the pint-size runways of hotel meeting rooms across the country.

Playing Dress-Up Meets Iris from Taxi

Child pageants fall into two categories—natural and glitz. Glitz pageants, like the ones JonBenét participated in, involve dressing young girls in makeup and clothing to mimic the appearance and movement of grown women as they walk down modeling runways and perform song and dance routines.

Many people view this as sexualization of the children involved. According to the 2007 Executive Summary of the American

Psychological Association Task Force on the Sexualization of Girls (https://www.apa.org/pi/women/programs/girls/report) report,

> Sexualization occurs when a person's value comes only from his or her sexual appeal or behavior, to the exclusion of other characteristics; ...and/or sexuality is inappropriately imposed upon a person.

The APA report goes on to describe cognitive and emotional impairments and multiple negative impacts on the physical, mental, and sexual health of the girl, including eating disorders, low self-esteem, and depression or a depressed mood.

The APA's definition of sexualization as sexuality that is inappropriately imposed upon a person sounds a lot like dressing five-year-olds up as grown women and having them perform suggestive moves on makeshift stages in the ballrooms of chain hotels, but that's just my opinion. However, it's hard to avoid that conclusion when, during one episode of *Toddlers & Tiaras*, a reality show featuring the pageant world, a three-year-old girl was dressed as Julia Roberts's character in the film *Pretty Woman*, prostitute Vivian Ward—complete with boots, miniskirt, bare midriff, and blond wig.

Children Can't Be Choosers

Since children by definition have no independent legal standing and cannot make decisions for themselves, it seems that participation in pageants, like any other choice in their lives, is imposed upon them by their adult decision makers. While some children appear to make certain decisions for themselves, like choosing their own clothing or picking their meals, this pseudoautonomy is actually granted to them by their adult caregivers, not taken as a right by the child. Moreover, these pseudochoices are made from a limited

Denise Diana Huddle

range of options offered by the adults. In any case, the child is by no means a free agent. So I take with a big grain of salt pageant moms' claims that their kids "choose" to participate. A young child's desperate need for approval and acceptance by the parental figure who is literally responsible for feeding and sheltering them often makes a child's "decision" to do whatever their parent wants nothing more than a survival tactic.

While the APA report was not an investigation into pageants or a direct indictment of them, the implications of the report for the quarter of a million children participating in these contests every year are staggering.

The tragic suicide of sixteen-year-old pageant star Kailia Posey, who hanged herself on May 2, 2022, is potentially an example of some of these harms. After a lifetime on the pageant circuit, including a stint on *Toddlers & Tiaras*, Posey ended her own life.

It was in this pageant world of helicopter moms swarming around child beauty contestants and that culture's inherent emphasis on outward appearances that six-year-old beauty queen JonBenét Ramsey lived her short life—until she was murdered on Christmas in 1996.

WHAT HAPPENED?

THE PLAYERS

The Patriarch

John Ramsey was born on December 7, 1943, in Nebraska. He graduated from Michigan State University with a BS in electrical engineering and an MBA and became a successful businessman. He founded a company that eventually evolved into Access Graphics, which he sold to Lockheed Martin in 1991. Ramsey stayed on as the president and chief executive officer of the new Lockheed subsidiary. He had three children with his first wife before their marriage ended in divorce.

Beauty and the Businessman

If John Ramsey was Ward Cleaver, Patsy Ramsey wasn't exactly his June. Patricia "Patsy" Paugh was thirteen years younger than John. She had been Miss West Virginia in 1977 and competed in the Miss America pageant, and she had a degree in journalism from West Virginia University.

The couple was married in 1980. They had two children born in Atlanta, Georgia: a boy, Burke Hamilton Ramsey, born January 27, 1987; and a girl, JonBenét Ramsey, born August 6, 1990. The Ramseys moved from Atlanta to Boulder, Colorado, in November 1991 for John Ramsey's business.

THE MURDER

Christmas

John and Patsy Ramsey enjoyed a traditional Christmas morning with six-year-old JonBenét and nine-year-old Burke. Around 4:30 that afternoon, the family left their house and went to the home of their close friends, Fleet and Priscilla White, for Christmas dinner. According to the Ramseys' account of the evening, the family returned home around 9:30 p.m. Burke and JonBenét reportedly fell asleep in the car, and their parents put them straight to bed. No one in the family reported hearing or seeing anything strange during the night.

December 26—The Crime Is Discovered

According to Patsy Ramsey, she got up early and came down the back stairs of the house (wearing the same clothes she wore to Christmas dinner) and discovered a ransom note on the steps. She called her husband, and they searched for but could not find JonBenét.

At 5:52 a.m. on December 26, 1996, a female caller contacted the Boulder Police Department's 911 service. The call originated from a landline at the home of John and Patsy Ramsey at 755 15th Street in Boulder. The woman, who identified herself as "Patsy Ramsey, I'm the mother," was frantic and indicated that her daughter had been kidnapped and a note had been left. The following is a transcript of the call:

911: 911 Emergency.

Patsy Ramsey: Police?

911: What's going on, ma'am?

Patsy Ramsey: 755 15th Street.

911: What's going on there, ma'am?

Patsy Ramsey: We have a kidnapping. Hurry, please!

911: Explain to me what's going on. Okay?

Patsy Ramsey: There… We have a—there's a note left and our daughter's gone.

911: A note was left and your daughter's gone?

Patsy Ramsey: Yes!

911: How old is your daughter?

Patsy Ramsey: She's six years old. She's blonde, six years old.

911: How long ago was this?

Patsy Ramsey: I don't know. I just got the note, and my daughter's gone.

911: Does it say who took her?

Patsy Ramsey: What?

911: Does it say who took her?

Patsy Ramsey: No! I don't know. There's a—there's a ransom note here.

911: It's a ransom note?

Patsy Ramsey: It says SBTC. Victory! Please!

911: Okay, what's your name? Are you Kath...?

Patsy Ramsey: Patsy Ramsey, I'm the mother. Oh my God! Please!

911: Okay, I'm sending an officer over, okay?

Patsy Ramsey: Please!

911: Do you know how long she's been gone?

Patsy Ramsey: No I don't! Please, we just got up and she's not here. Oh my God! Please!

911: Okay, cal...

Patsy Ramsey: Please send somebody.

911: I am, honey.

Patsy Ramsey: Please.

911: Take a deep breath and...

Patsy Ramsey: Hurry, hurry, hurry!

911: Patsy? Patsy? Patsy? Patsy?

Operator, Can You Help Me End This Call?

Apparently, at this point, Patsy Ramsey believed she had hung up the phone, as she quit communicating with the operator. However, the line was not disconnected, and some claim that garbled voices can still be heard in the background. Numerous attempts at enhancing the remaining audio have been made, and sources, including the 911 operator, have suggested that three voices were present, one of which might have been JonBenét's brother, Burke, who was reported by the Ramseys to have been asleep at the time. Burke Ramsey denies having been present during the call.

I've heard this recording along with alleged transcriptions, but, in my humble opinion, the content of the conversation is completely unintelligible. You can listen for yourself on YouTube: Patsy Ramsey 911 Call (Enhancement of Voices at the End) https://www.youtube.com/watch?v=hX-PSF80GYQ

Honesty—It's What the 911 Operator Needs from You

Now, let's think this through. Patsy Ramsey supposedly came down the back stairs and found the ransom note. She called for John, and they looked for JonBenét and couldn't find her. Patsy then made her hysterical call to 911, referencing the ransom note—the note that specifically warned her not to call the police. The note said:

Speaking to anyone about your situation, such as police, F.B.I., etc., will result in your daughter being beheaded. If we catch you talking to a stray dog, she dies. If you alert bank authorities, she dies. If the money is in any way marked or tampered with, she dies. You will be scanned for electronic devices and if any are found, she dies. You can try to deceive us but be warned that we are familiar with law enforcement countermeasures and tactics.

Yet, Patsy Ramsey never mentioned a single word to the 911 operator about having the police respond clandestinely. In fact, she repeatedly demanded that the operator send officers quickly. She mentioned the note three times during the 911 call and even quoted from it ("It says SBTC. Victory!"). I find it very strange that in a hysterical state of panic a mother would quote the nonsensical initials of the kidnappers' group name, but wouldn't think to mention a threat to behead her child if she called the police.

Immediately after phoning 911, at 5:54 a.m., Patsy Ramsey called family friends, including Fleet and Priscilla White and John and Barbara Fernie, and asked them to come to the house, again violating the kidnappers' warning not to speak with anyone—even a stray dog—about the situation.

AFTER THE POLICE ARE CALLED
Step Right Up! The Show Is About to Begin!

Like a ringmaster leading a circus parade down 15th Street, Boulder police patrolman Officer Rick French arrived at the Ramsey property at 5:59 a.m. and parked his patrol car in front of the house. Shortly after Officer French arrived, the Whites and the Fernies showed up along with the Ramseys' minister. These individuals were reportedly not present in the house between the time the family returned home from Christmas dinner and the time the ransom note was allegedly discovered and, therefore, served no legitimate investigative purpose at the scene. Yet, responding officers allowed them to enter the home (which was by any definition an active crime scene) and move about without restriction or supervision.

Can No One Here Read Directions?

Even after law enforcement had access to the note, other police arrived at the residence without any effort to disguise their presence, nor is there mention in the public record I've seen that the Ramseys expressed concern about the very visible presence of police or their friends and pastor. Either the cops and the Ramseys couldn't read, or on some level, no one involved believed the note was real.

Victims' Advocates—The Hostess with the Mostest or How to Cater a Crime Scene

To round out the parade, police summoned victims' advocates to the scene to provide crisis intervention services to the Ramseys. The advocates arrived with bagels and coffee, and after serving the snacks, they were joined by one of Patsy's friends in cleaning up the kitchen, including scrubbing a countertop. When police later determined that the ransom note was most likely written in the kitchen, the extent of the damage to the evidence became clear. The Boulder police essentially convened a morning coffee klatch at an active crime scene.

Burke Has Left the Building

Burke Ramsey was taken to the home of friends at some point during the morning. He was removed from the Ramsey house without having been questioned by police. John and Patsy Ramsey were never separated and were allowed to spend the entire morning together. No steps were taken to isolate them and get their individual stories on the record before they could be rehearsed and coordinated.

Have Your People Call My People

Not that it really mattered. John and Patsy Ramsey did not individually give formal statements to the Boulder police until April of 1997, despite having previously given two exclusive television interviews to discuss the death of their child. They did, however, give fingerprints and DNA.

The Police Who Bungle the Investigation...

Anyone who has seen even a single episode of *Law & Order* knows this is an absurd excuse for police procedure, never mind atrocious investigative technique. Aside from the statistical likelihood that they were involved in the crime, the Ramseys were, at the very minimum, critical witnesses, and their recollections were essential to nailing down the timeline of events leading up to their daughter's disappearance.

Any competent investigator would have secured the crime scene and immediately sequestered each of them at an alternate location, ideally at the police department, to prevent contamination of their recollections. Then, they should have each been questioned separately.

Miranda Isn't Just a Character from Shakespeare

Moreover, from the minute the 911 call reached the Boulder Police Department, John and Patsy Ramsey should have been considered possible suspects in JonBenét's disappearance. Stereotypical kidnappings for ransom are exceedingly rare. According to an article in the October 3, 2005 issue of *Parents* magazine, 49 percent of child abductions at that time were perpetrated by a family member. According to the Office of Juvenile Justice and Delinquency Prevention's October 2001 Juvenile Justice Bulletin:

> Most homicides of young children are committed by family members through beatings or suffocation. Although victims include approximately equal numbers of boys and girls, offenders include a disproportionate number of women.

In the early hours of the investigation, JonBenét was theoretically presumed to be alive and the victim of a kidnapping. So, any detective should have realized that there was basically a fifty-fifty shot that the parents were involved in her disappearance. After the body was discovered, the overwhelming statistical likelihood was that a family member was involved in the death. Suspects, especially those who could be accomplices, should immediately be questioned separately and never be given an opportunity to get their stories straight.

Does the Boulder PD Really Care What Time It Is?

The ransom note said a call would take place between 8:00 and 10:00 a.m., but when it failed to materialize, the two senior Boulder detectives left the Ramsey house and returned to the police station to conduct discussions with the FBI, leaving Detective Linda Arndt in charge.

Why the senior detectives left the crime scene is a mystery. The claim that they needed to meet with the FBI back at the office is absurd. It's hardly like the FBI doesn't make house calls to kidnapping scenes. If the detectives needed to speak with the FBI agents privately, why not conduct their conversations in a car so they would be available in the event a ransom call came through after the appointed time?

Bad enough that the most critical witnesses and possible suspects were either allowed to leave the location outside of law enforcement supervision (Burke Ramsey) or spend hours together collaborating on their version of events (John and Patsy Ramsey), but worse, the crime scene was not preserved.

Everyone should have been removed from the home as soon as the first officer arrived at the location. The crime scene should have been secured, and a careful log of every entry and exit from the location should have been kept starting from the very beginning of law enforcement's involvement. Instead, the Ramseys took Burke off the premises without even notifying the police, and John and Patsy were left together while a gaggle of friends milled around the house, contaminating evidence that could have potentially led police to the perpetrator.

Now John Has Left the Building

The chaos at the house on 15th Street came to a head around noon when Detective Linda Arndt called the police department and informed her colleagues that John Ramsey had been missing from the house since approximately 10:30 a.m. Mr. Ramsey reappeared at the home sometime before 1:00 p.m., claiming that he had gone to get the family's mail. Police later determined their mail was delivered through a slot in their front door.

But just think that through for a second—your six-year-old child is missing, theoretically in the hands of a group of kidnappers who are demanding a ransom. The call promised in the ransom note doesn't come at the appointed time. Wouldn't you be huddled with police, glued to the phone, praying every second that a call would come with instructions for retrieving your precious child? Or would you go off somewhere to get your mail—mail that's delivered through your door anyway? And do it without telling the cops where you were going—the cops your wife so desperately begged for help? This gap represents at least two hours that no one knew where John Ramsey was while his daughter was supposedly in the hands of a small foreign faction of kidnappers threatening to behead her.

CHAPTER 6

DISCOVERY OF THE BODY

Come Out, Come Out, Wherever You Are!

Apparently, Detective Arndt was never taught that kidnapping investigations are a lot more complicated than playing hide and seek. She allowed the contamination of the crime scene to continue throughout the morning and early afternoon as she permitted Fleet White to wander through the house, ostensibly looking for JonBenét, who he thought might be "hiding." When White discovered a broken window in the basement, he moved some of the glass shards and crawled around the area inspecting the damage, further contaminating potentially important pieces of evidence.

Again, this is absurd. Why would Fleet White think JonBenét was hiding when Patsy found a note explicitly stating that she had been kidnapped? It appears that Mr. White didn't believe the note was real, either.

Around 1:00 p.m., Detective Arndt instructed Fleet White and John Ramsey to conduct a "top to bottom" search of the house. It was during this unsupervised search that John Ramsey shouted out his discovery of the body of his dead daughter in a basement room the family referred to as the "wine cellar." He then removed the duct tape from her mouth, carried her body upstairs, and laid her on the floor.

For reasons that are still not clear, Detective Arndt then moved the child's body again, placing it next to the Christmas tree, where someone covered it with a sheet. Patsy Ramsey reportedly took her dead daughter in her arms and held her as she sobbed. This series of events further corrupted the collection and interpretation of potentially valuable forensic evidence on the child's body and clothing that could have possibly broken the case.

Again, what was Detective Arndt thinking? Why would she task a parent and one of his friends, both civilians without law enforcement experience, to search the house for a kidnap victim? If Detective Arndt felt a search of the residence was appropriate, why didn't she conduct it herself or call in other detectives to do it? At the very least, why didn't she accompany the men while they searched? Instead of this amateur-hour version of detection, from the very beginning, police should have secured the home and had a crime scene crew combing every inch of the house for clues.

Leaving on a Private Jet Plane

At 1:40 p.m., less than an hour after he discovered his daughter's dead body, John Ramsey was allegedly heard on the telephone calling his pilot and arranging for the family to travel to Atlanta via their private plane. Plans for the trip were canceled when law enforcement advised Mr. Ramsey that his family's presence was required in Boulder.

The Cause of Death

The autopsy report indicated that JonBenét had been bludgeoned in the head, resulting in an 8 ½" crack in her skull. Sometime after the poor child was struck, she was killed by strangulation accomplished with a garrote, which was still in place when her father brought her body up from the basement. The garrote was likely fashioned from part of the handle of a paintbrush the perpetrator may have found in the Ramsey basement.

Denise Diana Huddle

THE RANSOM NOTE

Ransom note found on back stairs of Ramsey home. (TheSmokingGun.com)

Transcript of the Note

Mr. Ramsey,

Listen carefully! We are a group of individuals that represent a small foreign faction. We do respect your bussiness [sic] but not the country that it serves. At this time we have your daughter in our posession [sic]. She is safe and unharmed and if you want her to see 1997, you must follow our instructions to the letter.

You will withdraw $118,000.00 from your account. $100,000 will be in $100 bills and the remaining $18,000 in $20 bills. Make sure that you bring an adequate size attache to the bank. When you get home you will put the money in a brown paper bag. I will call you between 8 and 10 am tomorrow to instruct you on delivery. The delivery will be exhausting so I advise you to be rested. If we monitor you getting the money early, we might call you early to arrange an earlier delivery of the money and hence a [sic] earlier delivery pick-up of your daughter.

Any deviation of my instructions will result in the immediate execution of your daughter. You will also be denied her remains for proper burial. The two gentlemen watching over your daughter do not particularly like you so I advise you not to provoke them. Speaking to anyone about your situation, such as Police, F.B.I., etc., will result in your daughter being beheaded. If we catch you talking to a stray dog, she dies. If you alert bank authorities, she dies. If the money is in any way marked or tampered with, she dies. You will be scanned for electronic devices and if any are found, she dies. You can try to deceive us but be warned that we are familiar with law enforcement countermeasures and tactics. You stand a 99% chance of killing your daughter if you try to out smart [sic] us. Follow our instructions and you stand a 100% chance of getting her back.

You and your family are under constant scrutiny as well as the authorities. Don't try to grow a brain John. You are not the only fat cat around so don't think that killing will be difficult.

Denise Diana Huddle

Don't underestimate us John. Use that good southern common sense of yours. It is up to you now John!

Victory!

S.B.T.C

The Handwriting on the Stairs

The ransom note was written on paper taken from a pad belonging to Patsy Ramsey, which was found in the kitchen of the Ramseys' Boulder home. The ink used to write the note was chemically determined to have come from a specific pen also found in the Ramsey kitchen. (Yep, that's the same kitchen that was scrubbed after the coffee and bagels were served.) Multiple handwriting samples were taken from John and Patsy Ramsey. Additionally, previous samples of Patsy's handwriting were confiscated from the family vacation home in Charlevoix, Michigan.

John Ramsey was eliminated by handwriting experts as the writer of the note, but Patsy Ramsey was determined to be a possible source of the writing. Many analysts are of the opinion that, especially on the first page of the note, there had been an effort by the writer to disguise their handwriting.

Handwriting analysis is much more of an art than a science. The practice is a subjective process in which the examiner searches the questioned document and identifies specific characteristics of the writing that are, in the examiner's view, unique to the writer. Then, exemplars and samples of writing from suspected writers are obtained and searched for these characteristics. Also, the questioned document is searched for unique characteristics identified by the examiner in the exemplars contributed by suspected authors. Scores of analyses have been made of this writing over the past twenty years, but no firm consensus has ever been reached regarding the author beyond saying that Patsy Ramsey may have written the note or could not be eliminated as the writer of the note.

All the House Is a Stage...and the Ramseys Are Merely Players

Other characteristics of the ransom note have contributed to the general conclusion that the note was part of a staging of the crime scene.

The note demanded a ransom of $118,000, the exact amount that John Ramsey had just been paid as an annual bonus. The Ramseys lived in a 7,000-square-foot home and had their own private jet. They were obviously wealthy. Why would a kidnapper ask for only $118,000? And why ask for such a specific amount?

Move Over, War and Peace

The note is much longer than traditional ransom notes. In a demonstration shown in the 2016 CBS documentary *The Case Of: JonBenet Ramsey*, four investigators handwrote the contents of the note as fast as they could and took approximately twenty-one minutes to accomplish the task. This time was required to simply copy the note. Composing it would have logically slowed down the process even more.

This means that an intruder would have supposedly spent at least half an hour in the Ramsey home composing the three-page ransom note either while two adults and at least one surviving child were asleep upstairs or while he or she was alone in the home awaiting the Ramseys' unscheduled return from Christmas dinner. Interestingly, after the note was written, the pad and pen were returned to their regular storage places. Why wouldn't the kidnapper simply bring the note with them or send the note later? This aspect of the intruder scenario seems highly unlikely to even the most casual observer.

Denise Diana Huddle

If the child was killed during what started as an actual attempted kidnapping for ransom, then why didn't the kidnapper take the child's body with them when they left the home? The perpetrator would have logically had a plan for removing the victim from the home and transporting her away from the scene. This plan should have worked equally well for a living or deceased victim.

The Bruno Hauptmann Playbook

Consider the case of the Lindbergh kidnapping. The Lindbergh child was killed in the course of the abduction or shortly thereafter, but Bruno Hauptmann hurriedly buried the child four and a half miles from the Lindbergh home, then proceeded with his plan to collect the ransom. The Lindbergh ransom was paid on April 2, 1932, forty-one days before the baby's badly decomposed body was discovered on May 12.

However, it is important to keep in mind that garrotes do not end up around the necks of six-year-olds accidentally. JonBenét's death was clearly intentional. Purposely killing the kidnap target before collecting the ransom is inherently illogical, as the victim's life is the leverage in the negotiation.

Any possibility of the kidnapper successfully obtaining the ransom would have been eliminated when the child was found dead. Placing JonBenét's corpse in the basement of her parents' home as opposed to removing it from the premises substantially reduced the chances that the ransom would be paid before the body was discovered.

On the other hand, if the kidnapper believed the body would not be found before the ransom was paid, why didn't they place the ransom call between 8:00 and 10:00 a.m. on December 26 as promised in the note—a note they supposedly spent at least a half hour at great peril writing inside the Ramsey home?

In fact, the body had not been found (or at least its presence in the wine cellar had not yet been revealed) and the cash to pay the ransom had already been prepared in time for the call that morning. The theoretical kidnapper would have likely gotten away with the cash just like Hauptmann did, but no call was ever forthcoming.

Maybe because there never was a kidnapping attempt.

THE PINEAPPLE

The Ramseys reported that JonBenét was asleep when the family returned from the Christmas meal at the Whites' and that John Ramsey carried her inside and took her straight to bed. Yet, the autopsy report refers to an undigested substance found in Jon-Benét's small intestine resembling pineapple. Here's an excerpt from the report:

> GI Tract: … The yellow to light green-tan apparent vegetable or fruit material which may represent fragments of pineapple.

Additionally, the crime scene photos show a bowl of pineapple chunks on the Ramseys' kitchen counter with a spoon in the bowl. The bowl, spoon, and a tea glass reportedly contained varying combinations of the fingerprints of Patsy and Burke Ramsey.

Household members leaving fingerprints on family cutlery and dinnerware is hardly remarkable or indicative of anything sinister. Burke Ramsey claims no memory one way or the other of pineapple that night. However, Patsy Ramsey categorically denied any knowledge of how the bowl of pineapple happened to be on the counter and surmised that the kidnapper must have served JonBenét a snack during the attempted abduction.

Mary Poppins and David Copperfield Were In on It Together

If those claims about the pineapple are true and John and Patsy Ramsey put both children straight to bed upon arriving home from the Whites', the same intruder who spent half an hour writing a ransom note before returning the pen and pad to their regular storage spots served JonBenét a snack from the refrigerator using the family's cutlery and dinnerware while her parents and brother slept upstairs—and managed to do it without disturbing anyone in the house, without JonBenét raising any kind of alarm, and without leaving either the perpetrator's or JonBenét's fingerprints on the bowl or spoon. Then that same intruder murdered the child, stuffed her body in the basement, and slipped away into the night, never to be heard from again. What possible motive could an intruder have for such a series of events?

BURKE RAMSEY

Burke Ramsey had previously struck JonBenét in the face with a golf club. During an interview with police, Patsy Ramsey reported that the incident took place on the lawn of their vacation home in Charlevoix, Michigan. According to Patsy, while Burke was swinging a golf club to hit a wiffle ball, JonBenét came up behind him apparently without his knowledge, causing him to accidentally strike her with the club during his backswing.

There are questions about the timing in Patsy Ramsey's telling, including a possible conflict between her alleged date of the incident and Burke's age at the time, with her stating that Burke would have been between two and three years old. It is unclear to me how Burke could have hit JonBenét with the club at that age when JonBenét was three years, six months, and ten days younger than he. A family friend stated in the press that Patsy told her that Burke struck JonBenét with the golf club out of anger and placed the event approximately eighteen months before the murder. During an interview with Dr. Phil in 2016, Burke described the incident as an accident and denied ever intentionally harming his sister.

Burke Ramsey reportedly had a history of scatological issues. When crime scene technicians visited JonBenét's bedroom after sealing it off on December 26, they found "feces smeared on a box of candy" she had received as a Christmas gift the day before. Previously, a housekeeper had reported finding feces in JonBenét's bed and on the walls of the bathroom.

In the intruder scenario, that made JonBenét's room a pretty busy place over the night of December 25 and the early morning of December 26. Since the candy could be pegged to the timeline on December 25, sometime in that period someone snuck into her room and smeared feces on her Christmas gift and someone likely entered her room and abducted her (though we don't actually know that she didn't leave the room of her own volition and encounter the killer elsewhere in the home).

I have found no information in the public record about DNA studies on the feces found on the candy. While it is not the optimal source for genetic studies, human DNA is found in fecal material, and a comparison of DNA from the candy box and the genetic material collected from JonBenét's clothes and fingernails could be helpful.

But any way you slice it, a lot was going on in that room over Christmas night and the early morning of December 26.

Denise Diana Huddle

FAMILY MEMBER VS. INTRUDER THEORY

While the initial suspicion fell on the family as a result of a lack of evidence of forced entry, law enforcement was aware that several windows had been left unlocked in the home. John Ramsey even admitted breaking a basement window weeks before when he had locked himself out of the house, stating that the broken glass remained unrepaired at the time of the murder. These possible points of ingress meant that the house was not secure, and an intruder could have theoretically entered without force.

The Investigative Pissing Contest

Fairly quickly after the child's body was discovered, a schism began to develop between the Boulder district attorney's office and the Boulder police. The police became convinced that JonBenét had been killed by a member of her immediate family. The DA's office held tight to what came to be called the "intruder theory" and, in March of 1997, hired Lou Smit, a retired El Paso County and Colorado Springs homicide detective, to investigate the death of JonBenét Ramsey on their behalf.

Lou Smit conducted his own investigation of the crime and came to the conclusion that the DA's version of events was the most probable—that JonBenét Ramsey had likely been killed by an intruder.

Smit believed the most likely scenario supported by the evidence was that an intruder entered the Ramsey home through the unlocked basement window while the family was at the Whites' house for Christmas dinner. Using the time while the family was absent, the intruder wrote the ransom note. The intruder then lay in wait until the family was asleep, went into JonBenét's bedroom, disabled her with a stun gun, and carried her to the basement, where he attempted to stuff her into a blue suitcase that belonged to the Ramseys. When the kidnapper was unable to fit the suitcase through the window, he became angry, killed JonBenét, and escaped through the same window.

Other forensic evidence collected during the investigation could have been interpreted to support the intruder theory. The end portion of the paintbrush that was used to fashion the garrote was never found on the Ramsey property. The rope used for the ligature and the wrist bindings was never linked to the Ramseys, nor was the duct tape found covering JonBenét's mouth.

Black animal hair found on JonBenét's hands did not match any hair found in the house. Animal hair thought to have come from a beaver was stuck to the adhesive of the duct tape removed from JonBenét's mouth by her father, but no beaver hair was found inside the Ramsey home.

The *Rocky Mountain News* later reported that investigators determined that the footprint found near the body actually belonged to her brother, Burke, and that a palm print was left by her adult half sister, Melinda—and that both prints were unrelated to the unsolved murder. Burke played in the basement regularly, and Melinda was proven to be out of state at the time of the killing.

While no seminal fluid was found anywhere on her body, a splinter of wood alleged to be from the paintbrush handle that was used to fashion the garrote was supposedly found inside Jon-Benét's vagina along with other evidence that she had been sexually assaulted. However, the nature and meaning of these findings have been widely debated.

CHAPTER 7

THE SUSPECTS

Robert Christian Wolf—Unlucky Taste in T-Shirts and Girlfriends

In their book, *The Death of Innocence: The Untold Story of JonBenét's Murder and How Its Exploitation Compromised the Pursuit of Truth*, the Ramseys named Robert Christian Wolf as one of five possible suspects in their daughter's death. Wolf subsequently sued the Ramseys for libel and slander and emotional distress from accusations they made against him in the book. A federal judge granted the Ramseys' motion for summary judgment, and the case was closed.

Wolf, a freelance journalist, became a suspect when his girlfriend reported that he left home Christmas night and didn't return until the next morning covered in mud. He owned a T-shirt from the Santa Barbara Tennis Club with the initials SBTC on the front (just as the ransom note had been signed). He had reportedly written one or more articles about John Ramsey's company, Access Graphics, and supposedly held a grudge against its parent company, Lockheed Martin.

Bill McReynolds—Intruder Who Came Down the Chimney with a Bag Full of Coincidences

Bill McReynolds was an associate of the Ramsey family. He had regularly played Santa Claus at the Ramseys' annual Christmas events, and he had what was described as a "special relationship" with Jon-Benét, who called him "Santa Bill." Oddly, McReynolds's daughter and her friend had been abducted twenty-two years to the day before JonBenét was murdered, and McReynolds's wife had written a play about a child murdered in a basement. However, McReynolds was alibied by family members and cleared as a suspect.

Michael Landon Helgoth—Conspiracy Theories and Magic Bullets

Michael Helgoth worked in his family's junkyard in Boulder, Colorado. He was twenty-six years old at the time of JonBenét's murder. Helgoth supposedly told a friend and former employee, John Kenady, that he and an unnamed colleague had a scheme to each make between fifty and sixty thousand dollars right at Christmas. At one point, Helgoth reportedly told Kenady that he was curious about what it would feel like to crack someone's skull. Kenady reported that Helgoth owned a pair of Hi-Tec boots. While a footprint from a Hi-Tec boot was found at the Ramsey crime scene, no information is available about a match or even a comparison between Helgoth's boots and the crime scene footprint. (According to the *Rocky Mountain News*, the boot print was attributed to Burke Ramsey, who frequently played in the basement of his own home, so Helgoth's ownership of Hi-Tec boots is probably irrelevant.)

Helgoth died of a gunshot wound in what was an apparent suicide on February 14, 1997. However, the gun was found on the right side of his body while the bullet apparently traveled from left to right. His friend and former employee, John Kenady, suspects

Helgoth was murdered by his accomplices in the Ramsey killing. Kenady claims a tape recording exists of Helgoth confessing to the crime, but Kenady believes the tape is in the possession of Helgoth's accomplices. Helgoth was dismissed as a suspect when his DNA did not match the DNA found on JonBenét's underwear or under her fingernails.

John Mark Karr aka Alexis Valoran Reich—Kiddie Porn and False Confessions

John Mark Karr was a married schoolteacher in San Francisco, California, when he was accused of the murder of Georgia Lee Moses of Santa Rosa. When police searched Karr's home, they found child pornography on his computer and arrested him. When authorities failed to bring a case against Karr, he moved to London, then to Bangkok, Thailand. In 2006, Karr sent emails to a documentary filmmaker claiming to have killed JonBenét Ramsey. The filmmaker, Michael Tracey, turned the emails over to the Boulder authorities, who had Karr returned to the US. However, Karr was cleared as a suspect when he was not a match to DNA found on JonBenét's body.

Karr now lives at an undisclosed location as a transgender woman going by the name Alexis Valoran Reich.

Gary Oliva—Known Paranoid Schizophrenic Pedophile Obsessed with JonBenét

Gary Oliva was a thirty-eight-year-old trespasser who was arrested on December 12, 2020, on the University of Colorado campus. Inside Oliva's backpack, police found a stun gun and a poem about JonBenét Ramsey. Oliva was a diagnosed paranoid schizophrenic and a convicted child sex offender who had tried to murder his mother by strangulation.

At the time of JonBenét's murder, Oliva had been receiving

services for the homeless at a church in Boulder located ten houses down from the Ramsey home. He was identified in video footage of the candlelight vigil held in Boulder on the one-year anniversary of JonBenét's death. Oliva admitted to having an obsession with JonBenét, and police found a shrine to her in the place where he was living at the time of his arrest in 2020. Oliva claimed the stun gun in his backpack was a gift from a friend.

He was cleared by comparison of his handwriting to the ransom note and by comparison of his saliva with DNA samples found on JonBenét's underwear.

THE DNA

Countless potential suspects have been cleared and excluded from the JonBenét Ramsey investigation based on comparisons to unidentified male DNA found mixed with tiny drops of blood on JonBenét's underpants and collected from her long johns and under her fingernails. This genetic material reportedly does not match anyone in the Ramsey family. It has been processed and reprocessed as forensic DNA technology has evolved over the past twenty-five years.

Various experts still hold to the belief that the DNA on her clothing could have been contributed by a source other than the perpetrator, such as a male factory worker who packed or folded the underwear or some other source of contamination. Questions about the validity of the samples and the completeness and accuracy of the profile are abundant. The technical aspects of the arguments are scientifically complex and beyond most laymen's understanding (especially mine). However, I can say, absent a clear-cut scientific consensus on the validity of the DNA as a tool of exclusion in this investigation, any suspect cleared solely based on comparison between their DNA and that collected from JonBenét's clothing or fingernails should be returned to the suspect pool.

SEXUAL ASSAULT

The autopsy report inferred but did not conclude that JonBenét Ramsey was sexually assaulted on the night of her death. The inference was based on the condition of her genital tissue and the presence of a wood splinter in her vagina that is assumed by some to have come from the paintbrush handle used in the garrote found around her neck. Yet, various forensic pathologists have taken issue with the possibility of sexual abuse, saying that the autopsy evidence of sexual assault was weak at best and open to multiple interpretations. The family pediatrician vehemently denied any evidence of sexual abuse prior to the murder.

THE GRAND JURY

In August 1998, the Boulder County district attorney, Alex Hunter, convened a grand jury to investigate the death of JonBenét Ramsey. They met for thirteen months before disbanding in October 1999. When the grand jury concluded its business, Alex Hunter appeared at a press conference and, in an oddly worded statement, said that no charges would be filed in the matter at that time, implying that the grand jury had not voted to indict any suspects in JonBenét's death. Hunter said:

> "The Boulder grand jury has completed its work and will not return. No charges have been filed. Yet, I must report

to you that I and my prosecution task force believe we do not have sufficient evidence to warrant the filing of charges against anyone who has been investigated at this time."

In October of 2013, fourteen years after Alex Hunter implied that the grand jury had disbanded without voting to indict, a court unsealed four pages of documents with the foreman's signature redacted. Two pages contained indictments by the grand jury against John Ramsey and two pages contained identical indictments against Patsy Ramsey. One set alleged that both parents had unlawfully, knowingly, recklessly, and feloniously permitted a child to be unreasonably placed in a situation that posed a threat of injury to the child's life or health, which resulted in the death of JonBenét Ramsey. The other set alleged that John and Patsy Ramsey unlawfully, knowingly, and feloniously rendered assistance to a person, with intent to hinder, delay, and prevent the discovery, detention, apprehension, prosecution, conviction, and punishment of such person for the commission of a crime, knowing the person being assisted had committed and was suspected of the crime of murder in the first degree and child abuse resulting in death.

The Police Who Bungle the Investigation...and the DA Who Won't Prosecute the Offenders

I have to say here that my years of training in statement analysis screamed at me when I first heard Hunter's statement.

Why say the jury won't return after already saying they have completed their work? Why would they keep meeting if they had finished their investigation? And what is with the "Yet"? Why say "Yet" if Hunter believed his decision not to file charges was consistent with the grand jury's findings? "Yet" implies conflict between the preceding and succeeding phrases. "I wanted to have ice cream, yet I didn't get any because I'm on a diet," or "I told you not to come, yet here you are."

A more genuine statement consistent with the message he was trying to convey would have been, "The grand jury has concluded its investigation without issuing any indictments. No charges have been filed yet because we do not have sufficient evidence to support charges against anyone at this time." Of course, Hunter couldn't say that…because it would have been a bald-faced lie. Instead, he attempted to imply that was the case.

Why not charge the Ramseys? Why convene the grand jury only to ignore their indictments? Imagine the true statement. "The Boulder grand jury has completed its work and indicted John and Patsy Ramsey on the charges of endangering their child and protecting the person who killed her. Yet, the DA's office has decided we don't have enough evidence to support the charges, so we're not going to file on the Ramseys." The media attention would have been unbearable, and the public would have come unscrewed.

When I heard the "Yet," I knew something was rotten in Boulder.

THE DA LETTER

On July 9, 2008, the Boulder district attorney, Mary T. Lacy, wrote a letter to John Ramsey clearing him and his entire family of any suspicion in the 1996 murder of his daughter, JonBenét, and apologizing for the pain and suffering his family experienced as a result of the umbrella of suspicion under which they had lived since the murder.

This letter has been highly controversial ever since it was written, particularly as questions still persist about the quality and interpretation of the DNA evidence in the case. I'm not a lawyer, but in my understanding of the system, DAs simply do not write this kind of letter. District attorneys evaluate evidence and grand jury indictments and file charges or don't file charges. They are not in the business of explaining themselves beyond their court filings. Finally, district attorneys are not juries. On the contrary, they are prosecutors. Why a district attorney felt it appropriate to make such a statement about any suspect in a case, particularly two people indicted by a grand jury, is beyond me.

CHAPTER 8

INVESTIGATOR'S COMMENTS

Unfortunately, the tragic death of JonBenét Ramsey remains an open case. The family's wealth, JonBenét's participation in the pageant system, the conflicting and often confusing evidence in the case, the botched investigation, and the internal discord of the Boulder authorities all conspired to reduce the poor child's life and death and the dynamics of her family to the tawdriest of tabloid fodder. Between the contaminated crime scene, the inconclusive forensics, the often freakish suspected intruders, and the bizarre ransom note, a perfect storm of red herrings has left a brutal murder unsolved.

My fondest hope is that, as the science of forensic genetics becomes more advanced and the database of possible links to the perpetrator increases, someday the killer will be conclusively identified. As in the D. B. Cooper case, I hope that DNA technology will eventually allow the authorities to generate a complete DNA profile appropriate for inclusion in the public databases, thus allowing the genetic genealogy community to suggest possible identities for the killer.

I am struck by the behavior of all those involved regarding the ransom note from the get-go. The Ramseys and the police apparently wholly discounted the threat to behead JonBenét if the family called law enforcement or discussed the matter with anyone. Why wasn't the FBI involved all along if anyone really believed the kidnappers were foreigners as the note claimed? Why didn't the kidnappers ever call and attempt to collect the ransom? And, if the author of the note was a foreigner, why was there no linguistic evidence of that in the note? I found nothing in the public record to indicate that even one single suspect from a small foreign faction or any group going by the initials SBTC was ever identified (beyond the Santa Barbara Tennis Club, which is surely not in the business of child murder). In my opinion, everyone involved treated the note as a sham.

I find it almost beyond credulity that a kidnapper would rummage through drawers to find paper and a pen, then sit in the kitchen of his victim's palatial home for at least twenty minutes in the middle of the night and write a note as lengthy as that, then carefully replace the pad and pen in the locations where he or she found them.

Even more absurd is the idea that the kidnapper would serve the victim a pineapple snack from the family's refrigerator and do it without the perpetrator or victim leaving a single fingerprint on the bowl or spoon. How reasonable is it to assume that two adults and a nine-year-old child would sleep through such activity, which involved turning on lights, opening and closing kitchen cabinets where the bowl and spoon were located, opening and closing drawers to find and obtain then later replace the pad and pen, and opening and closing the refrigerator door to access the pineapple. And all of this without JonBenét raising an alarm when a stranger was in the family home fixing her a snack in the middle of the night?

So, if the note was a sham, how could the intruder theory work? Someone came into the house for what purpose? To kidnap Jon-Benét? So the kidnapper snuck into the house, took JonBenét from her bedroom to the kitchen, fed her pineapple, then took her to the basement, bashed her head in, and killed her with a garrote, then snuck out of the house leaving her body behind?

I've seen no evidence in the public record that the head wound was considered to be the result of an accident. In any case, the death by garrote was surely intentional. So why intentionally kill the kidnap victim before even leaving the home? Did the intruder actually break into the house with the intent of murdering JonBenét? Why? She was a six-year-old baby pageant queen, not a capo in a Mafia crime family. No evidence in the public record implies that her parents had any criminal connections that could have led to a revenge murder.

If murder was the original intent, then why take the time and risk to leave the note? If the killer put forth this effort, why not take the body and hope for a reward as Hauptmann successfully did in the Lindbergh case? As far as I can see, if the note was bogus, its presence undermines the logic of any intruder scenario I can imagine.

If there was no intruder, then the crime had to have been perpetrated by a member of the household, a scenario supported by the statistics surrounding crimes such as this one. Unfortunately, there doesn't seem to be any physical evidence proving or disproving this scenario, either. The astounding lack of evidence may indicate a careful and sophisticated perpetrator or be the result of a crime scene so badly compromised due to mismanagement that any physical evidence was destroyed or contaminated. Moreover, if the crime was committed by someone with a legitimate reason for being in the house previously, finding that individual's DNA, fingerprints, or hair would be entirely inconclusive.

The Boulder DA cleared the entire Ramsey family in writing, complete with a public apology—and did so despite secret indictments of both John and Patsy by the Boulder grand jury. No charges have ever been filed against any member of the family. No one in the family has ever been tried, let alone convicted of any crime. Legally, they are all completely innocent of any involvement in JonBenét's death. When Patsy Ramsey passed away from ovarian cancer on

June 24, 2006, she died an innocent woman, and nothing will ever change that. John and Burke will remain so unless one or both of them is at some point in the future convicted by a jury of his peers.

John Ramsey had previously lost a child from his first marriage in a car accident. He then lost his youngest daughter to murder and his second wife to cancer. He is a man who has lived a tragic life of terrible loss who has never been convicted of anything. It is not my purpose to say who killed JonBenét. I am in no position to make that judgment. I am merely trying to work out the logic of various scenarios based on the limited evidence in the public record. I would remind everyone that the grand jury that indicted the Ramseys spent over a year looking at evidence most of which is likely not in the public arena.

As of Thursday, November 10, 2022, the Boulder Police Department announced that in 2023, they would be turning their records over to the Colorado Cold Case Team and asking for their assistance with reinvestigating the case. The Cold Case Team is a board under the Colorado Department of Public Safety. They welcome the public to review the materials they have for each case and contribute any help they might be able to offer.

INVESTIGATOR'S TIPS

Here are some quick tips from the Department of Justice for keeping your kids safe.

What you can do to help your child:

- Children should know their full name, home phone number, and how to use the telephone. Post your contact information where your children will see it: office phone number, cell phone, etc.

- Children should have an alternate trusted adult to call if they're scared or have an emergency.
- Choose babysitters with care. Obtain references from family, friends, and neighbors. Once you have chosen the caregiver, drop in unexpectedly to see how your children are doing. Ask your children how the experience with the caregiver was, and listen carefully to their responses.

How to prepare for an emergency:

- Keep a complete description of your child.
- Take full face color photographs of your child every six months.
- Keep copies of your child's fingerprints.
- Keep a sample of your child's DNA.
- Know where your child's medical records are located.
- Have your dentist prepare and maintain dental charts for your child.

What to do if your child goes missing:

- Immediately report your child missing to your local law enforcement agency.
- Ask the law enforcement agency to enter your child into the National Crime Information Center (NCIC) Missing Persons File.
- Limit access to your home until law enforcement arrives and has the opportunity to collect possible evidence.
- Give law enforcement investigators all the information you have on your child including fingerprints, photographs,

a complete description, and the facts and circumstances related to their disappearance.

For a free guide from the DOJ about what to do if a child goes missing, visit https://ojjdp.ojp.gov/sites/g/files/xyckuh176/files/pubs/childismissing/contents.html.

QUIZ

Test your knowledge about the JonBenét Ramsey case.

JonBenét Ramsey Case: The Quiz
https://www.playbuzz.com/aeiciy10/a-jonben-t-ramsey-case-the-quiz

SNARKY HUMOR

If I make you breakfast in bed, a simple "Thank you." is all I need.

Not all this "How did you get in my house?" business.

Source: Pinterest

Denise Diana Huddle

REFERENCES & COOL SITES

JonBenet Ramsey Case Encyclopedia
http://jonbenetramsey.pbworks.com

What's The History Of Child Pageants?
https://www.bustle.com/
articles/183975-whats-the-history-of-child-pageants

7 Ugly Truths About Child Beauty Pageants
https://web.archive.org/web/20171106084812/http://www.babygaga.
com/7-ugly-truths-about-child-beauty-pageants/

Inside $5bn Industry Of Child Beauty Pageants | US News |
Sky News
https://news.sky.com/story/
inside-5bn-industry-of-child-beauty-pageants-10334507

Report of the APA Task Force on the Sexualization of Girls
https://www.apa.org/pi/women/programs/girls/report

Top News Stories from 1996 | Infoplease
https://www.infoplease.com/year/1996

CNN - 1996 Year in Review
http://www.cnn.com/EVENTS/1996/year.in.review/

The JonBenet Ramsey Ransom Note - Statement Analysis®
https://statementanalysis.com/jonbenet-ramsey-murder/ransom-note/

Evidence - The Unsolved Murder of JonBenét Ramsey
http://www.jonbenetramsey.com/evidence/

Burke's Behavior – A Short Life in the Spotlight
http://sites.gsu.edu/moyasfinalproject/support-3-maybe/

The Murder of Jonbenet Ramsey – Forensic Pathology - 1979 Words | Research Paper Example
https://ivypanda.com/essays/
the-murder-of-jonbenet-ramsey-forensic-pathology/

Child Abduction Statistics for Parents
https://www.parents.com/kids/safety/stranger-safety/
child-abduction-facts/

New enhanced audio Patsy Ramsey 911 call | YouTube
https://www.youtube.com/watch?v=686Ic9-yIwo

Homicides of Children and Youth
https://www.ojp.gov/pdffiles1/ojjdp/187239.pdf

Behm Thesis - Final.pdf
https://cardinalscholar.bsu.edu/server/api/core/
bitstreams/3897ab6d-dbc7-4650-a146-39f3083728a1/content

What Did JonBenet Ramsey's Autopsy Report Say? It Prompted Even More Questions
https://www.romper.com/p/what-did-jonbenet-ramseys-autopsy-report-
say-it-prompted-even-more-questions-18586

JonBenet Ramsey autopsy report details brutal attack
https://www.tampabay.com/archive/1997/07/15/jonbenet-ramsey-
autopsy-report-details-brutal-attack/#:~:text=The%20report%20
said%20%22a%20deep,were%20based%20on%20anonymous%20
sources

Autopsyfiles.org - JonBenet Ramsey Autopsy Report
https://www.autopsyfiles.org/reports/Other/ramsey,%20jonbenet_
autopsy.pdf

Denise Diana Huddle

'The Case of: JonBenet Ramsey': Everything We Learned | Rolling Stone
https://www.rollingstone.com/culture/culture-news/the-case-of-jonbenet-ramsey-everything-we-learned-from-part-two-106495/

Investigators Identify Whose Feces Were Smeared All Over JonBenet's Room And Gifts | USA Daily Brief
https://usadailybrief.com/investigators-identify-whose-feces-were-smeared-all-over-jonbenets-room-and-gifts/

THROWBACK THURSDAY: Burke hits sister with golf club, is it an accident? : JonBenetRamsey
https://www.reddit.com/r/JonBenetRamsey/comments/jkfw06/throwback_thursday_burke_hits_sister_with_golf

The Death of Innocence : The Untold Story of JonBenet's Murder and How Its Explo: Amazon.com: Books
https://www.amazon.com/Death-Innocence-Untold-JonBenets-Murder/dp/B002J81N2A

Who killed JonBenet Ramsey? An investigator's dying wish keeps the search going with his family | ABC News
https://abcnews.go.com/US/killed-jonbenet-ramsey-investigators-dying-search-family/story?id=75186109

Seven unanswered questions in JonBenét Ramsey case - from intruder theory to who wrote the ransom | The US Sun
https://www.the-sun.com/news/4311920/seven-unanswered-questions-in-jonbenet-ramsey-case-from-intruder-theory-to-who-wrote-the-ransom/

Pedophile Confesses to Killing JonBenet Ramsey in Letters to Friend | Rolling Stone
https://www.rollingstone.com/culture/culture-news/
jonbenet-ramsey-murder-gary-oliva-confession-letters-778025/

Cold Case | Colorado Bureau of Investigation
https://cbi.colorado.gov/sections/investigations/cold-case

PART 3

WHO WAS D. B. COOPER?

CHAPTER 9

WHAT HAPPENED?

FBI artist's rendering of hijacker Dan Cooper. (FBI.gov)

On November 24, 1971, a man using the name Dan Cooper boarded Northwest Orient Flight 305 from Portland, Oregon, to Seattle, Washington. Once airborne, he passed the flight attendant a ransom note and showed her what he said was a bomb in his briefcase. He demanded $200,000 in cash and four parachutes. When the plane landed in Seattle, the hijacker collected the ransom and released the passengers and part of the crew. He instructed the remaining crew to fly him to Reno, but while the plane was somewhere between the towns of Woodland and Ariel, Washington, Cooper strapped on the parachutes, gathered his money, lowered the rear airstairs, and jumped out of the plane, never to be seen again.

BACKGROUND

The Rise and Fall of the Boeing Empire

Seattle was headquarters for the Boeing Company, which was by far the largest employer in the region. The market for commercial jet airliners, which had been booming since the late 1950s, drove huge growth at Boeing. During the 1960s, people in the area either worked for Boeing or knew someone who did.

Go, Godzilla! Go!

In 1963, President Kennedy introduced the National Supersonic Transport Program wherein the government would help fund the design and development of a supersonic passenger aircraft as the centerpiece of a major upgrade to American civil air travel. Boeing prevailed in a heated bidding war for the government contract and began designing the new plane. The supersonic project turbocharged Boeing's already breathtaking growth trajectory.

Losing Financial Altitude

Publicly, 1968 was a triumphant year for Boeing as the first 747 rolled out of its Everett assembly plant, which was, at the time, the largest building in the world. Yet, behind the scenes, executives at the aviation giant were beginning to worry—and with good reason. Costs associated with the development of the 747 were much higher than anticipated, putting a serious damper on profits. Meanwhile, the market for passenger aircraft was facing significant saturation issues, and orders for new planes were dropping.

To make matters worse, the supersonic program was bogging down. Cost overruns and design problems, which had plagued the project from the very start, were showing up on the bottom line. By 1969, the project was two years behind schedule. Both the

Denise Diana Huddle

Soviets and a UK/French cooperative had already rolled out their own supersonic passenger planes and had them in the air while Boeing was still mired in a failing development effort.

When it came to revenue, the Sexy Sixties were giving way to the Saggy Seventies.

The Death Spiral

While the magnitude of Boeing's financial tailspin first became apparent in 1970, the death knell came in early 1971 when Congress cut all funding for the supersonic project, and the program was canceled outright. Boeing had been running from debacle after debacle for years, but by 1972, they were maxed out on credit from borrowing a billion dollars to cover the 747 cost overruns, and there was nowhere left to hide.

Eject! Eject! Eject!

While Boeing staved off bankruptcy with a whip and a chair, the deadly claws of the layoff monster dug into every corner of the company, tearing the workforce apart. Sixty thousand employees were eventually laid off, leaving Seattle's unemployment rate almost three times the national average.

For victims of the layoff carnage at Boeing, there was a greater chance of being abducted by aliens than finding a new job in Seattle. The unemployment crisis morphed into a mass exodus from King County as laid-off workers left the area in search of jobs. The resulting glut of inventory led to a collapse of the area's housing market. A billboard near Sea-Tac Airport read, "Will the last person leaving Seattle — Turn out the lights."

It was into this dismal economic landscape of a town decimated by the poster child for everything wrong with corporate America that Dan Cooper hijacked a plane and literally disappeared into thin air with $200,000. While he never made any pretense of robbing the rich to support the poor, a significant slice of the public suffering through the disastrous repercussions of the Boeing Bust perceived Dan Cooper as a symbol of their clan, and to that extent, he became a Robin Hood figure.

Denise Diana Huddle

CHAPTER 10

THE HIJACKING

The plane ticket the hijacker bought under the name of Dan Cooper. (FBI.gov)

That's Not a Love Note

Once seated on the airplane, the passenger known as Dan Cooper handed one of the flight attendants on the short hop a note. (The name D. B. Cooper was misreported in a newspaper as the name given by the hijacker.)

In an era when female flight attendants were used by the air travel industry as the 1970s equivalent of clickbait, "stewardesses" were hit on more often than the backboard at the NBA finals. Since the airlines did nothing to help them, they learned to fend for themselves while still doing their jobs. Thinking that the man

97

with the note was just one more passenger propositioning her, the flight attendant, Florence Schaffner, took the piece of paper and pocketed it without reading it. Shortly after, the passenger known as Dan Cooper stopped her and said, "Miss, you better look at that note. I have a bomb."

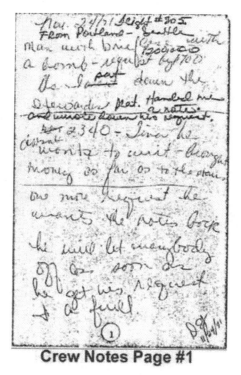

Crew Notes Page #1

Handwritten notes/dictation taken by the flight attendant.
(DBCooperHijack.com)

Take a Letter, Miss Hathaway

Apparently not having thought to bring paper and a pen for his fifteen pages of epistles to the pilots, the hijacker dictated his demands to flight attendant Schaffner, who wrote them on pieces of paper from her purse. Cooper demanded $200,000 in "negotiable American currency" in a knapsack, two chest parachutes, and two back parachutes. The loot was to be delivered to him before 5:00 p.m. when the plane landed in Seattle. He wanted a fuel truck standing by to refuel the Boeing 727 051. To preserve calm, Cooper instructed the crew to advise the passengers the plane was experiencing minor mechanical problems and promised, if his demands for money and parachutes were met, he would release the passengers after the plane was refueled.

Evelyn Wood Microfilming Dynamics

The president of Northwest Orient Airlines authorized the payment of the ransom from company funds. In the more common version of the story, the cash was gathered as quickly as possible from Seattle-area banks and microfilmed by the FBI before the plane landed. This was no mean feat since the ransom involved 10,000 twenty-dollar bills that had to be microfilmed with 1970s-era technology.

In another telling of the story, the money was obtained from a single bank, Seattle First National Bank. SeaFirst reportedly maintained an emergency stash of cash for just such a circumstance, the serial numbers of which had already been recorded ahead of time.

A memo on page 101 of Part 67 of the FBI vault of the Cooper case documents describes a film canister containing "the microfilm on which was recorded the serial numbers of all the bills given to the hijacker of Northwest Airline Flight #305, which was hijacked out of Seattle, Washington, on November 24, 1971. The film canister was obtained from Seattle First National Bank, Main Branch, Seattle, Washington, on November 25, 1971." Since the memo clearly states that the film was obtained from SeaFirst and contained the numbers of all the bills, I think it's fair to say that all the ransom money came from that one single source—Seattle First National Bank. The multiple bank reports are probably inaccurate.

Hijackers Can Be Choosers

Originally, the parachutes to be supplied to Cooper were military rigs provided by McChord Air Force Base in Tacoma, Washington. When word reached Cooper during the flight that military-style parachutes would be waiting for him, he refused them and demanded what were called free-fall rigs used in civilian or sport skydiving.

There is considerable controversy regarding the source of the free-fall parachutes and how they arrived at the airport. In one version, the manager of the Sea-Tac airport called his friend skydiver Earl Cossey about supplying the free-fall rigs. Variations on the theme include a version where Cossey called his office in Issaquah, Washington, and had a person staying there gather the equipment, which police retrieved and rushed from Issaquah to Sea-Tac International. Other versions say that the chutes were transported by taxi and private car. In yet another telling, the chutes were taken from Cossey's home.

The *Mountain News* reported in 2013 that federal documents revealed the chutes were actually owned by a man named Norman Hayden.

In a tragic turn of events, Earl Cossey was murdered Tuesday, April 23, 2013, in his home in Woodinville, Washington. He died of blunt force trauma to the head. A few days later, an envelope addressed to the decedent was forwarded to his son, Wayland Cossey. The envelope had no return address and contained Earl Cossey's driver's license, bank cards, and casino gaming card. As far as I can tell from the public record, the crime was never solved.

Coffee, Tea, or Two Hundred Grand?

Upon Flight 305's arrival in Seattle, Cooper instructed flight attendant Tina Mucklow to exit the plane, retrieve the money, and deliver it to him. He then demanded she make multiple trips out of the plane to retrieve the parachutes. The poor woman schlepped all of Cooper's ill-gotten gains up a flight of airstairs wearing a dress and high-heeled shoes while he sat comfortably in his seat, drinking bourbon and smoking filtered Raleighs. When she finished, the plane was refueled, and Cooper released the passengers and two of the flight attendants. But he didn't release Tina Mucklow. She was forced to stay on board for the duration of the hijacking.

Airport Meets *Sister Act*

Ms. Mucklow reported praying throughout the flight. I think I would have spent the time planning for my application to beauty college, but not Ms. Mucklow. Not only did she suck it up during the hijacking, but she bravely continued with her career as a flight attendant until her retirement in 1981, when she became a nun and entered the Maria Regina Convent, a Catholic nunnery outside Eugene, Oregon. She left the order after twelve years as a Carmelite nun.

Flying Down to Reno

After the passengers and flight attendants were released, the remaining crew were long-suffering flight attendant, Tina Mucklow, pilot, Captain William Scott, first officer, William Rataczak, and second officer, Harold Anderson. Cooper directed the pilots to fly a route that passed over Portland and Medford in Oregon, and Red Bluff, California, before landing in Reno, Nevada, to refuel. After the refueling stop in Reno, Cooper stated that the plane would be heading to Mexico City. The hijacker demanded that the aircraft remain below 10,000 feet, fly at a minimal airspeed not exceeding 200 mph, and keep flaps and landing gear lowered.

After the plane took off for Reno, Cooper ordered Ms. Mucklow to move into the first-class section of the jet and close the dividing curtain. Our gal Tina was no fool. Once she got behind that curtain, she raced into the cockpit and locked the door behind her, leaving Cooper alone in the back of the plane with the handset normally used to connect the flight attendants with the pilots.

Help! The Airstairs Are Stuck, and I Can't Get Out

Via that intercom, Cooper requested help from the crew when he was unable to lower the tail airstairs. The pilots leaped at the opportunity to get Cooper off their airplane and happily reduced their speed even more. That apparently did the trick because the crew felt and heard a bump, which they construed to be the airstairs bouncing into place for Cooper's exit.

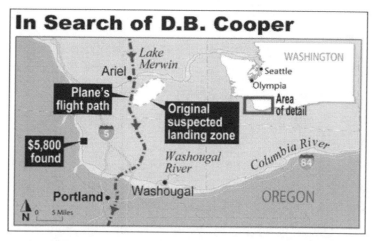

Locations where Cooper was originally thought to have landed and where some of the ransom money was later found. (FBI.gov)

Bye Bye Birdie!

The pilots marked their screens at that time to indicate the location where they believed Cooper parachuted from the plane. Flight recorder data indicated that Cooper likely jumped when the plane was between the towns of Woodland and Ariel in southwest

Denise Diana Huddle

Washington. While no one actually saw the hijacker make his jump, Cooper was nowhere to be found when the plane landed in Reno, and the cockpit indicator showed the airstairs were lowered at the time of the last intercom communication with Cooper.

CHAPTER 11

THE INVESTIGATION

Going Cold Turkey

The first question on the investigative decision tree was whether or not the hijacker could have survived the jump. Cooper parachuted out of the plane wearing only a lightweight men's business suit and a raincoat. At an altitude of 10,000 feet, that night the winds were estimated at over 100 miles per hour, and the temperature outside the plane was not more than 20°F.

Assuming he wasn't killed in the trees and actually made it to the ground safely, the real question regarding the weather is what Cooper did when he landed. The descent from the plane door to the ground probably took between three and four minutes. As if 20°F isn't bad enough, being wet makes the body lose heat twenty-five times faster, and wind makes that even worse.

Motel Wilderness—We Won't Leave the Heat On for You

On the ground, conditions were substantially better than at altitude, but were still more than sufficient to induce hypothermia. When he jumped at 8:13 p.m., in Woodland, Washington, it was about 46°F with light rain and a five-mile-per-hour wind. Still, Cooper was wet, and his body temperature would have already been lowered by the extreme conditions at altitude, putting him well on the road to hypothermia. It's fair to say Cooper would have required immediate access to shelter, heat, and warm, dry clothes when he landed if he was to avoid severe hypothermia.

To Live or Die in Washington State

Since the beginning, many in the FBI believed that Cooper could not have survived the jump due to darkness, rain, winds, low temperatures, lack of proper clothing, possible lack of experience, dangerous landing zone conditions, etc. In their book *Finding DB Cooper—Chasing the Last Lead in America's Only Unsolved Skyjacking*, authors Martin Andrade Jr. and his father take issue with the premise that Cooper likely didn't survive the jump out of the 727. In their book, they describe a study Andrade Jr. did looking at military pilots bailing out, particularly various WWII pilots who jumped out of planes at night in similarly challenging conditions with little or no prior parachuting experience. Those WWII pilots had a survival rate that Andrade calculates as over 90 percent.

Moreover, Andrade makes the case that Cooper actually exited the plane farther south than the FBI believed in 1971. Andrade believes Cooper landed in farmland about ten miles outside of Vancouver, Washington. While I don't feel qualified to evaluate the mathematic analysis or the choice of dataset he used, I think Andrade's study is interesting and probably points to a higher likelihood of survival for Cooper than the FBI assumed. You can read Andrade's risk analysis at https://martinandrade.files.wordpress.com/2014/12/dbcooperfinalupdated.pdf.

We're from the Government, and We're Here to Help You

Skyjacking is a federal crime, and the FBI was involved in the case from the time the crew became aware their plane was being hijacked. One of the first things they did was scramble chase planes to monitor Flight 305. Two Convair F-106 Delta Darts (the Air Force's primary all-weather interceptor aircraft) from the 318th Fighter Interceptor Squadron took off from McChord Air Force Base.

They were later joined by a Lockheed T-33. The T-33 was a single-engine two-seat jet trainer aircraft capable of flying lower than the F-106s. The plane in question had taken off from the Oregon Air National Guard Portland Air Base at Portland International Airport on a routine mission when the pilots were asked by air traffic control to join the F-106s. Eventually, the T-33 was called off the chase, leaving the two Darts as the only planes following the Northwest Orient 727 at the time Cooper supposedly exited the aircraft. The pilots of the chase planes did not see anyone parachute from the jet, but the jump took place under cover of darkness during a rainstorm.

Robert H. Edwards has written a book on D. B. Cooper and has a great blog entry about the chase planes at his author page at Goodreads. It's definitely worth checking out at https://www.goodreads.com/author_blog_posts/22541040-d-b-cooper-and-flight-305-the-chase-planes.

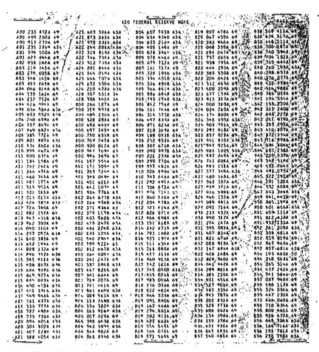

One of 34 pages on the list of the ransom bills released by the FBI

Page from the FBI's list of ransom note serial numbers. (Quora.com)

Shortly after the hijacking, a thirty-four-page list of serial numbers of each of the 10,000 twenty-dollar bills was circulated to banks and Federal Reserve offices across the country in hopes the money would show up in the banking system and could be traced. However, none of the bills was ever detected in circulation.

Investigative Crash and Burn

The FBI followed thousands of leads to dead ends between November 24, 1971, and July 12, 2016, when the agency officially closed the investigation, leaving the events of Flight 305 as the only unsolved hijacking of a commercial airliner in US history.

Denise Diana Huddle

That Wasn't in the Marketing Brochure...

At the time of the hijacking, a spokesman for Boeing indicated that the choice of a 727 for the target of the hijacking was likely not a coincidence. The Boeing 727 was the only commercial jetliner of that time from which a parachute exit was possible. The fact that the rear stairs descended vertically out of the tail allowed the hijacker to safely exit the plane during flight, protected from the flaps and engines.

This unique feature of the 727 made it likely that, in addition to experience with parachutes, Cooper had particular knowledge of passenger aircraft design, particularly that of the Boeing 727. This insight into the architecture of the 727 gave rise to the idea that Cooper might have been associated with Boeing in some way.

Viewing the hijacking in the context of the Boeing Bust and the desperate economic hardships it was causing people in the Northwest, it's not hard to imagine Dan Cooper as a man crushed by that economic disaster and striking out against the air travel industry.

Aviation Industry Baby-Proofs the Doors

Cooper vane that prevents airstairs from coming down in flight. (Wikipedia)

With the lightning-fast response speed typical of the federal government, after six more Cooper copycat hijackings, the FAA finally got hip to the problem, and an architectural change came to aviation. Since the whole idea of hijacking a plane and jumping out the door with the money Cooper-style was contingent on exiting the plane through rear (ventral) airstairs, the FAA decided it was time to block those doors during flight.

A device called a Cooper vane was mandated for the ventral airstairs of Boeing 727 and McDonnell Douglas DC-9 aircraft. The mechanism prevents the stairs from being lowered while the plane is in the air. A spring-loaded paddle interacts with the airflow to move a plate over the seam where the airstair module meets the rest of the fuselage, locking it shut when the plane is flying and releasing it when the plane is parked.

Three Cheeseburgers and a Rental Car

The Cooper vane combined with the universal security screening of all carry-on luggage stopped the parade of Cooper imitators—right up until July 11, 1980. That's when seventeen-year-old Glenn Kurt Tripp returned to the scene of D. B.'s crime and hijacked Northwest Orient Flight 608 from Seattle-Tacoma Airport to Portland. His initial demand was for $100,000, two parachutes, and (go big or go home) the assassination of his boss.

A sharp flight attendant spiked Tripp's alcoholic drink with Valium, and the plane never left the ground. A ten-hour standoff ensued, and Tripp reduced his demands to three cheeseburgers and a rental car. He released all fifty-two passengers and demanded the two pilots drive him out of the airport. The FBI brought the car to the base of the airstairs, but Tripp was jumped by agents hiding under the plane the second he hit the tarmac.

CHAPTER 12

THE SUSPECTS

During the almost forty-five years the D. B. Cooper case was open at the FBI, over a thousand possible suspects were considered. Here are three of the more interesting possibilities.

RICHARD McCOY—COPYCAT OR THE REAL McCOY

Mug shot of Richard McCoy (Wikipedia) and FBI artist's sketch of Dan Cooper (FBI.gov).

Richard McCoy lived in Provo, Utah. He was a member of the LDS church, a family man with two children, a Vietnam veteran, and a helicopter pilot in the 115th Engineer Group of the National

Guard. When McCoy returned from Southeast Asia, he faced considerable financial hardship, living on his meager National Guard stipend.

Disco Dick

On April 7, 1972, McCoy boarded the Boeing 727-22C operating as United Airlines Flight 855 from Denver to Los Angeles under the name James Johnson. According to a story about McCoy by Musika Farnsworth published at Parachutist.com on March 12, 2011, immediately after boarding, McCoy went into a lavatory to change into a disguise. While he was there, a flight attendant made an announcement asking if any passenger had left a manila envelope in the gate area. To his horror, McCoy realized, in his rush to board the plane after waiting in a long line at the ticket counter, he had left behind in an unsealed envelope the typed hijack instructions he was planning to pass to the crew.

Hearing the announcement, he peeked out of the lavatory door and saw a flight attendant walking down the aisle holding up the envelope for its owner to claim. He covered his face with a paper towel as though he were ill, waved to the flight attendant, and stuck his hand out of the lavatory door. The flight attendant passed him the envelope, and he retreated back into the toilet. Minutes later, after having been roused by a crew member for delaying their take-off with his lengthy stay in the bathroom, he came out wearing an ensemble worthy of *Saturday Night Fever*. Sporting a wig, mirrored sunglasses, dark-toned makeup, a green flowered shirt, a blue tie, and a blue-and-red-striped jacket, he returned to seat 20D, and the plane took off. Approximately twenty minutes later, he passed a two-page typewritten note to flight attendant Diane M. Surdham with instructions for her to deliver the envelope to the pilot.

The Devil Is in the Details—and the Explosives

To add a little punch to the message, the envelope also contained a bullet and a grenade pin. A FAA flight plan form directing the pilot to fly to San Francisco was included with the instructions. In a subsequent note, McCoy demanded $500,000 in ransom and four parachutes. He directed the pilots to have the plane refueled in San Francisco with fuel sufficient for six hours of flight. McCoy provided his luggage check ticket and demanded that his suitcase be retrieved from the cargo hold and delivered to him along with the ransom and parachutes.

My Bags Are Packed, I'm Ready to Jump

Once on the ground in San Francisco, McCoy ordered a passenger, a prisoner named William Richard Coggin who was being transported to San Quentin, to retrieve the luggage, ransom, and parachutes, which were delivered outside the plane by the airlines. After Coggin brought back the blue suitcase McCoy had checked, the parachutes, and two large briefcases containing the ransom money, McCoy handed the flight attendant another note ordering all the passengers off the plane.

Tehachapi to Tonopah

When the plane took off at 7:40 p.m., the flight attendant delivered another set of instructions directing the pilot to fly over Tonopah, Nevada. One of the notes said that if chase planes were observed following the airliner, the skyjacker would remotely detonate an explosive in the plane after he parachuted out.

The Price Is Right

Near Utah, McCoy ordered the plane to fly from the vicinity of Marysvale, Puite County, toward Salt Lake City International Airport. Near the town of Fairfield in Utah County, McCoy directed the pilot to fly easterly toward the town of Price. McCoy put on a jumpsuit from the blue suitcase, strapped on parachutes, and opened the rear door of the plane. He exited the aircraft a few minutes after the pilots turned toward Price.

Busted!

Apparently, Richard McCoy's wife wasn't thrilled about playing Bonnie to his Clyde. Around 11:30 p.m. on April 7, McCoy's sister-in-law called his best friend, Robert Van Ieperen, a Utah highway patrol trooper. She advised Van Ieperen that McCoy was not home and his wife was worried about him because he had enlisted her help in preparing for a skyjacking. Trooper Van Ieperen immediately called the FBI.

The Handwriting on the Wall

Unlike the Cooper hijacking, McCoy brought his own notes and didn't have to rely on a flight attendant to provide the paper and a pen and take his dictation. McCoy also ordered that all of his notes and flight plans be returned (just as Cooper took his original note with him). But Ms. Surdham managed to keep one note handwritten by McCoy without him noticing. This note was subsequently turned over to the FBI and proved a critical piece of evidence in the investigation.

After Van Ieperen identified McCoy as a suspect, the FBI retrieved McCoy's military record, and the handprinted skyjacker's note that Ms. Surdham secreted away was quickly compared with writing found in McCoy's personnel file. Experts declared that the note and the handwriting in McCoy's official records were written by the same person. Gotcha!

Death by a Thousand Clues

After the FBI had McCoy's name and knew where to look, the evidence against him piled up like snow ahead of a plow blade. William Coggin positively identified a photo of McCoy as the hijacker. The FBI established that McCoy was an experienced skydiver. As a helicopter pilot, he had access to FAA flight plan forms. He had several pistols, and his past military service made it possible for him to have gotten hold of a hand grenade.

Following his arrest, investigators found a bag containing $499,970 inside his house. That pretty well cinched it. McCoy was convicted of the United hijacking and was sentenced to forty-five years in prison.

Because the gods of law enforcement have a sense of humor, when McCoy was finally arrested, authorities learned he was on his way to National Guard duty where he was to fly a helicopter as part of the search for the man who skyjacked United Flight 855.

The Shawshank Destruction

On August 10, 1974, Richard McCoy escaped from the federal prison in Lewisburg, Pennsylvania. Using dental paste from the prison's medical facility, McCoy fashioned a fake gun. Lacking Andy Dufresne's sense of finesse, McCoy and some other prisoners used the fake gun to commandeer a garbage truck, which McCoy then crashed through the gates of the prison. Even though McCoy's escape was instantly detected, he managed to stay on the lam for three months.

But on November 9, 1974, the karmic boomerang struck with a vengeance when the cops who caught up with the fugitive were using real guns made of cold blue steel. McCoy was shot dead during an attempt to apprehend him in Virginia Beach.

Digging Up Dirt on the Bad Guys

Bernie Rhodes was the chief probation officer for the federal courts in Salt Lake City at the time of the McCoy trial. He was responsible for preparing the presentencing report (commonly called a PSR) for the judge's use in sentencing McCoy. These reports are generally considered to be among the most thorough background investigations in all of law enforcement, rivaled only by those done for top-level security clearances, and the probation officers who prepare them are among the best background investigators in the country. In the legal system, federal probation officers are the investigative equivalent of a whole body scanner.

The Devil in Disguise—If He Quacks like D. B. Cooper and Hijacks like D. B. Cooper...

After turning McCoy's life inside out in his investigation, Rhodes became convinced that McCoy was D. B. Cooper. Rhodes believed Cooper repeated his hijacking after having lost the money on the way down during the first attempt on the day before Thanksgiving of 1971. In the interview he gave for the HBO documentary *The Mystery of D.B. Cooper*, Rhodes pointed out that the FBI delivered the twenty-two pounds of twenty-dollar bills to Cooper in a plain canvas bag without handles for the express purpose of making it difficult to carry. Cooper apparently cut out the cords on one of the unused back parachutes to secure the money to his waist.

During Rhodes's interview with McCoy, McCoy insisted he was at home with his family in Provo, Utah, for the Thanksgiving holidays. However, authorities knew that McCoy was in Las Vegas, Nevada, the day after the hijacking. Phone records allegedly placed

McCoy in Las Vegas Thanksgiving night. Rhodes stated unequivocally that during an interview with McCoy, he found McCoy to be a dead ringer for the composite sketch of D. B. Cooper and had little if any doubt that Richard McCoy was D. B. Cooper.

LYNN DOYLE (L. D.) COOPER

L. D. and his four brothers were raised by their parents in a logging camp outside of Sisters, Oregon, run by the Brooks-Scanlon company. Friends from high school remembered the brothers as rambunctious, but hardworking. Shortly after graduating from high school, L. D. applied for work at Brooks-Scanlon, but he didn't get the job and left the area.

Little Red Riding Hood and the Big, Bad Hijackers

Marla Wynn Cooper of Oklahoma City came forward in 2011 with her recollection of a story about her father Don Cooper's brothers, Dewey and L. D. Cooper. Right before Thanksgiving of 1971, the family had gathered at her paternal grandmother's house in Sisters. While on a family walk in the woods, eight-year-old Marla overheard her paternal uncles, L. D. and Dewey, talking secretly about some mysterious plan they were making. She saw them with what she took to be sophisticated, expensive walkie-talkies just before the men left her grandmother's house, ostensibly to go turkey hunting.

Turkey Hunting at Ten Thousand Feet

When her uncles returned Thanksgiving Day (the day after the hijacking), L. D. was wearing a white T-shirt covered in blood. Despite being bruised and battered and barely able to walk, he refused medical help. He said his injuries were the result of a car accident. Before L. D. left her grandmother's house, Marla overheard

Dewey say to him, "We did it. Our money problems are over; we've hijacked an airplane."

After her uncles departed, Marla's father, Don Cooper, told her that his brothers had done something very bad and then swore her to secrecy about what she had seen, telling her it was a matter of life and death.

The Not-So-Invisible Man

Marla believes that L. D. and Dewey stayed with another uncle while L. D. recovered from his injuries. She saw her uncle L. D. twice in 1972, once midyear and then again at Thanksgiving, but she never saw him again after that. She regularly asked her family where her favorite uncle was, but no one would ever tell her, claiming they didn't know. From her perspective as a child, L. D. Cooper just disappeared.

However, when investigative journalist Bruce A. Smith interviewed several other members of the Cooper family, he learned that L. D. had gotten married sometime after 1972 to a woman named Marcia, who consistently refused to be interviewed about her life with L. D.

In addition to a six-month marriage I found for L. D. in Oregon from 1955–1956, I have also found a record of a Lynn Doyle Cooper (a resident of Oklahoma) marrying a Marcia K. Focsko (a resident of Nebraska) on October 11, 1973, in Virginia City, Nevada. This marriage took place almost two years after the hijacking of Flight 305. If L. D. Cooper was trying to fly under law enforcement radar, he needed some work on his technique. Going into the Virginia City courthouse and putting his real name on a marriage license was about as stealthy as the flashing signs in Times Square.

Dewey Cooper's widow, Janet Cooper, also told Smith that L. D. Cooper served as the best man at her wedding to Dewey Cooper in 1981, so apparently the brothers were still in touch. While Janet stated that the wedding was the first and only time she had met her brother-in-law in person, she said he called to offer her his condolences when Dewey died in 1985.

A Ramblin' Man

An article in the Bend, Oregon *Bulletin* on August 6, 2011, reported that property records showed L. D living in Reno in the early 1970s and stated that at various other times, he was living in California, Iowa, and other parts of Oregon. In addition to the marriage record, which listed him as a resident of Oklahoma, I also found a record indicating he lived in Sparks, Nevada, at one time.

Shortly before her father died, Marla asked him if he thought his brother L. D. was still alive. He said he did, but surmised that L. D. was still in hiding. When Marla asked why in the world her uncle would have been hiding, her father said, "You know—they hijacked that plane."

L. D. died April 3, 1999, and is buried in the Pilot Butte Cemetery in Bend, Oregon. His tombstone shows him to have been a seaman in the US Navy during the Korean War. According to an article in the *Seattle Times* on August 5, 2011, he was a engineering surveyor at the time of his death.

Not the Sharpest Axe in the Logging Camp

While Bud Keep, a high school friend of the Cooper brothers, admitted to seeing a certain resemblance between the D. B. Cooper sketches and the actual Cooper brothers, Doug Hockett, a former neighbor, said he "couldn't imagine L. D. enough on the ball to rob a plane." Meanwhile, Marla Cooper claims to have passed a polygraph test regarding her recollections about her uncles.

ROBERT RACKSTRAW—HERO TO ZERO?

FBI artist's sketch of Dan Cooper (FBI.gov) and Robert
Rackstraw's army ID photo (Wikipedia).

A team of retired FBI agents and other forensic experts calling
themselves the Case Breakers conducted an in-depth investigation into the D. B. Cooper case. They even sued and successfully
obtained documents from the FBI's case file on the matter through
the Freedom of Information Act. After years of investigation, they
are convinced that Robert Rackstraw was D. B. Cooper.

Move Over, Rambo

Rackstraw was a Vietnam veteran with Special Forces experience.
He attended the US Army Airborne School at Ft. Benning, Georgia,
where he had parachute training. At Ft. Bragg, North Carolina, he
trained at the Special Forces school with the Green Berets where he
learned to fly planes and helicopters and perform HALO jumps.
(HALO stands for high altitude, low opening.) These are com-
mando drops where the parachutist jumps out of a plane at a very
high altitude and free-falls, only opening their parachute at the
last possible moment to avoid detection. In Vietnam, Rackstraw

received two Distinguished Flying Crosses, Bronze and Silver Stars, and thirty-seven air medals.

An Officer and a Con Man

But, in spite of his exemplary service as a combat soldier, Rackstraw was forced to leave the military for falsifying his educational credentials and lying about his combat record and true army rank. His exit from the armed services came just five months before the hijacking.

Folsom Prison Blues

The same character flaws that derailed Rackstraw's military career plagued him in his civilian life. He had a long criminal record that began when he was charged in the murder of his stepfather in Calaveras County, California. He was tried for the death of Philip Rackstraw, his mother's third husband, but was acquitted at trial. In February 1978, Rackstraw was arrested in Iran, where he was working as a pilot for hire. He was deported to the US to face charges related to the possession of explosives.

While out on bail, Rackstraw tried to fake his own death by radioing a false mayday call that he was bailing out of a rented plane over Monterey Bay. He was subsequently arrested in Fullerton, California, and an additional charge of forging federal pilot certificates was added to the list. The plane he claimed to have ditched was found repainted and hidden in a hangar. He served a year in Folsom State Prison and was released in 1980.

He Wears the Rose of Youth upon Him

Rackstraw's name came up in the original FBI investigation in 1978 when two Stockton, California detectives holding Rackstraw on state charges notified the FBI that he might be a Cooper suspect.

The FBI didn't consider him seriously because he was twenty-eight at the time and was considered too young to be D. B. Cooper, who witnesses placed in his forties.

What's My Line?

According to the *Stockton Record*, Rackstraw admitted to the FBI to being in the Northwest area at the time of the hijacking. A Los Angeles news station arranged to have two interviews with Rackstraw while he was in jail in Stockton. According to the Case Breakers' website for their book *The Master Outlaw*, in archived news video of the Stockton interviews, when the reporter asked, "Do you think it's legit that you could be one of the [Cooper] suspects?" Rackstraw responded, "Oh yes, if I was an investigator, definitely so. I wouldn't discount myself…or a person like myself."

When a *Courthouse News Service* journalist interviewed Rackstraw in 2018 about the Case Breakers' latest revelations and pressed him to confirm or deny that he was the mysterious skyjacker, the four-time convicted felon was unequivocal in his answer: "There's no denial whatsoever, my dear."

Rackstraw waffled more than a Rooty Tooty Fresh 'N Fruity breakfast when it came to whether or not he was D. B. Cooper. In some interviews, he danced within a hair's breadth of admitting it. Other times, he issued cryptic semidenials. He remained a cipher until he died of a long-standing heart condition on July 9, 2019, at his home in the Bankers Hill section of San Diego.

CHAPTER 13

DAN COOPER COMICS

Dan Cooper was a Canadian cartoon character first drawn by the Belgian artist Albert Weinberg in 1954. In the French-language stories, Dan Cooper was a daring test pilot in the Royal Canadian Air Force. According to the FBI website, one issue released around the time of the hijackings had a cover illustration of the hero, Dan Cooper, parachuting out of a plane. (You can see the comic cover at FBI—In Search of D.B. Cooper at https://archives.fbi.gov/archives/news/stories/2009/march/in-search-of-d.b.-cooper. I can't show it here because it's copyrighted.)

The idea of D. B. Cooper as a Canadian is further supported by the language he used in his instructions to Florence Schaffner that the ransom be paid "in negotiable American currency." This is not generally how an American would refer to US dollars. Others see the comic inspiration as a possible indicator that D. B. Cooper had lived or served abroad or overseas, thus giving him an opportunity to be exposed to the Dan Cooper comics in Canada or Europe. Marla Cooper recalled her uncle being a fan of the stories and having a Dan Cooper comic tacked to his wall.

THE TIE

Never in the history of modern fashion has so much attention been paid to a polyester clip-on tie. The FBI described the tie as "A black clip-on tie which contained a tie clip, yellow gold in color, with a round, white pearl in the center. ... The tie bore the label 'Towncraft,' a trademark of the J.C. Penney Company."

Hijacker's clip-on tie from JCPenney left on board the airplane. (FBI.gov)

Tacky as it may have been, when it comes to the Cooper hijacking, the tie is haute couture. It may well hold the clues that could eventually break the case.

DNA Testing—Garbage In, Garbage Out

A possible partial DNA profile for the hijacker has been derived from a sample taken from the black clip-on tie from JCPenney the man calling himself Dan Cooper left on board the airplane. Several Raleigh cigarette butts smoked by the hijacker during the flight were recovered by the FBI but were, unfortunately, lost before DNA testing became a known forensic technique. The loss of the cigarette butts is an event that has waved a red flag before the conspiracy theory fringe who claim the FBI was covering up the hijacking. Additionally, fingerprints assumed to belong to the subject were recovered from the plane.

Denise Diana Huddle

However, the FBI reportedly had concerns about whether the prints and DNA were actually left by the hijacker, since a commercial passenger jet is a high-traffic public location exposed to the DNA and fingerprints of many individuals coming and going every day. Astonishingly, despite these concerns, over and over the FBI has cleared possible suspects based on this DNA profile.

Worse, there is no evidence I could find in the public domain indicating that the partial profile was ever run through public genealogical databases. If the sample is sufficient to generate the necessary information for entry in the databases, that approach would give the investigators a fighting chance of using genetic genealogy to identify the donor of the DNA.

If it turns out that the DNA found on the tie belonged to a member of the cleaning crew or a loader from the catering service, then all of those possible suspects eliminated from the investigation based on the DNA profile can be thrown back into the suspect pool.

On the other hand, if the DNA could be traced to a relative of someone on the FBI's actual suspect list, that individual would rocket up the chart to the number-one position on the list of D. B. Cooper top-forty hits.

Metal Particles Found on the Tie—Cooper Kryptonite?

A more interesting aspect of the tie is what the Citizen Sleuth group found when the FBI gave them access to it. (The Citizen Sleuths are a team of citizen scientists investigating the Cooper hijacking.) Independent researcher Thomas G. Kaye of the Foundation for Scientific Advancement is the group's primary researcher. Kaye used scanning electron microscopy to determine that, among other metals, the tie contained particles of pure titanium.

Following Bread Crumbs through a Chemical Forest

Titanium is a metal with a wide variety of industrial uses. However, almost all of those uses involve titanium alloys, not pure titanium. Pure titanium is used in chemical manufacturing environments where extreme corrosion protection is required. So, Kaye concluded that the tie had to have been present either in a chemical manufacturing plant or in a metal fabrication plant where chemical manufacturing equipment was made.

Kaye also found particles of pure titanium embedded with stainless steel. The only place such a particle would be found is in a metal fabrication facility. Spiral chips of 500 series cast or 5000 series wrought aluminum were also present on the tie. The only way that aluminum is rendered into a spiral shape is as a shaving from the work of a metal lathe, drill press, or other similar equipment—again pointing to a metal fabrication plant producing equipment for use in chemical manufacturing.

In January 2017, Kaye reported that he and his team had discovered particles containing the rare earth minerals cerium and strontium sulfide on the Cooper tie. These minerals were used in a variety of aerospace applications in the era of the Cooper hijacking, including Boeing's supersonic transport development project. This suggested that Cooper could have either been a Boeing employee or a contractor who was present around the supersonic project.

Three Specs and a Patent

More recently, a Cooper researcher named Eric Ulis in Arizona made sense of another element found on Cooper's tie. Kaye's team found three specs of a titanium-antimony alloy in their analysis of the tie. Ulis discovered that a metallurgical company headquartered in Midland, Pennsylvania, called Rem-Cru Titanium, Inc., received a patent in 1957 for a titanium-antimony alloy. Ulis says that the alloy was never sold by the company, leading him to believe that the only place that alloy could have been found was inside of the Rem-Cru facility where it was developed.

Of further interest is the fact that Rem-Cru Titanium was a Boeing contractor, and representatives from Rem-Cru regularly traveled to Boeing's facility in Seattle to conduct business. These visits may have offered the hijacker an opportunity to learn about the rear stairs of the 727. It also could explain the familiarity of the hijacker with the Northwest region of the United States.

Kaye observed that metal workers in fabrication facilities did not wear ties. In 1971, the only employees in those facilities who wore ties were either executives or engineers. While clip-on ties have long been the stuff of children's clothes and cheap men's attire, there is one group who have always worn clip-on ties—professional men who work around industrial equipment. If a traditional necktie were to become caught in machinery, the wearer could be seriously injured or even killed. Yet, a clip-on tie will safely snap off. An engineer working in or around a metal fabricating plant who encountered industrial equipment as part of his job would most likely have worn a clip-on tie. Better to be a fashion disaster than to be choked to death by a Louis Vuitton.

THE RECOVERED MONEY

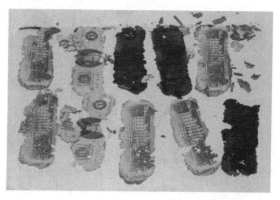

Hijacking ransom bills recovered at Tena Bar. (FBI.gov)

Babe in the Woods

On February 10, 1980, nine years after the hijacking, eight-and-a-half-year-old second grader Brian Ingram of Vancouver, Washington, was helping his father lay wood for a fire during a family outing to the Tena Bar stretch of the Columbia River when he discovered a packet of soggy, buried twenty-dollar bills totaling $5,800. When the family returned to their home in Vancouver, Brian's parents set the badly decomposed cash on the counter to dry.

Do the Feds Take Trade-Ins?

During a break at his job the next day, Brian's father called his bank to see if the soggy bills could be replaced with fresh cash. The bank advised Mr. Ingram that the exchange could be made if the serial numbers on the bills were still legible and did not appear on any of the bank's lists of stolen money.

The next day, Mr. Ingram called the FBI about the cash. The agents soon discovered that the few serial numbers still legible were on the list of bills provided to D. B. Cooper during his hijacking of Flight 305. The FBI began an exhaustive search of the area where

Brian found the cash, but found only tiny bits of bills. Funny how a second grader accomplished more in fifteen minutes than the entire federal law enforcement establishment had been able to do in nine years of working on the case.

Money, Money...You're Out of Time

The working theory was that the cash had been buried by Cooper upon his landing then dislodged by the dredging of the Columbia River by the Army Corps of Engineers. However, the engineers hadn't dredged that stretch of the river since October of 1974. The money was discovered above the dredge layer in the soil and depositional profile, indicating that the money was deposited at the location on Tena Bar sometime substantially later than 1974—at least three years after the hijacking.

In 1980, Thomas Kaye and his coauthor, Mark Meltzer, discovered a discreet selection of algae particles (diatoms) on one of the Cooper bills discovered by Brian Ingram. In the conclusions section of their paper published in the journal *Nature*, they describe how the genera, abundance, and elemental signatures of the algae particles found on the bills indicate the money was not submerged during November, but was more likely put in the water during May or June. Also, their research indicated that a human burial of dry bundles of cash was unlikely. In summary, the researchers stated, "Finding summer diatoms rules out the theory that Cooper landed in the river in November, soaking the money and then buried some of it on shore." Their conclusion: the hijacking of the plane and the burial of the money did not take place at the same time.

CHAPTER 14

THE CODED NOTES

Hey, Mr. Postman—Is There a Letter to the Editor in Your Sack for Me?

In the months and years following the hijacking, at least six notes and letters were sent to various news outlets, primarily on the West Coast, claiming to be from the hijacker. Considerable energy has been applied to discerning hidden codes within these communications that might expose the identity of Dan Cooper. However, there has never been any conclusive proof the letters actually came from the hijacker, let alone that they contained hidden or encoded messages. Nonetheless, some of the code-breaking efforts have shown interesting results.

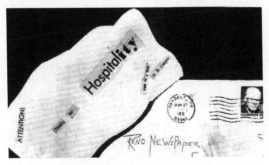

Thanks for the Hospitality note sent to the *Reno Gazette*.
(*Reno Gazette*, November 29, 1971)

FIRST NOTE TO THE RENO GAZETTE, *RENO, NEVADA (#1)*

A pasted-up note received on Monday, November 29, 1971, read:

> ATTENTION: Thanks for the hospitality.
>
> was in a rut.
>
> D.B. Cooper

The letter was postmarked November 27, 1971, in Oakdale, California, a small town fifteen miles northeast of Modesto. The *Modesto Bee* confirmed that four of the eight words were cut from the Friday, November 26, 1971 issue of their paper.

LETTER TO THE PROVINCE, *VANCOUVER, BC, CANADA (#2)*

A handwritten note was received December 1, 1971, by the chief editor of *The Province*, a newspaper in Vancouver, BC, Canada. The note read:

> Chief Editor,
>
> The Province
>
> The composite drawing on Page 3 as suspected by the FBI does not represent the truth.
>
> I enjoyed the Grey Cup game. Am leaving Vancouver.
>
> Thanks for your hospitality.
>
> D.B. Cooper

The letter was postmarked in Vancouver, Canada, on November 30, 1971.

SECOND NOTE TO THE RENO GAZETTE, *RENO, NEVADA (#3)*

Another pasted-up note was received by the *Reno Gazette* on December 2, 1971. It read:

> plan ahead for Retirement Income
>
> D.B. Cooper

The note was postmarked in the Sacramento area on December 1, 1971.

FIRST NOTE TO THE OREGONIAN, *PORTLAND,* OREGON (#4)

The hand-printed note read:

> I am right here in Portland! And the $200000 is for revolution.
>
> D.B. Cooper

The note was postmarked on December 3, 1971.

LETTER TO THE SEATTLE TIMES, *THE* LOS ANGELES TIMES, *THE* NEW YORK TIMES, *AND THE* WASHINGTON POST *(#5)*

(Typewritten.)

Sirs,

I knew from the start that I wouldn't be caught.

I didn't rob Northwest Orient because I thought it would be romantic, heroic or any of the other euphemisms that seem to attach themselves to situations of high risk.

I am no modern day Robin Hood. Unfortunately do have only 14 months to live.

My life has been one of hate, turmoil, hunger and more hate, this seemed to be the fastest and most profitable way to gain a few fast grains of peace of mind.

I don't blame people for hating me for what I've done nor do I blame anybody for wanting me to be caught and punished, though this can never happen.

Here are some (not all) of the things working against the authorities:

I'm not a boasting man

I left no fingerprints

I wore a toupee

I wore putty make-up

They could add or subtract from the composite a hundred times and not come up with an accurate description; and we both know it.

I've come and gone on several airline flights already and am not holed up in some obscure backwoods town. Neither am I a psycho-pathic killer. As a matter of fact I've never even received a speeding ticket.

Thank you for your attention.

D.B. Cooper

Denise Diana Huddle

ccccccc

Wash Post – 717171684*

New York Times –

Seattle Times –

Los Angeles Times – 7698QA2753

The typed letter received by the *Seattle Times* was postmarked on December 11, 1971, somewhere in the Seattle area.

SECOND NOTE TO THE OREGONIAN, *PORTLAND, OREGON (#6)*

The *Oregonian* received another typewritten letter purporting to be from D. B. Cooper.

March 28, 1972

The Portland Oregonian Newspaper

Portland, Oregon

Gentlemen:

This letter is to let you know I am not dead but really alive and just back from the Bahamas, so your silly troopers up there can stop looking for me. That is just how dumb this government is. I like your articles about me but you can stop them now. D.B. Cooper is not real.

I had to do something with the experiences Uncle taught me, so here I am, a very rich man. Uncle gave too much of it to world idiots and no work for me. I had to do it to relieve myself of frustration. I want out of the system and saw a way through good old Unk. Now you know. I am going around the world and they will never find me because I am smarter than the system's lackey cops and lame duck leaders. Now it is Uncle's turn to weep and pay one of it's own some cash for a change. (And please tell the lackey cops D.B. Cooper is not my real name.)

Sincerely,

A Rich Man

The letter was postmarked in Jacksonville, Florida.

DECODING THE LETTERS

Over the years, countless attempts have been made to decode the letters and evaluate their contents. Were they really sent by the hijacker? If so, what clues did they contain to his identity? Unfortunately, there have never been satisfactory answers to these questions. The most recent and widely publicized is the effort by the Case Breakers.

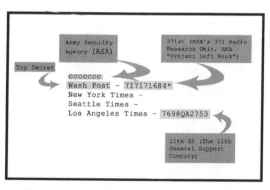

Bottom section of the letter to the *Seattle Times* with Sherwood's interpretation. (Denise Huddle)

The Case Breakers received a tip that the hijacker was a former pilot for the Army Security Agency in Vietnam named Robert W. Rackstraw. Former government codebreaker Rick Sherwood (a member of the same unit as Rackstraw) used a mathematical method of assigning numerical values to letters, and using this method, he determined that "please tell the lackey cops" from the sixth letter has a numerical total of 269. He then determined that using the same values for the letters of "I'm Lt. Robert W. Rackstraw" also equals 269. Sherwood applied the same methodology to link other parts of the letters to various designations and inside information from their unit in Vietnam.

While some modern cryptographers applaud Sherwood's work, one skeptic in the field complained that the method Sherwood used is not conclusive, is easily manipulated, and is highly subjective, pointing out that, using Sherwood's method, "I am SpongeBob SquarePants" also equals 269.

CHAPTER 15

INVESTIGATOR'S COMMENTS

My favorite of the currently known suspects is Richard McCoy. First and foremost, McCoy demonstrated he could successfully exit a 727 through the ventral stairs and parachute safely to the ground and get back to civilization in one piece with his loot. Not only was he was a highly accurate copycat, but he seemed to learn from Cooper's previous experience, and I'm not sure how much of that learning could have been done from the information publicly available at the time.

McCoy brought his own notes with him and skipped the problems associated with dictating his demands to the flight attendant who just happened to have paper and a pen in her purse. He also brought warm jump clothes packed in a checked bag that he had the airlines deliver to the base of the airstairs. He threatened to remotely detonate a bomb after he jumped if he saw chase planes following the 727 as they had done during the Cooper hijacking, thus eliminating the risk of a chase plane breaking off after he jumped and pinpointing his landing spot. Perhaps most importantly, he chose a route that did not involve jumping into rocky terrain in a dense forest.

While McCoy was a masterful hijacker, he wasn't so skilled in the getting-away-with-it component of the crime. He was arrested at 5:30 a.m. on Sunday, May 21, 1972, just forty hours after the hijacking. Held without bail, he was captured as a result of his wife's concerns over her own involvement in the scheme that ultimately led to his sister-in-law calling his best friend, a state trooper, who then alerted the FBI.

If McCoy was Cooper, then one might wonder where his wife was during the planning and execution of the first hijacking and why he made the fatal error of involving her in the second crime. Furthermore, if you believe the letters to the press were actually written by the Cooper hijacker, then it is unlikely that McCoy was Cooper because he was in jail when many of the notes were written and mailed.

While Marla Cooper strikes me as a credible and honest person, her claim (or at the very least insinuation) that L. D. Cooper disappeared after the hijacking seems questionable to me. Ms. Cooper implies that this disappearance indicated a consciousness of guilt on her uncle's part. Yet, Ms. Cooper even admits seeing L. D. herself twice during the year following the crime when the hijacker should have been the most vigilant about laying low. If I can find multiple past addresses and vital records for L. D. Cooper using nothing but my Ancestry.com subscription, I doubt he was actually hiding at all.

In the end, I believe that it is the metal particles from the tie that will ultimately solve the puzzle. While the DNA and fingerprints collected from the Cooper plane could have come from an infinite number of sources, the pure titanium didn't come from inside the 727, and it strains credulity to believe it was contamination from touch transfer during the flight. If the Cooper hijacker purchased the tie at Goodwill, then the particles could be attributable to activities of the tie's previous owner. But if the tie was originally purchased and worn only by the hijacker, then I believe the titanium-antimony alloy particles will eventually lead investigators to the perpetrator.

So who was D. B. Cooper? Maybe he was one of the countless suspects that the FBI ruled out...or maybe he was someone who never so much as blipped any law enforcement radar. While many

Denise Diana Huddle

said the hijacker could not have survived the jump, no body was ever found. Maybe his remains are just waiting for a hiker or hunter to discover them. Or maybe he hit the ground running and walked out of the woods and into the ether. None of the ransom money was ever reported in the banking system, and besides the $5,800 found by Brian Ingram, none of it was ever recovered. By now, over fifty years later, whoever he was, he's probably gone to that big airport in the sky, so we may never know for sure who he was and what happened to him after the airstairs went bump in the night.

Meanwhile, I'll be glued to Eric Ulis's website (EricUlis.com) for details about where the titanium-antimony alloy particles take him on one more man's search for Dan Cooper.

INVESTIGATOR'S TIPS

After talking about Cooper's hijacking, I thought this might be a good time to focus on a few tips for flying safe. Professor Ed Galea, a fire and evacuation expert and founding director of the Fire Safety Engineering Group at the University of Greenwich in London, conducts research on the topic. Professor Galea has some tips for surviving an air disaster:

- Sit close to the exits as every second counts in the event of an emergency. He suggests being within five rows of the nearest exit. More distance from the exit equals less chance of survival after a crash.
- Keep your shoes on in preparation for an escape. There may be dangerous debris on the plane's floor during a crisis.
- Recognize those seat belts aren't exactly like the ones in your vehicle. Airplane seat belts release by lifting a lever, not depressing a button. It's easy to revert to common muscle memory under extreme stress.

- Before takeoff, count the number of seat rows from yours to the nearest exit in case the plane cabin fills up with smoke or the lights go out in the event of a crash.
- Remember the "plus three, minus eight" rule: Close to 80 percent of all plane crashes occur during the first three minutes after takeoff and the last eight minutes before landing. Be extra vigilant during these times. Don't sleep, keep your shoes on, and be on the lookout for trouble and ready to react.

QUIZ

Test your knowledge about the D. B. Cooper case.

D B Cooper, Where Are You? Quiz | U.S. History | 10 Questions
https://www.funtrivia.com/trivia-quiz/History/D-B-Cooper-Where-Are-You-343995.html

SNARKY HUMOR

I found this at EAA.org. There are a bunch of funny announcements on their Jokes page.

This is a transcript of a Southwest flight attendant doing the preflight safety briefing. I think it's a scream.

"In the event of a sudden loss of cabin pressure, masks will descend from the ceiling. Stop screaming, grab the mask, and pull it over your face. If you have a small child traveling with you, secure your mask before assisting with theirs. If you are traveling with more than one small child, pick your favorite."

REFERENCES & COOL SITES

The Notes & Letters

Technology: D.B. Cooper Letters
https://ronmilione.blogspot.com/2011/11/db-cooper-letters.html

Skyjacker D.B. Cooper revealed real identity in 1972 letter to The Oregonian, code-breaker claims | OregonLive.com
https://www.oregonlive.com/news/erry-2018/06/cc9c62a1082655/the_real_db_cooper_provided_en.html

FBI Credible Lead DB Cooper Suspect Print May Confirm Ransom Man Dead | Wacktrap
https://www.wacktrap.com/events/unusual-events/fbi-credible-lead-db-cooper-suspect-print-may-confirm-ransom-man-dead

Were These Taunting Letters Really from D.B. Cooper, the Mysterious 1971 Hijacker? | HISTORY
https://www.history.com/news/db-cooper-case-fbi-letters

The Hunt for DB Cooper – letter sent by "DB Cooper" in 1971 is now causing a flap | The Mountain News – WA
https://themountainnewswa.net/2012/06/18/the-hunt-for-db-cooper-letter-sent-by-db-cooper-in-1971-is-now-causing-a-flap/

D.B. Cooper 'secret ciphers' released, point to key suspect; cryptology experts say, Not so fast | OregonLive.com
https://www.oregonlive.com/news/erry-2018/08/76268e4b361333/db-cooper-secret-ciphers-relea.html

DB Cooper Sleuths Tout New Evidence on Infamous Hijacking | Courthouse News Service
https://www.courthousenews.com/db-cooper-sleuths-tout-new-evidence-on-infamous-hijacking/

Crew Notes
https://website.thedbcooperforum.com/Crew-Notes-More/

PowerPoint Presentation | DBCooperHijack.com
https://dbcooperhijack.com/wp-content/uploads/2022/06/Crew-Notes-1.pdf

The Ransom Money

Diatoms on DB Cooper's Cash | ERIC ULIS :: The Official Site
https://ericulis.com/pages/diatoms-on-db-coopers-cash

D B Cooper's Loot
https://www.check-six.com/lib/DBCooperLoot.htm

DB Cooper ransom money found buried along Columbia River entered the water months after skyjacking | Daily Mail Online
https://www.dailymail.co.uk/news/article-8589339/DB-Cooper-ransom-money-buried-Columbia-River-entered-water-months-skyjacking.html

DB Cooper Money Serial Number Search
http://www.hcscapps.com/dbcoopermoney/Default.aspx

DB Cooper case gets new clues in tiny algae found on ransom money, study says | Fox News
https://www.foxnews.com/science/db-cooper-case-new-clues-tiny-algae-ransom-money

Diatoms constrain forensic burial timelines: case study with DB Cooper money | Scientific Reports
https://www.nature.com/articles/s41598-020-70015-z

The Vault — D.B. Cooper Part 67 | FBI
https://vault.fbi.gov/D-B-Cooper%20/d.b.-cooper-part-67/view

The Tie

The Tie - D.B. Cooper
https://dbcooperhijack.com/the-tie/

Titanium Particles from Cooper's Tie
https://citizensleuths.com/titaniumparticles.html

ERIC ULIS' COMPLETE DB COOPER THEORY IN 9 MINUTES | YouTube
https://www.youtube.com/watch?v=jFkssI_CmwQ

DB COOPER Investigation Update | YouTube
https://www.youtube.com/watch?v=zxh3UNMOA8g

The Cooper Vortex E11 - DB Cooper Wore a Tie - Tom Kaye | YouTube
https://www.youtube.com/watch?v=zphHuKBU8xQ

Tie Clip | CitizenSleuths.com
https://citizensleuths.com/tie-clip.html

The Suspects

D.B. Cooper suspect was surveyor; brother worked for Boeing | The Seattle Times
https://www.seattletimes.com/seattle-news/
db-cooper-suspect-was-surveyor-brother-worked-for-boeing/

Mystery of DB Cooper: What The HBO Film Left Out About LD Cooper
https://screenrant.com/
mystery-d-b-cooper-hbo-documentary-l-d-cooper-leaves-out/

The Odd Story of Richard Floyd McCoy Jr | Fear of Landing
https://fearoflanding.com/history/
the-odd-story-of-richard-floyd-mccoy-jr/

Richard Floyd McCoy, Jr. | FBI
https://www.fbi.gov/history/famous-cases/richard-floyd-mccoy-jr

Mystery of D.B. Cooper: What The HBO Film Left Out About Richard McCoy
https://screenrant.
com/d-b-cooper-hbo-documentary-richard-floyd-mccoy-leaves-out/

Skyjacker—The Richard McCoy Jr. Story
https://parachutist.com/Article/skyjackerthe-richard-mccoy-jr-story

Who was L.D. Cooper? | Local&State | BendBulletin.com
https://www.bendbulletin.com/localstate/who-was-l-d-cooper/
article_8c861ce7-9696-53d0-bf56-642014234d5c.html

Cold Case Team | The Case Breakers
https://thecasebreakers.org/

DB Cooper suspect Robert Rackstraw, 75, dies nearly 48 years after the legendary hijacking | Daily Mail Online
https://www.dailymail.co.uk/news/article-7230447/DB-Cooper-suspect-Robert-Rackstraw-75-dies-nearly-48-years-legendary-hijacking.html

DB Cooper: Robert Rackstraw, Accused in History Channel Show, Denies Accusation | People
https://people.com/crime/db-cooper-robert-rackstraw-accused-in-history-channel-show-denies-accusation/

Rackstraw: 5 Fast Facts You Need to Know | DB Cooper
https://dbcooper.com/robert-rackstraw-5-fast-facts/

The Stairs & The Cooper Vane

The Problem With The Boeing 727's Rear Door
https://simpleflying.com/boeing-727-rear-door-problem/

How one elusive man changed aircraft design: The D.B. Cooper story | AeroTime
https://www.aerotime.aero/articles/24238-db-cooper-story

History

Boeing Bust (1969-1971) | HistoryLink.org
https://historylink.org/File/20923

General

Timeline of D.B. Cooper | New York Magazine
https://nymag.com/news/features/39617/

D.B. Cooper | Crime Museum
https://www.crimemuseum.org/crime-library/cold-cases/d-b-cooper/

Research Conclusions
https://citizensleuths.com/summary.html

The D.B. Cooper Hijacking And The Haunting Mystery Behind It
https://allthatsinteresting.com/db-cooper

D.B. Cooper | Hijacking, Investigation, Parachute, Money Serial Numbers, Suspects, & Facts | Britannica
https://www.britannica.com/biography/D-B-Cooper

DB Cooper – Parachute Conundrum Still Unresolved | The Mountain News – WA
https://themountainnewswa.net/2021/01/31/
db-cooper-parachute-conundrum-still-unresolved/

DB Cooper case heats up again with controversy over parachutes | The Mountain News – WA
https://themountainnewswa.net/2011/10/25/
db-cooper-case-heats-up-again-with-controversy-over-parachutes/

Tina Mucklow Now: Where is DB Cooper's Stewardess Today? Update
https://thecinemaholic.com/
where-is-db-coopers-stewardess-tina-mucklow-now/

dbcooperfinalupdated.pdf
https://martinandrade.files.wordpress.com/2014/12/
dbcooperfinalupdated.pdf#

Finding DB Cooper: Chasing the Last Lead in America's only Unsolved Skyjacking: Andrade Jr, Martin, Andrade Sr, Martin G | Amazon
https://www.amazon.com/Finding-DB-Cooper-Americas-skyjacking/
dp/1539694429/

DB Cooper news: Interview with author Martin Andrade | The Mountain News – WA
https://themountainnewswa.net/2017/11/08/
db-cooper-news-interview-with-author-martin-andrade/

Flight Path
https://website.thedbcooperforum.com/Flight-Path/#

Robert H. Edwards's Blog: Great 20th century mysteries - D.B. Cooper and Flight 305: the chase planes - May 16, 2022 23:21
https://www.goodreads.com/author_blog_posts/22541040-d-b-cooper-and-flight-305-the-chase-planes

D.B. Cooper: Flight Attendant Tina Mucklow Opens Up | Rolling Stone
https://www.rollingstone.com/culture/culture-features/db-cooper-tina-mucklow-untold-story-1111944/

In Search of D.B. Cooper | FBI
https://archives.fbi.gov/archives/news/stories/2009/march/in-search-of-d.b.-cooper

DB Cooper - Google Docs
https://docs.google.com/document/d/1tS_XP7GekGlB8idOZUK3ffGgcdUyfe3ipR5hFm0p3vY/edit#!#

A tale of the '70s: When D.B. Cooper's plane landed in Reno
https://www.rgj.com/story/news/2014/11/24/reno-retro-db-coopers-plane-landed-reno-airport/70049690/

Tips

How to Survive a Plane Crash: 10 Tips That Could Save Your Life | The Art of Manliness
https://www.artofmanliness.com/skills/outdoor-survival/how-to-survive-a-plane-crash-10-tips-that-could-save-your-life/

How to survive a plane crash | BBC NEWS | Magazine
http://news.bbc.co.uk/2/hi/uk_news/magazine/5402342.stm

PART 4

WHO WAS THE ZODIAC KILLER?

CHAPTER 16

WHAT HAPPENED?

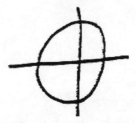

The Zodiac symbol. (Denise Huddle image)

Between December 20, 1968, and October 11, 1969, the killer known as the Zodiac attacked at least seven victims, killing five of them. The Zodiac operated in the town of Vallejo and in rural Napa County, California, in the northern part of the Bay Area before moving into one of the priciest neighborhoods in San Francisco. The killer sent multiple communications to the media and the police after the murders, four of which contained coded messages. As of today, only two of the four ciphers have been broken.

BACKGROUND

It was the time of change, and it was the time of fighting to keep things the same. In short, 1968 was a year of social and political chaos. Widely considered to be a critical societal turning point in American history, 1968 saw the very fabric of American society fraying around the edges. Evening news broadcasts were filled with images of that fabric in flames as radicalized college students burned flags and draft cards during protests against the Vietnam War.

The Age of Aquarius

Hair! opened on Broadway in April of 1968 as the first rock musical to ever see a Broadway stage. But, despite a theme song that won two Grammy awards and topped the charts, the sympathy and understanding promised by the lyrics were definitely not abounding in America. Racial tension, radical feminism, and escalating antiwar sentiment mixed together to create a perfect storm of social revolution across the country—and much of the counterculture that drove that revolution was born and incubated in the Bay Area of Northern California. The University of California at Berkeley, Golden Gate Park, and the Haight-Ashbury District of San Francisco were at the forefront of the movement.

In 1968, 549,500 American soldiers, sailors, and Marines were fighting in the jungles of Southeast Asia, and 16,592 of them died there in that year alone. Racial tensions boiled over in the streets and on college campuses across the country while women demanded their own place at the American table. Tommie Smith and John Carlos raised black-gloved fists in the Black Power salute during their medal ceremony at the Olympics in Mexico City a month after 200 protesters gathered outside the iconic Miss America pageant in Atlantic City, New Jersey, and stuffed brassieres, girdles, and makeup into flaming Freedom Barrels, giving birth to the era of bra burning.

Cascading Dominoes of Disaster

Every month of 1968 brought a new crisis. The year began with the Tet Offensive that changed the entire dynamic of the war in Vietnam. In February, Walter Cronkite, beloved newscaster and one of the most trusted voices in American media, ended his evening news broadcast with a blistering editorial about Vietnam, concluding that the war was unwinnable.

On the heels of Cronkite's commentary, in March 1968, word began to seep out of Vietnam about an incident in the remote hamlet of My Lai. In what came to be called the My Lai Massacre, US Army soldiers killed at least 347 unarmed civilians in cold blood. The Pentagon's initial lies about the incident and subsequent whitewash and sham investigations were ultimately unmasked in 1969 when a former soldier wrote letters describing the incident to several members of Congress, the chairman of the Joint Chiefs of Staff, and the president. The story escalated into a full-scale disaster for the military, ultimately leading to the conviction of Lt. William Calley for multiple counts of murder. Calley's trial inflamed the nation and undermined most of the remaining vestiges of support for the Vietnam War.

April brought the assassination of civil rights leader Martin Luther King Jr. in Memphis. As news of the assassination filled the airwaves, riots broke out across the country. Conditions in the US capital were so bad that the Marines and the National Guard were called in to restore order.

With the country still reeling from the death of Dr. King, in June, Robert Kennedy was assassinated in Los Angeles while leaving a campaign event, transforming the upcoming presidential election into a political tinderbox. The rapidly escalating national tension culminated in August when a riot erupted outside of the Democratic National Convention in Chicago. Republican Richard Nixon was elected as the thirty-seventh president of the United States on November 5, further polarizing the country.

By the end of the year, America was angry, divided, exhausted, and on a hair trigger.

It was in this tense and violent atmosphere that on December 20, on a dark road in the rural Northern California town of Benicia, the Zodiac struck for the first time. The murder site was a half hour north of the Haight-Ashbury District of San Francisco, where the social revolution was boiling over. That night was the beginning of a year-long reign of terror perpetrated by a bizarre killer whose identity remains a mystery to this day.

The Zodiac's random and grotesque murders seemed to embody the violent and chaotic times of 1968 and 1969. Ever since, America's fascination with the mystery of the Zodiac murders has manifested itself throughout modern culture. The world has paid approximately two billion 2022 US dollars at the box office to see the five major blockbuster films inspired by the killings: *Dirty Harry* (1971), *Exorcist III* (1990), *Seven* (1995), *Zodiac* (2007), and *The Batman* (2022). The website Goodreads lists fifty-four full-length books on the subject, and a Google search for "zodiac killer" yields almost fourteen million results. Fifty-five years later, people are still fascinated by the Zodiac.

As with the senseless carnage of the Vietnam War and the tragic deaths of Martin Luther King Jr. and Bobby Kennedy, when it comes to the Zodiac, for over half a century, America has longed to know "Why?" Amateur and professional cryptographers have spent countless hours trying to break the Zodiac's ciphers, while retired detectives and criminal profilers have scoured every available piece of evidence—all in search of answers about who he was and what drove him to kill.

CHAPTER 17

THE CRIMES

THE JENSEN/FARADAY MURDERS—SLAUGHTER OF THE ALL-AMERICAN KIDS

BETTILOU JENSEN, 16, AND DAVID FARADAY, 17
Young couple were slain on first date near Vallejo

Betty Lou Jensen and David Faraday.
(San Francisco Examiner)

David Faraday and Betty Lou Jensen were high school students who had met a few weeks prior at a church youth group function. When Betty Lou's parents agreed to let her go on her very first date ever on December 20, 1968, David, an Eagle Scout, promised to have her back by 11:00 that evening. They never made it home.

Shortly after 11:00 p.m., witness Stella Medeiros was driving down rural Lake Herman Road when she discovered David and

Betty Lou lying in the road by David's Rambler station wagon. The terrible scene was tucked into a secluded spot near the gate to a pumping station on the outskirts of Benicia, California, just outside the city limits of the town of Vallejo.

Ms. Medeiros sped toward town, where she found a Benicia policeman and summoned aid. Benicia officers raced to the location. Betty Lou was already dead when police arrived, shot five times in the back. David was found next to the Rambler still alive with a bullet wound in his head, but he died at the scene.

Betty Lou was buried in Skyview Memorial Lawn cemetery in Vallejo. David Faraday's body was cremated after a funeral service where he was saluted by a full honor guard of his fellow Boy Scouts.

The Murder Weapon from Sears

In the late 1960s, Sears, Roebuck and Company evolved from the down-home, all-American mail-order catalog where mostly rural America had shopped since 1892 into a fresh, hip, more urban version of itself, offering new departments like the Junior Bazaar where young women could purchase go-go boots, miniskirts, and bell-bottoms.

Yet, despite these concessions to the fads of the time, the Sears catalog was still the consumer's bible, and their core customer base was still rural America.

Between 1908 and 1962, Sears marketed a line of sporting goods manufactured for the company under the J. C. Higgins brand. John Higgins was a real Sears employee who hired on with the company in 1898 and worked there his entire career before retiring as the company's head bookkeeper in 1930.

The gun used to kill Jensen and Faraday was identified as possibly being a J. C. Higgins Model 80 semiautomatic pistol. The J. C. Higgins Model 80 was manufactured by the High Standard Firearms company exclusively for Sears, Roebuck and Company.

Super-X shell casings found at the Jensen/Faraday crime scene.
(Police photo/ZodiacKillerFacts.com)

Using shell casings found at the crime scene, police identified the ammunition used as Winchester Western Super-X copper-coated. Ballistic evidence indicated that the killer used a .22-caliber hand gun.

The Witnesses

One witness driving in the area between 9:30 and 10:00 that night reported passing a blue sedan, possibly a Valiant, coming from Benicia toward Vallejo. The vehicle passed the witness, stopped, turned around, and drove behind them at a high rate of speed. The witness took the turnoff to Benicia, and the blue car continued ahead. The witness reported seeing two white subjects in the blue car.

David Faraday's Rambler station wagon.
(Crime scene photo/ZodiacCiphers.com)

Baa, Baa, Black Sheep, Have You Any Clues?

A sheep herder named Bingo Wesner who was working in the area reported seeing the station wagon and another car parked abreast of it at the entrance to the pumping station at 10:00 p.m. He described the other car as a white Chevrolet Impala sedan.

Around 11:00 p.m., a couple drove through the area so the husband could check on equipment and pipe on-site for a construction project. They reported seeing two people in the station wagon twice— on their way to check on the equipment and upon returning from the inspection. The male driver was sitting upright and the female passenger was sitting next to him with her head on his shoulder.

According to the police report, the couple checking the construction site also stated that the only other vehicle they saw was one red pickup truck with wooden sideboards parked next to the gate. They described a man about twenty-eight years old in dark clothes standing next to the gate with a long-barreled gun in his hand while an older man exited the truck.

These men in the red pickup were subsequently identified as raccoon hunters named Frank Gasser and Robert Connelly. They were interviewed, and their weapons were checked for ballistics and cleared. The hunters reported seeing a white four-door 1959 or 1960 model Chevrolet Impala parked a few feet from the station wagon driven by the murder victims when the hunters arrived at the location around 9:00 p.m.

The raccoon hunters and another witness all reported seeing the Rambler parked facing one direction at 10:15 p.m. and then facing the opposite direction at 10:30 p.m.

Later on in the investigations, a fourteen-year-old witness came forward and reported that while traveling to Blue Rock Springs on Columbus Parkway, he saw a blue 1963 Impala with two people inside turn onto Columbus Parkway toward Blue Rock Springs at 10:30 p.m.

Will the Real Impala Please Stand Up

It is not clear to me if the white four-door 1959 or 1960 model Chevrolet Impala seen parked by the Rambler at 9:00 p.m., the blue maybe-a-Valiant that chased the witness between 9:30 and 10:00 p.m., the white Impala seen parked by the Rambler at 10:00 p.m., and the blue 1963 Impala with two people inside seen turning onto Columbus Parkway at 10:30 p.m. are the same vehicle.

As an investigator, I find the description of the "white four-door 1959 or 1960 Chevrolet Impala" given by the raccoon hunters to be the most credible. The amount of detail and the mention of "1959 or 1960" implies to me that the witnesses could differentiate between model years of Impalas and were communicating a degree of certainty and specificity about what they saw.

I am most suspicious of the description of the "blue car, possibly a Valiant" because the vehicle was chasing the witness on remote roads in the dark. A moving vehicle seen by a driver under stress in their rearview mirror at night would likely be difficult to identify accurately.

I am also curious as to how the fourteen-year-old witness came to be at the location—was he a passenger in a vehicle? Was he walking, riding a bicycle, or driving illegally? And how could a kid that young say with certainty he saw a 1963 Impala? While it's entirely possible his account was accurate, I would want further information on the witness before assigning his statement a particular weight in my evidence pool.

Once in a Blue Moon

The moon was in a waxing crescent phase with only 1 percent illumination on the night of December 20, 1968. In Vallejo that night, sunset was at 4:52 p.m., so it would have been full dark by no later than 6:00 p.m. According to historical weather records, the night was clear. It's reasonable to assume the site where the Rambler was parked was used as a lovers' lane in part because of its relative lack of artificial lighting.

In evaluating the witness sightings and various descriptions of cars seen that night, I wonder about the available lighting at the locations where the vehicles were encountered by the witnesses. Certain types of lighting change the appearance of vehicle colors, so I would want to explore what lighting was present at each location to determine if white cars in one location could have taken on a blue cast at another before deciding that the white and blue vehicles were not the same car. In any case, in my opinion, investigators would have been reasonable searching for a blue or white 1959–1963 Impala.

FERRIN/MAGEAU ATTACK—BLUE-COLLAR VICTIMS AT BLUE ROCK SPRINGS

Darlene Ferrin and Michael Mageau. (ZodiacKiller.com)

Chevrolet Death Trap

Ralph Nader released his book *Unsafe at Any Speed* in 1965, condemning the American automobile industry for design flaws that Nader viewed as potentially life-threatening to consumers. His book focused on the dangers he saw in the suspension of the 1963

Chevrolet Corvair. The Corvair became a symbol of Nader's consumer rights movement targeting iconic American car companies and corporate disregard for consumers in general—a movement that occupied a prominent place in the tapestry of the '60s social revolution. But the awful harm that came to Darlene Ferrin and Mike Mageau in Darlene's 1963 Corvair had nothing to do with her car's controversial suspension system. Instead, the danger they faced came from a mysterious killer armed with a 9mm Lugar.

Unlike Betty Lou Jensen, who was killed while out on her very first date with a boy she met at church, Darlene Ferrin was a twenty-two-year-old waitress living with her second husband and infant child. During her marriage to Dean Ferrin, Darlene was frequently seen in the company of other men. While David Faraday was a seventeen-year-old high school student and an Eagle Scout, Mike Renault Mageau was a nineteen-year-old laborer who had been arrested for petty theft on September 6, 1968.

In the early hours of July 5, 1969, after the fireworks displays were over and the holiday celebrations were winding down, Darlene and Mike were parked at the Blue Rock Springs Golf Club in Vallejo in Ferrin's brown Corvair when they were shot multiple times. Darlene Ferrin was killed, but Mike Mageau survived multiple gunshot wounds.

The Witching Hour

Officer Richard Hoffman of the Vallejo Police Department reported checking the parking lot at the Blue Rock Springs Golf Club at around 11:55 p.m. on July 4, 1969. At that time, he found the lot empty. At 12:10 a.m. on July 5, a female citizen called the Vallejo Police Department and reported that two juveniles were being shot in the Blue Rock Springs parking lot. Officer Hoffman returned to the lot and found the victims near Ferrin's Chevrolet.

Hoffman called Solano Ambulance to transport the victims and rode with them to the Kaiser Foundation Hospital. Darlene Ferrin was pronounced dead on arrival. Officer Hoffman spoke to Mike Mageau while he was being treated. Mageau told Hoffman a white man older than Mageau drove up in a car, got out, walked up to Darlene's Corvair, shone a flashlight inside, and started shooting.

Living to Tell the Tale—The First Zodiac Survivor

Later on, while he was recovering, Mageau gave a more detailed account of the shooting. Mageau reported that Ferrin picked him up in her car at around 11:30 p.m. July 4. While on their way to get something to eat, Ferrin told Mageau she had something she needed to discuss with him, and he directed her to pull over into the Blue Rock Springs Golf Club parking lot. Mageau reported that Darlene turned the ignition off and extinguished the car's headlights, but left the radio playing. When the victims were discovered, the car's engine was running and the headlights were on.

Shortly after the couple's arrival in the empty parking lot, a group of rowdy young kids arrived at the same time in three separate cars, laughing and shooting off fireworks. The group departed just minutes after they got there.

About five minutes after the rowdy kids left, another car pulled into the lot coming from the direction of Springs Road and Vallejo. The car parked six to eight feet from Ferrin's Corvair and cut its lights. Over various interviews, Mageau described the car as similar in shape to Ferrin's vehicle, either a late-model Corvair or Ford Mustang, brown, but lighter in color than Ferrin's car.

Baby, Let Me Be Misunderstood

Mageau asked Ferrin if she recognized the car and reported her response as "Oh, never mind." He never understood whether that meant Ferrin did or did not recognize the brown car. Mageau stated that shortly after pulling in and parking next to them, the car exited the parking lot and sped off toward Vallejo.

He's Baaaack

Approximately five minutes later, the car returned and parked about ten feet behind Ferrin's Corvair. This time, the driver left the lights on as he exited the vehicle and approached Ferrin and Mageau with a high-powered flashlight. Both Ferrin and Mageau perceived the man as a policeman.

Mageau reported he heard muffled shots and felt pain then tried unsuccessfully to climb into the back seat for protection. The shooter turned the gun on Ferrin and fired multiple shots before walking back toward his car. When Mageau made a noise, the shooter returned to the Corvair and shot the victims two more times each before casually heading back to his vehicle.

Mageau opened his door and fell out of the car as the shooter was backing up and turning to exit the parking lot. He reported the rear of the car bore California license plates. Mageau saw the assailant leave the parking lot and speed on Blue Rock Springs Road toward Springs Road and Vallejo and described the attacker as a white male, twenty-six to thirty years old, five-eight, heavyset and beefy without being "blubbery," weighing 195–200 pounds with short, curly light brown or blond hair and wearing a short-sleeved blue shirt. The man had a "large face" that Mageau saw only from the side.

He told police he had not been involved in any recent conflicts, and that Ferrin had not mentioned any similar problems to him, either.

Dial M for Double Murder

At 12:40 a.m., an anonymous male caller contacted the Vallejo Police Department and confessed to the crime to dispatcher Nancy

Slover. The police report said the substance of the call was: "I want to report a double murder. If you will go one mile east on Columbus Parkway to the public park, you will find the kids in a brown car. They were shot with a 9mm Luger. I also killed those kids last year. Goodbye." The call was traced to a gas station pay phone at Joe's Union at the intersection of Springs Road and Tuolumne in Vallejo. You can see a talk by Ms. Slover about the call on YouTube at https://www.youtube.com/watch?v=-kDPcR9VYN8.

Two partial fingerprints were lifted from the right door handle, and one was taken from the back of the front seat on the driver's side of Ferrin's Corvair.

The Mystery Man in the Pink Truck

Darlene Ferrin's sister, Linda Doris del Buono, told police about a part-time bartender named "George." According to del Buono, George unsuccessfully pursued a romantic relationship with Darlene Ferrin. Ms. del Buono thought that George had a pink pickup truck and a brown car that was possibly a Corvair. She described George as a short and stocky man with brown hair and a volatile personality who didn't like it at all when Darlene didn't pay enough attention to him. Ferrin told her sister that she was afraid of George and only acted friendly toward him to placate him. Ferrin also told del Buono that George had threatened to rape her, but she had been able to talk him out of it. Ferrin's husband, Dean, told police that he had met George once and sold him his 1951 Ford half-ton faded red pickup truck.

On July 11, 1969, Vallejo police detectives John Lynch and Clarence "Ed" Rust located George (last name redacted from police report) in Yountville, California, and interviewed him. George denied ever threatening Darlene and stated that he had been at a softball game for a team he managed around 10:30 a.m. on July 4. After the game, he came home and took a nap then went to Calistoga for a fair. That night, around 7:00 p.m., he and his wife went to see fireworks and returned home around 11:00 p.m. and did not leave the house after that. He stated that he was a citizen of the Philippines and did not own a gun. I found nothing in the public records available online indicating if the police verified this alibi.

A Suspect Seed Is Planted

The police report is chock full of suspects reported by citizens and acquaintances of the victims, all of whom seem to have been tracked down and eliminated by police. Of particular interest, though, is the brief mention of an interview with one Arthur Leigh Allen. Arthur Leigh Allen later became one of the primary suspects in the Zodiac murders.

SHEPARD/HARTNELL ATTACK—THE EXECUTIONER & THE PICNICKERS

Police sketch of Lake Berryessa attacker based on Bryan Hartnell's description. (ZodiacKiller.com)

In 1847, the town of Monticello sprung up on a Mexican land grant originally made to brothers José de los Reyes and Sexto "Sisto" Berelleza. (The Berelleza name was pronounced "Berryessa" by local non-Spanish speakers.) For a hundred years, the town prospered, and its three hundred or so citizens farmed the fertile soil of Napa County's Berryessa Valley along the banks of Putah Creek.

In 1953, after a lengthy battle to save their homes failed, a successful condemnation proceeding allowed the government to force sales of the land on which the town was built for the construction of the Monticello dam. The entire community of Monticello was leveled in the name of progress. The graves of the Monticello cemetery were disinterred and moved to a new location. But the grave of Sexto Berelleza could not be found, and his remains were left to rest under the lake—and to bear silent witness to the terrible events that took place on its banks.

Controversy continued to plague the project as the government granted leases to seven concessionaires to develop park and recreation facilities around the new lake—facilities that had been promised to the public to ease opposition to the condemnation process. In spite of their commitments to build recreational infrastructure, the concessionaires built trailer parks instead, citing better cash flow from the leased trailer spaces.

It was next to this symbol of progress and the devastating toll it can take on people who get in its way that on September 27, 1969, Cecelia Ann Shepard and Bryan Calvin Hartnell drove in Hartnell's white 1956 Karmann Giah to Lake Berryessa. Shepard, twenty-two, from Loma Linda, California, was a student at the University of California at Riverside and a former girlfriend of Hartnell's. Hartnell, twenty, from Troutdale, Oregon, was a student at Pacific Union College in Angwin.

Shepard and Hartnell were picnicking near the lake when Shepard noticed a strange man observing them from behind a tree. After having been noticed, the man walked away. Around 6:15 p.m. they noticed a man approaching them wearing a black executioner's hood and dark clothing with a white symbol of a cross over a circle on the chest. He was carrying a gun in a holster on his right hip and had a long-blade knife in a sheath on his left hip. Bryan Hartnell described the man as over six feet tall with a heavy build, weighing between 200 and 250 pounds.

The man claimed he was an escapee from a prison in Deer Lodge, Montana, and said he was robbing them for money to fund his escape to Mexico. Hartnell offered the man his wallet and keys, but the man didn't take them. He tied the couple up with precut lengths of plastic line and stabbed them with the long-blade knife, attacking Hartnell first, then Shepard.

A man named Ronald Fong at the nearby Rancho Monticello Resort overheard the couple screaming and called park rangers. Rangers responded and summoned Napa County sheriff's deputies and an ambulance from the Piner Ambulance Company. Both victims were transported to the Queen of the Valley hospital.

Shepard died there from her wounds two days later on September 29, 1969. Shepard's funeral services attracted a huge crowd of mourners, and she was buried at Saint Helena Cemetery in Napa County. Hartnell recovered from his wounds and is now an attorney in Southern California. While Bryan Hartnell gave many interviews in the first few years after the attack, he is no longer discussing the case with the news media.

I just called to say I killed someone.

An hour and ten minutes after the Lake Berryessa attack, the Zodiac killer called the Napa County Sheriff's Office. When dispatcher Dave Slaight answered the call, the man said, "I want to report a murder, no, a double murder. They are two miles north of Park Headquarters. They were in a white Volkswagen Karmann Ghia. I'm the one that did it." The caller stopped communicating with the dispatcher but left the receiver lying on the shelf beneath the phone. With the help of the telephone company and local media, the pay phone from which the call was made was located at the Napa Car Wash near the corner of Main and Clinton Streets in Napa. Fingerprints were retrieved from the pay phone.

The Handwriting on the Car Door

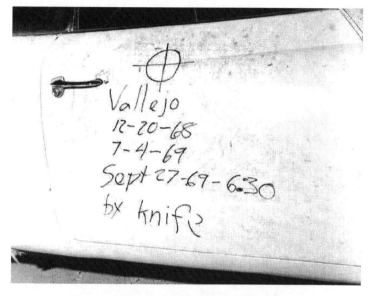

Message left by the Zodiac on Bryan Hartnell's car.
(FBI.gov/Wikimedia Commons)

Responding officers found a message left for them by the perpetrator as evidence that the murder was the work of the killer calling himself the Zodiac. The message was written in black marker on the door of Hartnell's Karmann Ghia. Under the distinctive symbol of the Zodiac, he listed the dates of the Jensen/Faraday murders, the Ferrin/Mageau attack, and the Shepard/Hartnell attack.

Police photograph of boot print left at the Lake Berryessa site.
(Napa County Sheriff's Office/ZodiacKiller.com)

These Boots Are Made for Wing Walkin'

Shoe prints recovered at the Lake Berryessa crime scene indicated a suspect weighing more than 210 pounds. A probation officer recognized a cast of one of the prints as having been derived from a type of boot associated with the US Air Force. The probation officer put detectives in contact with a mechanic from Travis Air Force Base who advised that the boot was called a chukker, issued to members of the USAF during basic training at Lackland Air Force Base in San Antonio, Texas. The mechanic advised that both military and civilian employees at the nearby Travis Air Force Base frequently wore the boots, which were government issue sometimes sold as surplus and were designed primarily for use while walking on the wings of airplanes. Further investigation determined that the print was made by a size 10 ½ R in the military version or 10 ½ D in the civilian version of a boot commonly referred to as a Wing Walker.

Police sketch of Lake Berryessa attacker.
(ZodiacCiphers.com)

See the USA in Your Chevrolet

Tire tracks indicated the killer had parked behind Hartnell's car. Multiple witnesses at the Lake Berryessa park reported seeing a tall, heavy-set white male driving a silver-blue late-model two-door Chevrolet coupe with California plates in the immediate area of the attacks the afternoon before the crime.

The investigator in me is remembering the white or blue Chevy Impalas seen at and around the Lake Herman crime scene. I'm still curious about the lighting effects on the vehicles seen making the color fluctuate between blue and white. And don't forget Mike Mageau's description of the Chevrolet Corvair with California plates at the Blue Rock Springs scene.

Denise Diana Huddle

Heard It through the Grapevine...or the Newswire

Convicts Escape

DEER LODGE (AP) — Two prisoners escaped late Sunday from the medium security compound at the state prison near Deer Lodge.

They were identified as Carl Pierce, 27, and Ronald Woods, 22. Acting Prison Warden Charles Dell said the two men cut the fence behind the baseball backstop at Rothe Hall, about 9 p.m. Sunday.

He said Pierce, who had been in the prison since Nov. 5, 1968, was serving an eight-year sentence from Custer County for robbery. He was a miner by occupation.

Woods was serving a 15-year sentence for first-degree assault from Lewis and Clark County. A brick layer by occupation, he has been in the prison since July 12, 1960.

Dell said the escapes are the first since he took over Aug. 19 after the Board of Institutions discharged the former warden, E. C. Ellsworth.

Security guards were searching the area around the compound in the Deer Lodge Valley. Dell said there were no immediate reports of stolen vehicles.

Article about Deer Lodge prison break.
(*Helena Independent-Record*/Newspapers.com)

In an excellent piece of forensic archival research, the host of the website ZodiacKiller.com, Tom Voigt, has recently made an important discovery. He found newspaper articles describing an escape from the state prison right outside of Deer Lodge, Montana, on September 21, 1969, just six days before the Berryessa attacks. The fugitives were subsequently arrested a little over a month later on October 28 in Portland, Oregon.

It is unlikely that the Zodiac was one of the escapees as he claimed, because the men were either incarcerated at the time of the previous Zodiac attacks (Lake Herman Road and Blue Rock Springs) or had been captured before the last murder (Stine killing). However, I find it fascinating that the Zodiac knew about this obscure prison break.

According to the 1970 census, Deer Lodge was home to 4,681 people—hardly a bustling metropolis. Voigt discovered that the article about the prison break was an AP story that was picked up by only four newspapers he could find, all of them in Montana.

Since there was no such thing as the internet or an online newspaper archive in 1969, Voigt reasons that the Zodiac either had some connection to Deer Lodge, Montana, through which he could have heard about the prison break, or had access to the AP wire where he could have learned about it. Of all the case materials I've read, I find this information about the Deer Lodge prison escape to be one of the most significant clues in the case data pool.

THE STINE KILLING—DEATH OF THE SCHOLAR CABBIE

In the 1960s and '70s, the Tenderloin District of San Francisco was a crime-infested nest of vice and graft. A concentration of single-room occupancy hotels catered to residents paying by the day as they teetered on the precipice of homelessness. The district was also a haven for San Francisco's gay and lesbian community. Ironically, the gritty neighborhood was wedged between some of San Francisco's most exclusive communities. It was at the northeastern border of the Tenderloin that the Zodiac encountered his seventh victim.

Twenty-nine-year-old graduate student Paul Stine was scheduled to receive his PhD in English from San Francisco State in January 1970. The San Francisco State English department was at the epicenter of the longest student strike against an academic institution in US history. Students from the Black Students' Union, the Third World Liberation Front, and other student organizations went on strike from November 6, 1968, to March 21, 1969, demanding more representation for students of color within the university. The catalyst for the strike was the firing of Stine's classmate, George Murray, a graduate student and instructor in the English department and a high-ranking member of the Black Panther party.

Stine drove a taxi part-time to support himself and his wife while he was in graduate school. On October 11, 1969, at around 9:45 p.m., Stine picked up a fare at Mason and Geary Streets in the Tenderloin in Yellow Cab #912. The passenger directed Stine to an address in the prestigious Presidio Heights neighborhood located a little over three miles away near the southeastern corner of the army post, the Presidio of San Francisco.

A representative from the Yellow Cab company told investigating officers that Stine's last fare was dispatched to him at 9:45 p.m. to pick up a passenger at 500 9th Avenue, Apartment 1, approximately three and a half miles due west of the Mason and Geary pickup. Stine never showed up at the 9th Avenue address.

At the northeast corner of Washington Street at the intersection of Washington and Cherry, Stine stopped the cab, and the passenger shot Stine once in the head behind the right ear.

After Stine's body was discovered, the meter on his taxi was running and had a fare of $6.25 showing at 10:46 p.m. The taxi company and police interpreted this information from the meter to mean that Stine had picked up the killer on his way to the 9th Avenue assignment.

The Three Kids in the Window

Three teenagers were watching the scene from the window of the house directly across the street, approximately fifty feet from where Stine's taxi was parked. They reported never hearing the shot, but watched as the killer sat in the front passenger's seat of the taxi doing something they interpreted as rifling Stine's pockets.

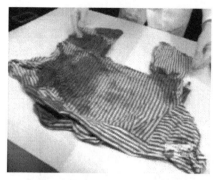

Evidence photo of Paul Stine's shirt.
(San Francisco Police Department)

In fact, the killer cut pieces from Stine's shirt and took his wallet and taxi keys. The witnesses watched as the attacker wiped down the inside of the taxi with a white cloth before exiting the front passenger's door and walking around to the driver's side where he wiped off the exterior of the car then casually walked down Cherry Street toward the Presidio. The witnesses called the police, and an ambulance was summoned by responding officers. Upon its arrival, Stine was pronounced dead at the scene at 10:10 p.m.

Denise Diana Huddle

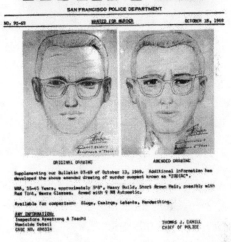

Wanted poster for the Zodiac suspect for Paul Stine's murder.
(San Francisco Police Department)

The witnesses described the killer to police. The following is an excerpt from the police report:

WMA [WHITE MALE ADULT], in his early forties, five-eight, heavy build, reddish-blond "crew cut" hair, wearing eyeglasses, dark brown trousers, dark (navy blue or black) "Parka" jacket, dark shoes. Suspect should have many bloodstains on his person and clothing, suspect may also be in possession of the keys to the Yellow Cab, possibly has wallet belonging to the victim. Suspect is armed with a gun. Last seen walking north on Cherry St. from Washington St.

Ebony Is Not Ivory

Somehow, the message broadcast to law enforcement immediately after the murder described the suspect as a Black male, not a white male. In a painful irony, Officers Donald Fouke and Eric Zelms spotted a male subject who Donald Fouke later described as a white male adult, thirty-five to forty-five years old, five-ten, 180–210 pounds. Thinking they were looking for a Black male, the officers continued their search. When the officers learned that the subject was in fact white, not Black, they proceeded onto the army post and searched in the direction where they had last seen the white subject, but they were not able to locate him again.

There is controversy to this day about what exactly transpired between Fouke, Zelms, and the white male subject they saw near the crime scene that night. The Zodiac later reported in a letter that he actually spoke to the officers and sent them in the wrong direction. Fouke and Zelms deny having had a conversation with the man they admit seeing but were never able to find again.

Bloody fingerprints were collected from Stine's taxi. While a taxi is a high-traffic public area, it is very likely that fingerprints left in blood belonged to the perpetrator. However, the fingerprints have never led authorities to the killer.

Until the Zodiac letter arrived in the mail weeks later, law enforcement treated the Stine killing as a robbery murder.

CHAPTER 18

THE LETTERS & CIPHERS

Between July 31, 1969, and July 8, 1974, the Zodiac sent twenty letters to various news outlets and one attorney in the San Francisco Bay Area that are generally considered to be legitimately attributed to the killer. Four of these letters contained ciphers. As of today, two of those encrypted messages have been decoded. The most critical of these twenty letters are discussed in detail below. A complete set of the images can be found on the website Zodiac Killer Letters and Ciphers—Codes, Cryptography at https://zodiackiller.com/Letters.html.

The July 31, 1969 Letters

Shortly after the Ferrin/Mageau attack, the Zodiac mailed three separate letters to news organizations in Northern California—the *San Francisco Examiner*, the *San Francisco Chronicle*, and the *Vallejo Times*. Postmarked in San Francisco on July 31, 1969, the letters contained essentially the same message in which the author took responsibility for the Jensen/Faraday killings (Christmas) and the murder of Ferrin and the attempted murder of Mageau (Fourth of July). Each letter contained one-third of what is known as the "408 cipher" for its 408 characters. The author demanded that the cryptograms included with each letter be published on the front pages of the respective newspapers within the coming week, threatening to go on a murdering rampage if the papers refused to comply with his demands.

Vallejo Times *Letter & Cipher Decoded by Don and Bettye Harden*

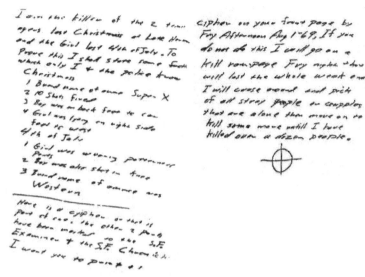

Published in the *Vallejo Times* on August 1, 1969;
decoded cipher from ZodiacKiller.com

Denise Diana Huddle

San Francisco Examiner *Letter & Cipher Decoded by Don and Bettye Harden*

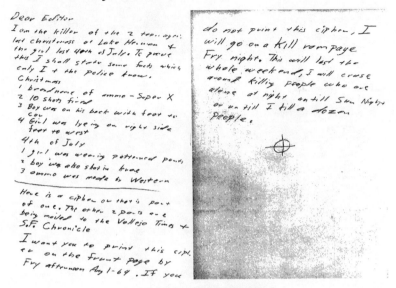

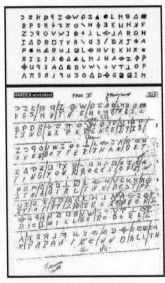

Published in the *Vallejo Times* on August 2, 1969, and
in the *SF Examiner* on August 4, 1969;
decoded cipher from ZodiacKiller.com

San Francisco Chronicle *Letter & Cipher Decoded by* Don and Bettye Harden

Dear Editor

This is the murderer of the 2 teenagers last Christmoss at Lake Herman + the girl on the 4th of July near the golf course in Vallejo To prove I killed them I shall state some facts which only I + the police know.

Christmoss
1 Brand name of ammo Super X
2 10 shots were fired
3 the boy was on his back with his feet to the car
4 the girl was on her right side feet to the west

4th July
1 girl was wearing patterned slacks
2 The boy was also shot in the knee.
3 Brand name of ammo was Western

Over

Here is part of a cipher the other 2 parts of this cipher are being mailed to the editors of the Vallejo times + SF Examiner.

I want you to print this cipher on the front page of your paper. In this cipher is my identity.

If you do not print this cipher by the afternoon of Fry. 1st of Aug 69, I will go on a kill rampage Fry. night. I will cruise around all weekend killing lone people in the night then move on to kill again, untill I end up with a dozen people over the weekend.

Published in the *Vallejo Times* and the *San Francisco Chronicle* on August 2, 1969; decoded cipher from ZodiacKiller.com

Despite the failed efforts of the CIA, FBI, and NSA, the three-part cipher was cracked by a Salinas, California couple a week after it was published. The cipher is what professional cryptographers call a "homophonic substitution cipher." What this means is that while symbols and letters are substituted directly for the actual letters in the original text, more than one symbol or letter is substituted for the same original letter at different points in the message. For example, four different letters and symbols are substituted for the letter *A* at different points in the original text, and seven different letters or symbols are substituted for the letter *E* in the 408 cipher.

Here is the key:

Key to homophonic substitution system used
on 408 cipher. (Denise Huddle image)

Here is the actual translation discerned by high school teacher Donald Gene Harden and his wife, Bettye June:

I LIKE KILLING PEOPLE BECAUSE IT IS SO MUCH FUN IT IS MORE FUN THAN KILLING WILD GAME IN THE FORREST BECAUSE MAN IS THE MOST DANGEROUE ANAMAL OF ALL TO KILL SOMETHING GIVES ME THE MOST THRILLING EXPERENCE IT IS EVEN BETTER THAN GETTING YOUR ROCKS OFF WITH A GIRL THE BEST PART OF IT IS THAE WHEN I DIE I WILL BE REBORN IN PARADICE AND THEI HAVE KILLED WILL BECOME MY SLAVES I WILL NOT GIVE YOU MY NAME BECAUSE YOU WILL TRY TO SLOI DOWN OR ATOP MY COLLECTIOG OF SLAVES FOR MY AFTERLIFE EBEORIETEMETHHPITI

The final eighteen letters (underlined for identification) have never been interpreted in a manner agreed upon by experts. While the FBI confirmed that the Hardens' decoding of the cipher was correct, to this day no one has conclusively determined the meaning of the final eighteen characters. Various individuals have suggested that they are an anagram of some sort for the Zodiac's name or that the letters need to be further decoded before being interpreted as an anagram.

August 4, 1969 Letter (The Debut Letter)

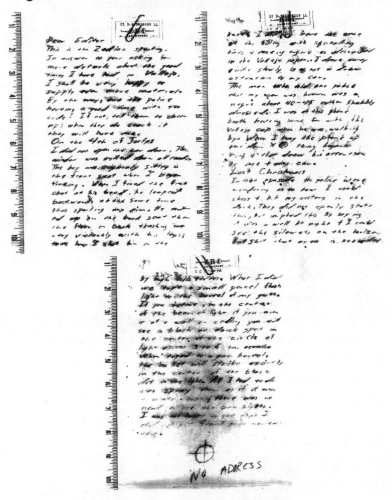

August 4, 1969 letter. (FBI.gov and ZodiacKiller.com)

On August 4, 1969, the *San Francisco Examiner* received a letter from the killer postmarked in San Francisco. This letter is referred to as the Zodiac Debut Letter because it is the first time the killer referred to himself as the Zodiac. In the letter, he provides more detail about the Jensen/Faraday murders and the Ferrin/Mageau attack as proof that he is the actual killer. The FBI determined that the letter was printed on paper watermarked "Fifth Avenue." This is the watermark of the F. W. Woolworth Company. The letter is difficult to read, so here is a transcription:

Dear Editor

This is the Zodiac speaking.

In answer to your asking for more details about the good times I have had in Vallejo, I shall be very happy to supply even more material. By the way, are the police haveing a good time with the code? If not, tell them to cheer up; when they do crack it they will have me.

On the 4th of July:

I did not open the car door, The window was rolled down all ready. The boy was origionaly sitting in the front seat when I began fireing. When I fired the first shot at his head, he leaped backwards at the same time thus spoiling my aim. He ended up on the back seat then the floor in back thashing out very violently with his legs; thats how I shot him in the knee. I did not leave the cene of the killing with squealling tires & raceing engine as described in the Vallejo paper,. I drove away quite slowly so as not to draw attention to my car.

The man who told the police that my car was brown was a negro about 40–45 rather shabbly dressed. I was at this phone booth haveing some fun with the Vallejo cops when he was walking by. When I hung the phone up the dam X@ thing began to ring & that drew his attention to me & my car.

Last Christmass

In that epasode the police were wondering as to how I could shoot & hit my victoms in the dark. They did not openly

Denise Diana Huddle

state this, but implied this by saying it was a well lit night &
I could see the silowets on the horizon. Bull Shit that area is
srounded by high hills & trees. What I did was tape a small
pencel flash light to the barrel of my gun. If you notice,
in the center of the beam of light if you aim it at a wall or
celling you will see a black or darck spot in the center of the
circle of light about 3 to 6 in. across. When taped to a gun
barrel, the bullet will strike exactly in the center of the black
dot in the light. All I had to do was spray them as if it was
a water hose; there was no need to use the gun sights. I was
not happy to see that I did not get front page coverage.

NO ADDRESS

October 13, 1969 Letter (The Stine Letter)

On October 13, 1969, the Zodiac killer sent a letter to the *San
Francisco Chronicle* in which he took credit for the Stine killing,
which, up to that point, had been construed as a robbery murder
of the taxi driver. To authenticate his claims, the killer included a
piece of Paul Stine's blood-soaked shirt. He criticized the police for
their search technique after the discovery of Stine's body and, worst
of all, threatened to attack a school bus full of children.

This is the Zodiac speaking.
I am the murderer of the
taxi driver over by
Washington St & Maple St last
night, to prove this here is
a blood stained piece of his
shirt. I am the same man
who did in the people in the
north bay area.
The S.F. Police could have caught
me last night if they had
searched the park properly
instead of holding road races
with their motorcicles seeing who
could make the most noise. The
car drivers should have just
parked their cars & sat there
quietly waiting for me to come
out of cover.
School children make nice targets, I think I shall wipe out
a school bus some morning. Just
shoot out the front tire & then
pick off the kiddies as they come
bouncing out.

Letter sent to the *San Francisco Chronicle* on October 13, 1969.
(San Francisco Police Department and ZodiacKiller.com)

This is the Zodiac speaking.

I am the murderer of the taxi driver over by Washington St &
Maple St last night, to prove this here is a blood stained piece
of his shirt. I am the same man who did in the people in the
north bay area.

The S.F. Police could have caught me last night if they had
searched the park properly instead of holding road races with
their motorcicles seeing who could make the most noise. The
car drivers should have just parked their cars and sat there
quietly waiting for me to come out of cover.

School children make nice targets, I think I shall wipe out
a school bus some morning. Just shoot out the front tire &
then pick off the kiddies as they come bouncing out.

Denise Diana Huddle

November 8, 1969 Letter (The Dripping Pen Card & the 340 Cipher)

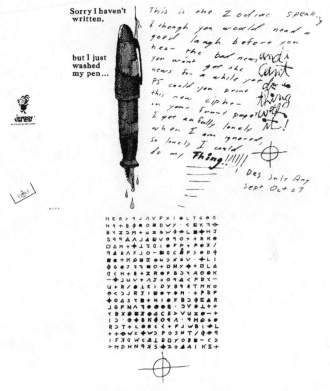

Dripping pen card with message and accompanying 340 cipher. (*Napa Valley Register*)

A greeting card postmarked in San Francisco on November 8, 1969, was mailed to the editor of the *San Francisco Chronicle*. The envelope included a new cipher, now generally referred to as the "340 cipher" because of its 340 letters and symbols. The 340 cipher remained unbroken for fifty-one years and one month until December 11, 2020, when David Oranchak (a software developer from Virginia), Sam Blake (an applied mathematician from Australia), and Jarl Van Eycke (a warehouse operator and computer programmer from Belgium) publicly released the solution to it.

> I HOPE YOU ARE HAVING LOTS OF FUN IN TRYING TO CATCH ME - THAT WASN'T ME ON THE TV SHOW - WHICH BRINGS UP A POINT ABOUT ME - I AM NOT AFRAID OF THE GAS CHAMBER BECAUSE IT WILL SEND ME TO PARADICE ALL THE SOONER BECAUSE I NOW HAVE ENOUGH SLAVES TO WORK FOR ME WHERE EVERYONE ELSE HAS NOTHING WHEN THEY REACH PARADICE - SO THEY ARE AFRAID OF DEATH - I AM NOT AFRAID BECAUSE I KNOW THAT MY NEW LIFE IS LIFE WILL BE AN EASY ONE IN PARADICE DEATH.

In a video describing the process the trio used to break the code at https://www.youtube.com/watch?v=-1oQLPRE21o, David Oranchak describes the three phases of deciphering the message. First, when the team began their work in 2006, they hypothesized that the Zodiac scrambled the original message in some way before substituting the symbols. This meant that the letters and symbols were going to have to be reordered prior to being deciphered.

Sam Blake divided the cipher into three sections: lines 1–9, lines 10–18, and lines 19–20 and then generated approximately 650,000 different ordered permutations of the letters and symbols while Van Eycke wrote a computer program called AZDecrypt to be used in the actual decryption of the reordered cipher. Oranchak began running each of Blake's reordered cryptograms through Van Eycke's program.

On December 3, 2020, one more pass through AZDecrypt yielded a result that was mostly meaningless—except that Oranchak spotted the phrases "hope you are," "trying to catch me," and "the

Denise Diana Huddle

gas chamber" buried in the gibberish of lines 1 through 9 of one of Blake's reordered samples. In the end, the letters and symbols in the first nine lines of the original cipher had to be reordered using a diagonal pattern, starting by writing down the letter or symbol in the upper left-hand corner of the matrix then moving down one and right two symbols, writing that letter or symbol and repeating the process, eventually wrapping over to the lower left corner until all of the symbols had been reordered.

Using a feature of Van Eycke's program that basically forced the program to reexamine the cipher while honoring the letters and symbols assigned to the nongibberish phrases Oranchak had discerned in the previous run, the team was able to refine the decryption process of the top nine lines of the newly ordered cipher.

The team then skipped to the last two lines and applied the same key. While certain words emerged clearly, others appeared to be trash until the team realized the trash was actually words written backward. When these letters were reversed, the words emerged, and the section made sense.

While using the key on lines 10 through 18 yielded some legitimate words, the decipherment was clearly not as complete as it was in first and third sections. The team eventually realized that if the reordering rule applied the same pattern as they used on the first nine lines but first shifted the top left character to the end and the entire reordered cipher was shifted one spot to the right, most of the remaining spelling errors were corrected.

Oranchak knew the team was on the right track when mention of a TV show appeared in the partially deciphered text. On October 22, 1969, a man claiming to be the Zodiac had called into a talk show on ABC hosted by Jim Dunbar. The caller said he was afraid of going to the gas chamber. In the deciphered 340 message, the Zodiac makes it clear that the caller was an imposter.

Here's the final key derived by Oranchak, Blake, and Van Eycke:

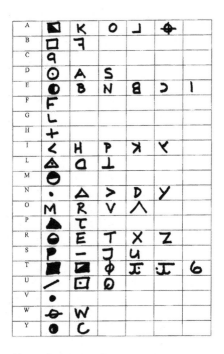

Key to 340 cipher. (Denise Huddle image)

What an amazing effort by three brilliant and creative computer scientists and mathematicians—postulating that the symbols and letters in the cipher matrix had to be reordered before a homophonic substitution cipher could be discerned and applied then plowing through 650,000 permutations until they hit pay dirt. Great work, guys! I highly recommend watching the video where they describe their work.

Slaves in the Afterlife—It's So Hard to Get Good Help in Hell

In the one of the police reports, an investigator described information received from an unnamed expert at the Stanford Research Institute at Menlo Park stating that the idea of slaves serving the dead in the afterlife is a feature of certain Southeast Asian death traditions with particular origins on the Philippine Island of Mindanao. The

Denise Diana Huddle

unnamed expert believed that the author of the ciphers had some exposure to this culture.

Malcolm W. Mintz discussed this idea of slaves in the afterlife in more detail in his monograph *The Philippines at the Turn of the Sixteenth Century*. The concept of slaves accompanying their masters into the afterlife can also be found in texts about Viking death traditions and ancient Egyptian death rituals.

I find it interesting that George, the driver of the faded red pickup truck he purchased from Darlene Ferrin's husband and the same man Darlene Ferrin's sister said Darlene was afraid of, stated that he was a citizen of the Philippines.

November 9, 1969 Letter (The Bus Bomb Letter)

On November 9, 1969, the Zodiac wrote to the editor of the *San Francisco Chronicle* again, this time taunting police about his techniques for evading detection. He stated that a police car stopped him and asked if he had seen anything suspicious immediately following the Stine murder. He went on to gloat about pointing the officers in the wrong direction while he calmly walked away. The policemen involved were supposedly Officers Donald Fouke and Eric Zelms. While these officers acknowledged seeing the suspect (shown with glasses in the famous wanted poster drawing above), they denied ever having stopped and questioned him.

In the November 9 letter, the Zodiac threatened to bomb a school bus. He even included a diagram of the bomb, which explosives experts advised investigators would actually function just as described in the letter. However, no bomb ever went off, and in the April 20 letter, the Zodiac stated that the bomb failed because it was damaged in a heavy rain.

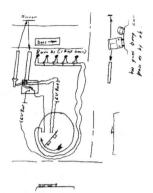

Diagram from the Bus Bomb Letter.
(San Francisco Police Department/ZodiacCiphers.com)

April 20, 1970 Letter (My Name Is Cipher)

This is the Zodiac speaking
By the way have you cracked
the last cipher I sent you?
My name is —

A E N ✦ Ø K ⊖ M ⊖ ⅃ N A M

I am mildly cerous as to how
much money you have on my
head now. I hope you do not
think that I was the one
who wiped out that blue
meannie with a bomb at the
cop station. Even though I talked
about killing school children with
one. It just wouldnt doo to
move in on someone else's teritory.
But there is more glory in killing
a cop then a cid because a cop
can shoot back. I have killed
ten people to date. It would
have been a lot more except
that my bas bomb was a dud.
I was swamped out by the
rain we had a while back.

My Name Is Cipher and letter.
(San Francisco Police Department/ZodiacKiller.com)

In the April 20 letter, the Zodiac claims to have provided his name in a thirteen-character cipher written near the top of the letter. Numerous attempts have been made to decode the name cipher. However, none to date have met with any widespread acceptance. Generally speaking, the longer a cipher, the greater the chance it can be conclusively decoded because there are statistically fewer options in which consistent application of the proposed key will generate a message that makes sense.

Some observers have suggested that the repeating symbol that appears like a figure 8 inside a circle might be a period, and the AEN might be decoded by the words written underneath it "I am," yielding a sentence: "I am Zodiac." However, there is no saying that this is the case because the cipher is too short and the *E, N,* and Zodiac symbol don't occur elsewhere in the cipher.

In 2021, French engineer Fayçal Ziraoui claimed to have cracked the Zodiac killer's final two ciphers. Using the key developed by Oranchak, Blake, and Van Eycke combined with several iterations of systems of substituting numbers for letters then applying what is called a trifid cipher—developed by Félix Delastelle at the turn of the twentieth century—Ziraoui decodes the name to be "KAYR." He takes this to be close to "KANE," which is the surname of one of the police's prime Zodiac suspects. However, many call this likely a false positive, and the FBI has yet to confirm this as a valid result.

June 20, 1970 Letter (Button Letter, Cipher, and Map)

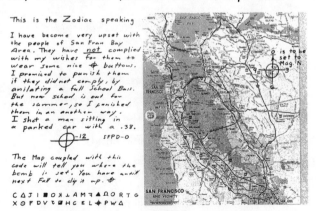

June 20, 1970 Button Letter, Cipher, and Map.
(San Francisco Police Department/ZodiacKiller.com)

Here, the Zodiac says that he has buried a bomb that will blow up a school bus. He has offered the authorities the period of the summer school break to find and disable the bomb, claiming that the location of the device is encoded in the cipher at the bottom of the letter and the attached map.

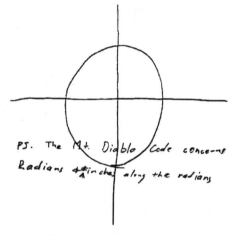

who, but the task of filling up the blanks I rather leave up to you. But it really doesn't matter whom you place upon the list, for none of them be missed, none of them be missed.

PS. The Mt. Diablo Code concerns Radians +#inches along the radians

Last page of the July 24, 1970 letter. (San Francisco Police Department/ZodiacKiller.com)

On July 24, 1970, the Zodiac provided another clue saying that the "code concerns radians and inches along the radians." Despite multiple theories as to the content of the cipher, the device has never been found and no school bus was ever bombed.

Fayçal Ziraoui's interpretation of the cipher reads "LABOR DAY FIND 45.069 NORT 58.719 WEST." which Ziraoui interprets to be a location near a school in South Lake Tahoe. Again, the FBI has not validated this interpretation of the cipher.

CHAPTER 19

SUSPECTS

Over the years, literally thousands of suspects have been considered and dismissed. Of the remaining subjects whose names are bandied about as possible suspects today, most of them are being linked to other crimes that have not been confirmed as Zodiac events. While the Zodiac boasted of many more murders than the five confirmed kills and two attempted murders discussed here, there is no conclusive evidence that these other cases are attributable to the Zodiac.

As far as suspects directly related to the confirmed crimes, in the end, the police mainly focused on two men—Arthur Leigh Allen and Lawrence Kane.

Arthur Leigh Allen—Trailer Park Taxidermist

Arthur Leigh Allen was the most prominent of Zodiac suspects. He was a peculiar man who lived in a trailer filled with dissected specimens of small animals. He was a disgraced sailor and convicted child molester who wore a watch with the Zodiac symbol on it. He confided in his friend, Don Cheney, that he wanted to write a book about a killer who would murder couples, taunt the police with letters, and call himself Zodiac. He was described as being nearly obsessed with a 1924 short story by Richard Connell called "The

Most Dangerous Game" in which a villain named General Zaroff lures sailors to shipwreck then rescues them only to hunt them like animals on his remote island. The story contains language almost identical to that in one of the Zodiac communications. If you'd like to read the short story, you can find it at http://www.dukeofdefinition.com/dangerous_game.pdf.

The Vallejo police report mentioned an initial interview with Allen, who described his actions on September 26 and 27, 1969, at the time of the Berryessa attacks. Allen reported skin diving at Salt Point Ranch and then returning home, where he lived with his parents, on September 27 somewhere between 2:00 and 4:30 that afternoon. He reported staying home the rest of the day and could not recollect if his parents were home or not.

Arthur Leigh Allen eventually became the prime suspect in the series of murders. Yet, in the end, police determined that he did not contribute the DNA collected from the backs of the stamps on the Zodiac letters. His palm print did not match one collected from a Zodiac letter, and his fingerprints did not match the bloody prints taken from Paul Stine's taxi, Yellow Cab #912. Law enforcement regrettably had to dismiss Arthur Leigh Allen as a viable suspect.

Allen died of natural causes on August 26, 1992, in his home at 32 Fresno Street in Vallejo, California.

Lawrence Klein aka Lawrence Kane

US Naval Reserve mug shot of Lawrence Kane, 1943 (LawrenceKane.Wordpress.com) and Identikit composite of Lake Berryessa suspect (ZodiacKillerInfo.com).

Lawrence Kane not only matched the physical description of the Zodiac, but he was known to Darlene Ferrin. Kane was identified in a lineup by both of Darlene Ferrin's sisters as a man who Darlene knew and was afraid of. Darlene told others that she had seen Kane kill someone.

Kane had serious neurological and psychiatric problems. He was involved in a motor vehicle accident in 1962 wherein he sustained major brain damage that significantly impaired his impulse control. He had a lengthy criminal record, including peeping tom and prowling charges, one of which was in Redwood City only four months before the first killing. An only child raised by a single mother, he had documented psychiatric issues related to his relationship with his mom—problems serious enough they led to his separation from the Navy. Kane lived two and a half blocks from the spot where Paul Stine picked up the Zodiac the night he was murdered.

Substantial circumstantial evidence linked Kane to later murders that may or may not have been perpetrated by the Zodiac in Lake Tahoe and Las Vegas.

This is the Zodiac speaking

I am rather unhappy because
you people will not wear some
nice ⊕ buttons. So I now
have a little list, starting with
the woeman + her baby that I
gave a rather interesting ride
for a coupple howers one
evening a few months back that
ended in my burning her
car where I found them.

Kathleen Johns letter.
(San Francisco Police Department/ZodiacKiller.com)

A woman named Kathleen Johns identified Kane as the man who kidnapped her and her daughter on March 23, 1970. Johns stated that Kane sabotaged her vehicle on a dark road just west of Modesto on Highway 132 then drove her and her daughter around the outskirts of Tracy, California. Subsequently, Johns's car was found burned where she had left it by the side of the road.

Initially, at the police station, Johns saw a flyer with the artist's sketch of the Zodiac and immediately said that was the man who had kidnapped her. Years later, she picked Kane out of a six-photo lineup. In a letter mailed to the *San Francisco Chronicle* on July 24, 1970, the Zodiac took credit for the Johns kidnapping.

Lawrence Kane (also spelled Cane) aka Lawrence Klein aka Lawrence Kaye died May 19, 2010, in Reno, Nevada. By virtue of his service in the US Navy, he was interred in the Northern Nevada Veterans Memorial Cemetery in Fernley, Nevada.

I did not find any mention in the record of attempts to match fingerprints and DNA from the Zodiac crime scenes and correspondence to Kane, so I have no idea if this has been done or not. That said, all other things being equal, I like Kane as a suspect.

CHAPTER 20

INVESTIGATOR'S COMMENTS

As an investigator, I'm always asking myself why subjects do the things they do and why they do them in the way they do. This information is a function of a subject's identity, background, and personality. More importantly, often these motivations and methodologies are so second nature to the subject that they cannot or do not even think to disguise their manifestations.

Symbology of the Zodiac Ciphers—And Now, with the Weather...

The origin of the symbols used by the Zodiac is a topic of considerable interest. Of all the symbols in the world, why did the Zodiac use the ones he chose? Many of the symbols are frequently used in road maps, geologic maps, and weather maps. For example, the triangle with a dot in the center substituted for the letter *S* in the 408 cipher is used as a symbol for sleet or ice pellets in weather mapping and an indicator of a survey marker on geologic maps.

I have not yet discovered any one single set of map symbols that includes all of the symbols used by the Zodiac. However, in the macro sense, it seems reasonable to postulate that the killer borrowed map symbols for use in his ciphers. In any case, the symbols

the killer chose were somehow significant in his world of meaning...
a world we may never fully understand.

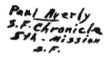

Avery envelope, October 27, 1970. (San Francisco
Police Department/ZodiacKiller.com)

48	60	61	62	63	64	65
Fog, depositing rime ice, sky visible.	Rain, not freezing, intermittent (slight at time of observation).	Rain, not freezing, continuous (slight at time of observation).	Rain, not freezing, intermittent (moderate at time of observation).	Rain, not freezing, continuous (moderate at time of observation).	Rain, not freezing, intermittent (heavy at time of observation).	Rain, not freezing, continuous (heavy at time of observation).

NOAH weather symbols for fog and rain. (Station
Model Chart/WeatherBriefing.com)

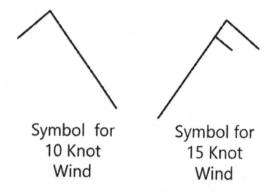

Symbol for
10 Knot
Wind

Symbol for
15 Knot
Wind

Weather symbols for wind speed and direction.
(Station Model Chart/WeatherBriefing.com)

Denise Diana Huddle

Of particular interest to me is the symbol found on the envelope of a letter sent on October 27, 1970, to Paul Avery, a reporter for the *San Francisco Chronicle*. It appears to me that the symbol in the upper left-hand corner of the envelope is closely associated with the weather map symbol groups for fog, for wind speed and direction, and for rain.

Meteorologists utilize a complex notation system for simultaneously indicating various aspects of the current weather conditions. I think it would be well worthwhile to have a meteorologist knowledgeable about the 1960s style of this notation system evaluate the Zodiac writings for general impressions.

Also, the Zodiac marks the map in the June 20, 1970 letter with "0 is to be set to Mag. N." Magnetic north is a different point from geographic north. This is a relatively sophisticated earth science concept. In the July 24, 1970 letter, the Zodiac provides another clue to the June 20 cipher saying that the "code concerns radians and inches along the radians." Radians are an alternative to degrees as a unit of measure for angles. Check out the drawings on page 204 to convince yourself that these concepts are not common knowledge.

The codes, the symbols, and the maps point to earth science and mathematics to me. There's clearly a military flavor with the ciphers and the Wing Walker boots. Exposure to the culture of the Philippines also could point toward military service. I'm not sure what that gets anyone, but I'll bet that the Zodiac had some experience beyond that of the average citizen with science, math, maps, and the military.

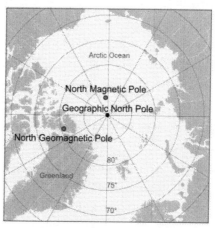

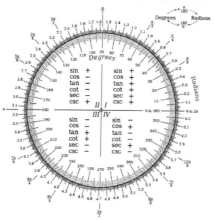

Map showing geographic vs. geomagnetic north and tool
for converting degrees to radians. (Wikipedia)

We can only hope with the advancement of DNA technology and the explosion of participation in the family history DNA databases that someday the Zodiac can be identified from genetic material found in the saliva on the backs of the postage stamps on his correspondence. Possibly the new insights into the Zodiac's cryptographic techniques revealed by the amazing work done decoding the 340 cipher will lead to a conclusive decipherment of the remaining two coded messages, one of which supposedly is the killer's name. Maybe someday, someone cleaning out an attic will discover decades-old evidence that conclusively identifies the Zodiac.

Until then, we will be left to wonder about the identity of the killer who embodied the chaos and violence of the late 1960s on a year-long killing spree perpetrated at the epicenter of the social revolution.

INVESTIGATOR'S TIPS

Since we have been talking about murders that took place in public venues in or around cars, I thought it might be a good time for a few personal safety tips for drivers. First, here are some handy pointers from the Washington DC Metro Police:

- Drive in the center lane to make it harder for potential carjackers to approach your car.
- Avoid driving alone. Travel with someone whenever possible, especially at night.
- When you are coming to a stop, leave enough room to maneuver around other cars, especially if you sense trouble and need to get away.
- Always drive with the doors locked.
- Don't stop to assist a stranger whose car has broken down. Instead, keep on going and use your cell phone to call the police for help.
- Park in well-lit areas, near sidewalks or walkways.
- Avoid parking near dumpsters, large vans or trucks, woods, or anything else that limits your visibility.
- Try to park in a garage with an attendant. Leave only the ignition key, with no identification.

- Even if you're rushed, look around before you get out of your vehicle and stay alert to the surroundings.
- Trust your instincts. If the situation doesn't "feel right," get to safety.

Here are a few tips from me:

- If you feel uncomfortable, do whatever you have to do to be safe. If you make a scene and the other party is completely innocent, apologize and they should understand. If they don't, well…screw 'em. It's better to have some stranger pissed at you than to be in the trunk of a maniac's car.
- Don't confuse feminist independence with foolhardy risk-taking. Just because you are a self-determined, professional woman fully equipped with your own set of big-girl panties does not mean that you should ever go into any situation where you don't feel safe. There is no shame at all in retreating back into that garage elevator and getting the security guard from the lobby to escort you to your car. That bad vibe you felt could well be a life-saving message from your subconscious telling you to get the hell out of Dodge.
- Keep your car in tip-top shape. Make certain that all routine maintenance is done in a timely manner. Find a shop you trust that won't milk you and be certain they check the whole vehicle over every time you take it in for oil changes and tire rotations. Don't ignore check engine lights, strange noises, or odd behaviors in your car. In a pinch, you may be trusting your life to that machine. You need to be able to rely on your equipment.
- Don't get in the car without your cell phone. Make sure you have a fully charged backup battery and working charging cable inside the car within easy reach and ready to go. Plug your phone into the car to charge as soon as you get in so

Denise Diana Huddle

it's not low if you encounter trouble. If you have to use your backup battery, be sure you charge it fully and put it back in the car as soon as you get home.

- Always have a plan. Driving on the highway alone after dark? Be aware of your surroundings and make sure you have a plan in case of car trouble or someone trying to run you off the road, ram you, or block you. Watch the mile markers so you know where you are in case you have to transmit your location. If your car has the option of an on-board emergency button, pay the subscription fee and be sure the service is working.

QUIZ & FUN

Try this quiz to see how much you know about the Zodiac now.

Unsolved: The Zodiac Killer Quiz | Criminals | 10 Questions
https://www.funtrivia.com/trivia-quiz/People/Unsolved-The-Zodiac-Killer-299289.html

Would you like to encipher your own message into Zodiac code? Here is an incredibly fun site where you can do just that:

Zodiac Killer Cipher - Online Decoder, Solver, Translator
https://www.dcode.fr/zodiac-killer-cipher

SNARKY HUMOR

I'm not big on talking politics in public, but I am from Texas… and this was just too good to pass up. I had no idea until I searched "Zodiac memes" on Pinterest that there is an entire genre of

Senator-Ted-Cruz-as-the-Zodiac-killer memes. It's obviously a joke since Cruz wasn't even born until 1970—over a year after the murders took place. But, he really does look kind of like the Lake Berryessa drawing… Sorry, Senator Cruz.

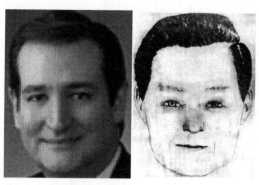

REFERENCES & COOL SITES

The Ciphers

Zodiac Letters & Ciphers — The Zodiac Killer
https://www.zodiackiller.com/Letters.html

Zodiac Killer's Final Two Ciphers Claimed To Be Solved By Amateur Sleuth
https://allthatsinteresting.com/zodiac-killer-cipher-solved

The Zodiac Ciphers: What We Know | HISTORY
https://www.history.com/news/the-zodiac-ciphers-what-we-know

Zodiac Killer's cipher has been solved by amateur code breakers | CNN
https://www.cnn.com/2020/12/11/us/zodiac-killer-cypher-340-code-trnd/index.html

Denise Diana Huddle

Let's Crack Zodiac - Episode 5 - The 340 Is Solved! | YouTube
https://www.youtube.com/watch?v=-1oQLPRE21o

Zodiac Killer Cryptogram Z-340 Decrypted News | HYPEBEAST
https://hypebeast.com/2020/12/
zodiac-killer-cypher-51-years-decrypted-news

The Zodiac Killer's Cipher Is Finally Cracked After 51 Years |
WIRED
https://www.wired.com/story/
zodiac-killers-cipher-finally-cracked-after-51-years/

Cryptologists Crack Zodiac Killer's 340 Cipher | Threatpost
https://threatpost.com/cryptologists-zodiac-killer-340-cipher/162353/

The Zodiac Ciphers | Boxentriq
https://www.boxentriq.com/code-breaking/zodiac-ciphers

Unsolved! The History and Mystery of the World's Greatest Ciphers
from Ancient Egypt to Online Secret Societies - sample chapter
http://assets.press.princeton.edu/chapters/s10949.pdf

1968

1968: The strike at San Francisco State
https://sfbayview.com/2018/12/1968-the-strike-at-san-francisco-state/

The Martin Luther King Assassination Riots (1968)
https://www.blackpast.org/african-american-history/
martin-luther-king-assassination-riots-1968/

The 1968 San Francisco Student Strike | Speak Out Now
https://speakoutsocialists.org/the-1968-san-francisco-student-strike/

All US Top 40 Singles For 1968 | Top40Weekly.com
https://top40weekly.com/1968-all-charts/

1968: The Year That Changed America Forever
https://www.usnews.com/news/national-news/
articles/2017-12-31/1968-the-year-that-changed-america-forever

Symbols

Weather Map Symbols Chart
https://www.weatherbriefing.com/observing-forms

weather_symbols.gif (3259×2055)
https://cdn2.hubspot.net/hubfs/604407/weather_symbols.gif

Petroleum Style Contents
http://downloads.esri.com/support/documentation/ao_/Petroleum.pdf

General

Vallejo Police Department Report (97 pages) - VPD 12 - Redacted
- Zodiac Killer Facts Image Gallery
https://zodiackillerfacts.com/gallery/displayimage.
php?album=48&pid=462

Zodiac Killer Police Reports | Case Files
https://www.zodiackiller.com/ZodiacPoliceReports.html

Vallejo police dispatcher Nancy Slover / Zodiac telephone call |
YouTube
https://www.youtube.com/watch?v=-kDPcR9VYN8

The Zodiac Killer - The Zodiac Killer: Police Reports, FBI Files and Other Official Documents from the Original Investigation
https://zodiackillerfacts.com/PoliceReports.htm

Blue Rock Springs Report, Page 10
https://www.zodiackiller.com/DFR10.html

Zodiac Killer FACTS - The Zodiac Letters
https://zodiackillerfacts.com/Zodiac%20Letters.htm

THE JULY 5TH 1969 PAYPHONE CALL | ZODIAC CIPHERS
https://www.zodiacciphers.com/zodiac-news/
the-recollection-of-the-july-5th-1969-payphone-call

THE PAYPHONE CALL AT MAIN STREET | ZODIAC CIPHERS
https://www.zodiacciphers.com/zodiac-news/
the-payphone-call-at-main-street

Why the Zodiac Killer Has Never Been Identified | Biography
https://www.biography.com/crime/zodiac-killer-murder-identity

David Faraday and Betty Lou Jensen Wiki & Bio
https://everipedia.org/wiki/lang_en/david-faraday-and-betty-lou-jenson

Blue Rocks Spring, July 4, 1969 -- The Quester Files Zodiac Killer Investigation
https://www.thequesterfiles.com/blue_rocks_spring__july_4__196.html

Lake Herman Murders | ZODIAC CIPHERS
https://www.zodiacciphers.com/lake-herman-murders.html

Deer Lodge: Narrowing the List of Suspects? - The Zodiac Killer -- Unsolved & Unforgotten
https://www.tapatalk.com/groups/zodiackillerfr/deer-lodge-narrowing-the-list-of-suspects-t9853.html

Zodiac - Blue Rock Springs
https://www.zodiackillerinfo.com/blue-rock-springs

"Today in True Crime" October 11, 2019: Paul Lee Stine (Podcast Episode 2019) | IMDb
https://www.imdb.com/title/tt20669616/

The Horrifying Murders Of The Zodiac Killer
https://www.buzzfeed.com/ryanbergara/
these-guys-went-to-the-murder-sites-of-the-infamous-zodiac-k

Breaking Blue | Freaky Friday: Zodiac Unmasked?
https://breakingblue.org/6427/freaky-friday/
freaky-friday-zodiac-unmasked/

The Zodiac Killer: A Timeline | HISTORY
https://www.history.com/news/the-zodiac-killer-a-timeline

Miscellaneous

Intersections: The Philippines at the Turn of the Sixteenth Century.
http://intersections.anu.edu.au/monograph1/mintz_status.html

Zodiac Fonts - The Zodiac Revisited
http://zodiacrevisited.com/zodiac-fonts/

Zodiac Killer Font, Pt. I | Phil's Blog
https://web.archive.org/web/20151007001318/http:/blog.philstrahl.
com:80/2007/08/31/zodiac-killer-font-part-1/

Why Hasn't the Tenderloin Gentrified Like the Rest of San Francisco? | KQED
https://www.kqed.org/news/11665527/
why-hasnt-the-tenderloin-gentrified-like-the-rest-of-san-francisco

Denise Diana Huddle

PART 5

WHO KILLED THE BLACK DAHLIA?

CHAPTER 21

WHAT HAPPENED?

Elizabeth Short photo from LAPD information poster. (FBI.gov)

On January 15, 1947, a body was discovered in a vacant lot in the Leimert Park neighborhood of Los Angeles (the area now known as Crenshaw). The body had been cut in two between the L1 and L2 vertebrae, eviscerated, and drained of blood. The woman's face had been mutilated, and her neck and wrists were marred by ligature marks. She died from a blow to the head and blood loss associated with multiple cuts on her face. Her body had been cut in two after she died.

After the FBI used fingerprints to identify the victim as Elizabeth Short, the LAPD launched one of the most extensive homicide investigations in the history of the department. In spite of thousands of leads and multiple confessions, the murder of Elizabeth Short has never been solved. Or has it?

BACKGROUND

There are many tales about Elizabeth's family, several of which would have had Jerry Springer's producers racing to the phones to book them. Her parents were Cleo and Phoebe Short. In some renditions, Cleo Short was a designer of miniature golf courses who lost everything in the stock market crash of 1929. Stories that he faked his own death sometime around 1930 and then reappeared a couple of years later are also widespread.

The Traveling Wilburys

The real story begins when Cleo Alvin Short married Phoebe Mae Sawyer on April 11, 1918, in Portland, Maine. Between 1920 and 1929, the couple bounced between Maine and Massachusetts and had five daughters along the way: Virginia Mae (later the wife of Adrian C. West), Dorothea (later the wife of Norman F. Schloesser), Elizabeth (never married, later the Black Dahlia), Elnora (later the wife of Duncan Chalmers), and Muriel Arlene (later the wife of Earle Ira McNair).

Elizabeth Short was born July 29, 1924, in Medford, Massachusetts. She was the third child born to the couple.

As a forensic genealogist, I can't resist digging into the old records about the characters in true crime stories, and this case is no exception. In the interval between 1920 and 1930, I found Cleo and Phoebe in various census records and city directories. Cleo's occupation was always listed as some variety of salesman or mechanical engineer. Zippo on miniature golf.

Don't Fear the Reaper

Whatever shenanigans went on between 1930 and 1940, by the enumeration of the 1940 census, Phoebe was calling herself a widow, and Cleo was off the radar, having managed to successfully dodge the census taker altogether. Yet, in 1942, Cleo Short was alive and well, registering for the draft in Robstown, Texas, and saying that his daughter Virginia (who was living with Phoebe on Salem Street in Medford, Massachusetts) would always know where he was. Phoebe's marital status had changed from widowed to separated by 1950.

I believe this evidence in the public record supports the assertion that Cleo Short faked his own death sometime after the 1930 census was taken. Either that, or he did a damn good impression of Lazarus rising from the dead. In any case, Cleo Short deserted his family, leaving Phoebe alone with five children at the height of the Great Depression.

Suffice it to say, the Shorts were hardly rivaling the Cleavers for middle-class stability and apple pie perfection.

The Black Dahlia in Hollywood website (https://www.The-BlackDahliaInHollywood.com) contains an amazingly detailed chronology of Elizabeth's life and times. It's a great site and definitely worth reviewing. Working from that and other resources along with some genealogical research thrown in, I have discerned the following summary of Elizabeth's life after she left home.

Breathing Easy in the Land of Oranges and Alligators

Elizabeth Short left Medford in 1939 at the age of fifteen and went to Florida, ostensibly to escape the brutal winter months in Massachusetts and the effect of the cold on her severe asthma. Asthma or not, it's easy to envision a teenage girl wanting to get the hell out of Dodge when the house on Salem Street was such a dysfunction junction. The stories vary between sources as to whether she went to live with "family friends" during these winters or if she simply left home at fifteen and went to Florida to shift for herself. My impression from the whole of the research materials I've read is that Elizabeth dropped out of school and amscrayed on her own, bouncing between Florida and Massachusetts from 1939 to the end of 1942.

Daddy Dearest Meets Californication

While the reports of his death were greatly exaggerated, Cleo Short left the East Coast in his rearview mirror and, by way of Texas, eventually landed in California, where the tourist brochures promised endless sunshine and infinite possibilities. Unfortunately, those promises often amounted to nothing more than tawdry living conditions and tarnished dreams. In poor Elizabeth Short's case, they ultimately amounted to murder.

In December of 1942, Elizabeth's father, Cleo, sent her a letter and offered for her to come live with him and a woman named Mrs. Yankee in Vallejo, California. The letter contained $200 to cover Elizabeth's travel costs. She accepted the invitation and headed west.

But, like so many other situations in her life, the living arrangement didn't last long. After a few weeks, Daddy Dearest, disapproving of her lifestyle, threw her out of his apartment and severed his newly rekindled relationship with her for good.

Camp Cutie to AWOL Patootie

In need of money and a place to live, on January 28, 1943, Elizabeth started work at the post exchange at Camp Cooke (now known as Vandenburg Air Force Base) near Lompoc, California. While at Camp Cooke, she was named "Camp Cutie" in a base beauty contest. But she quit the post exchange job after only a couple of weeks, leaving Lompoc on February 15, 1943.

On the Road Again

After spending the summer of 1943 in a cabin in luxurious Casmalia, California, Elizabeth returned to her mother's house in Medford for a brief stay before moving on to Miami Beach where she worked at Big Dave's Rosedale Delicatessen & Restaurant on Washington Avenue.

With the exception of the month of March in 1944, which she spent in Atlanta, Elizabeth stayed in Miami Beach.

Fickle on Fickling

In September of 1944, Elizabeth met and had a brief affair with a soldier named Gordon Fickling. But, by December of 1944, Fickling was out of the picture, and Elizabeth started seeing Matt Gordon, a pilot in the Army Air Corps. They fell deeply in love, but shortly after their relationship began, Matt Gordon shipped out.

By March of 1945, Elizabeth was back in Massachusetts, working at St. Clair's restaurant in Boston. Elizabeth and Matt Gordon wrote to each other frequently, and the couple had agreed to marry when Matt returned from the war. But, on August 10, 1945, Matt Gordon was killed in a plane crash in India. His mother sent Elizabeth a telegram dated August 22, 1945, telling her of Matt's death.

Between December 1945 and January 1946, we know that Elizabeth was living at the Colonial Inn on Riverside Avenue in Jacksonville, Florida, because her mother sent money to her at that address. By February 1946, Elizabeth was back in Medford, living with Phoebe again.

California, Here I Come!

In June of 1946, Elizabeth shipped trunks via Railway Express and bought herself a bus ticket to Indianapolis. But, for some reason that is not clear, she ended up in Chicago instead. Between June 24 and July 12, 1946, Elizabeth was registered as a guest at the Park Row Hotel in Chicago.

Selling Fake Mortgages on Swampland in Florida

According to the good folks at The Black Dahlia in Hollywood, Elizabeth then spent the next ten days in the Blackstone Hotel (also in Chicago) registered as the guest of a man named Jack Chernau.

While I can't find mention of the Park Row Hotel in current records, the Blackstone is one of America's iconic hotels. Interested in what penniless Elizabeth Short would be doing in a landmark of luxury like the Blackstone, I did some digging of my own. In public records of that era, I found only one Jack Chernau—Hyman Jack Chernau, to be exact. While there is no way to prove for certain that this man is the same Jack Chernau who Elizabeth was shacked up with at the Blackstone, the facts seem to fit.

Jack Chernau was born on December 13, 1912, as Hyman Rosenblum, but the name on his Social Security number was subsequently changed to Hyman J. Chernau. All of the historical addresses I found for him were in and around Miami, Florida (where Elizabeth had been living during the last part of 1945 and the first half of 1946).

The December 24, 1966 edition of the *Miami Herald* described Chernau's conviction on twelve counts of securities fraud. Chernau helped run a Ponzi scheme selling interests in fake mortgages that bilked the public out of 9.5 million dollars, leaving almost 2,000 investors without a chair in 1962 when the music stopped and the company folded like a cheap suit. In March of '67, Chernau was sentenced to six months in federal prison and three years' probation for his role in the scheme.

Elizabeth Short didn't have great taste in men.

After her sojourn in Chicago with conman Jack Chernau,

Elizabeth finally made it back to California. Gordon Fickling picked her up at the Long Beach bus station on July 22, 1946, thus beginning the death spiral that ended with her gruesome murder 176 days later.

It Wasn't Schwab's

Upon her arrival in Long Beach, Elizabeth was registered as a guest at the Washington Hotel from July 22 until August 3. During this time, she frequently hung out at Lander's Drug Store. It was reportedly at Lander's where other customers nicknamed her the "Black Dahlia" (a take on the popular 1946 film noir *The Blue Dahlia*) either because of her propensity to dress in black or, some say, because of her jet-black hair.

Still Fickle on Fickling

On August 4, Elizabeth took the Pacific Electric trolley to Hollywood and most likely lived at the Sunset Motel there until August 20, when she and good old Gordon Fickling registered as husband and wife at the Brevoort Apartments on Lexington Avenue. The couple stayed at the Brevoort until August 27, when the arrangement ended under unknown circumstances.

Funny Meeting You Here

After her cohabitation with Fickling fizzled out, while shopping at a dime store in Hollywood, Elizabeth ran into a woman she knew from back home in Massachusetts, and they struck up a conversation. When Elizabeth mentioned not having a place to live, the woman, Marjorie Graham, invited Elizabeth to stay at her apartment at the Hawthorne Hotel at 1611 North Orange Drive in Hollywood. Elizabeth stayed two nights with Marjorie and her roommate, Lynn Martin, before getting her own apartment at the Hawthorne.

Strike Three, You're Outta Here!

The women stayed at the hotel until the manager asked all three of them to leave on September 20, 1946. Elizabeth and Marjorie moved to the Hotel Figueroa at 939 South Figueroa Street in Los Angeles and stayed there for the next week. Lynn Martin did not join them.

Tot in Tinseltown

Only after the murder when the former roommates were being questioned did police discover that "Lynn Martin" was actually a fifteen-year-old girl named Norma Lee Myer who had run away from her adoptive home in Long Beach. After police learned her true identity, she was turned over to the proper juvenile authorities.

Are we to believe that Elizabeth and Marjorie couldn't tell that their roomie was a child? Norma Lee Myer should have been in ninth grade reading *Great Expectations*, not roughing it in Hollywood on her own. While this kind of atrocity is shamefully commonplace in the twenty-first century, it certainly was not in 1946. The tale of poor Norma Lee Myer lets us know what a social cesspool Elizabeth Short was living in during the last days of her life.

And the Band Played On…but Not for Long

On September 28, Elizabeth and Marjorie moved into the home of band leader Sid Zaid on Windsor Road in Los Angeles. After two nights in the cramped quarters of Zaid's small home, the band leader was ready to make his needy guests someone else's problem. He took the women to meet his friend and associate, Mark Hansen, at Hansen's home at 6024 Carlos Avenue in Los Angeles.

Hansen's Harem

Hansen owned a chain of movie theaters and managed a nightclub called the Florentine Gardens on Hollywood Boulevard. Hansen was married but separated from his wife, who lived in the Hollywood Hills. Hansen frequently had young single women staying at the house on Carlos Avenue. Elizabeth and Marjorie stayed with Hansen until October 10, when he threw them out, reportedly over Marjorie's drinking.

Cruisin' the Boulevard

After their eviction from Hansen's home, Elizabeth and Marjorie met Bill Robinson and Marvin Margolis on Hollywood Boulevard. Elizabeth and Marjorie apparently knew the men from their visits to Mark Hansen's house. Learning that the women were fresh out of a place to live, Robinson invited them to come stay with him and Marvin Margolis at the Guardian Arms complex on Hollywood Boulevard. The women accepted the offer and stayed at the apartment for about two weeks, during which time Marjorie reportedly slept with the two men in one bed (how cozy), and Elizabeth slept on the couch, or so the story goes.

Hansen's Harem, V. 2.0

Around October 22, Elizabeth left the Guardian Arms with a man named Glen Sterns (or Stearns), leaving her suitcases behind. Sterns described to investigators how he met Elizabeth on Hollywood Boulevard and convinced her to allow him to photograph her. The pair went to Marshall High School to take the pictures. Afterward, Sterns drove Elizabeth around the San Fernando Valley overnight looking for a place for her to stay. When she couldn't find one, he finally took her back to the Guardian Arms, where she retrieved her suitcases. Sterns then drove her back to Mark Hansen's house on Carlos Avenue. Elizabeth stayed with Hansen until he threw her out for a second time on November 13.

Relying on the Kindness of Semi-Strangers

When she was evicted from Hansen's house, once again Elizabeth had nowhere to go. Anne Toth was another single woman who lived at 6024 Carlos Avenue and was the closest thing Elizabeth had to a friend. In an effort to help Elizabeth get on her feet, on November 13, Toth helped Elizabeth move her things to the Chancellor Apartments at 1842 North Cherokee Avenue, where Toth paid Elizabeth's first week's rent.

There's No Place like San Diego for the Holidays

By December 7, Elizabeth was already behind on her rent at the Chancellor. After crying to Juanita Ring, the Chancellor's manager, about her financial woes, she finally paid her arrearage and left, saying she was going to visit her sister in the Bay Area for the holidays. Like the countless other lies Elizabeth told, she never went to her sister's house. When she was interviewed after the murder, Elizabeth's sister Virginia West said she had not heard from Elizabeth in some time and certainly didn't expect her for Christmas.

Elizabeth was picked up at the Chancellor by a man named Carl Balsiger. I found only one Carl Balsiger in Los Angeles at that time. H. Carl Balsiger, originally of Kansas City, Missouri, had been a captain in the US Army Quartermaster Corps during the war. In 1942, an article in the *Pasadena Star-News* described his work leading a field bakery in the Los Angeles area, overseeing the production of 4,000 loaves of bread per day. Assuming this is the same man who picked Elizabeth up at the Chancellor (which I can't prove but seems likely), by 1952 he was back in Kansas City working as a supervisor for Trans World Airlines.

Balsiger told investigators that he took Elizabeth with him on a business trip, driving them to Camarillo in a 1940 Oldsmobile. He claimed to have rented her a room at an unnamed motel on Yucca Street at some point on December 7. Where he spent the night is not clear, nor was his explanation of what happened between them on the trip. According to Balsiger, on December 8, he drove Elizabeth back to Hollywood, where he dropped her off at the bus station so that she could go to Berkley to see her sister.

But, instead of heading north to the Bay Area, Elizabeth bought a bus ticket south to San Diego. She arrived at the San Diego bus station on December 9. With no money for a room, she purchased a ticket at the Aztec Picture Theater, where she fell asleep in her seat. Dorothy French, a twenty-one-year-old cashier, invited Elizabeth to come home with her to the house Dorothy shared with her mother, Elvira French, in the Pacific Beach neighborhood of San Diego. Elizabeth stayed with the Frenchs until January 8, 1947.

Houseguest from Hell

While Dorothy French had intended, out of the goodness of her heart, to give a poor traveler a place to sleep for the night, she and her mother ended up with a stranger living in their house for a month. Elizabeth lounged around during the day then disappeared at night with a litany of different men who came to call on her. Elizabeth hadn't been gone from the French home for a week when the women, finally relieved of their hostlessly burden, were thrust into one of the largest homicide investigations in American history.

After the murder, the French women were questioned at great length by investigators regarding Elizabeth's activities and contacts while she was living in their house in Pacific Beach.

Elizabeth's Revolving Door of Love

The French women gave a detailed account of Elizabeth's activities with different men during her time with them. They reported that sometime between December 10 and 15, 1946, Elizabeth dated a naval officer whose name they never knew. (How lovely to have a strange man coming to your house to pick up the strange woman who's living with you for free.) Between December 17 and 20, Elizabeth had four dates with Robert "Red" Manley. On December 22, Elizabeth received a $100 money order from Gordon Fickling. On December 24, Elizabeth went on a date with a man named Frank Dominguez, and on the twenty-sixth, she went out with Robert Manley again. On the twenty-seventh, she had a date with another unidentified suitor. On the thirty-first, she had a second date with Frank Dominguez. On January 7, she received a telegram from Robert Manley before going out on a date with a man named Sam Navarra.

Elizabeth Short took gross advantage of Dorothy and Elvira French's goodwill. She overstayed her welcome and brought all manner of strange men to their home while she was hitting long-suffering Gordon Fickling up for cash. (The $100 he sent her in 1946 was roughly equivalent to $1,500 in today's money.) She was spending Fickling's money at the same time she was sponging off the Frenchs and dating a platoon of men.

On January 8, Elizabeth finally left the French home with Robert Manley and went to a motel with him. The next day, January 9, 1947, Manley drove her to the Biltmore Hotel in Los Angeles. That was the last confirmed sighting of Elizabeth Short alive.

Just for the record, in the 176 days that Elizabeth Short was known to be in California before her death, she lived at a minimum of eleven different addresses. That averages a new location every sixteen days.

She also spent the night with at least seven different men that researchers are aware of during this interval. What went on during those nights is anyone's guess, but at the very least Elizabeth Short was in a hotel, house, car, or apartment overnight with Gordon Fickling, Sid Zaid, Mark Hansen, Bill Robinson, Marvin Margolis, Glen Sterns, and Robert Manley at some point before her death. She may have also spent the night at a motel with Carl Balsiger. Additionally, the Frenchs reported her having at least one date with an unidentified naval officer, a man named Frank Dominguez, and another man named Sam Navarra while she was living at the French house in San Diego. The record is not clear if she stayed out over-night with these men.

CHAPTER 22

THE INVESTIGATION

Polansky Wasn't Kidding about Chinatown

In the late 1930s, corruption in the Los Angeles mayor's office and the LAPD escalated to a dramatic crescendo. In 1937, Los Angeles restaurateur and political activist Clifford E. Clinton's home was bombed. In 1938, private investigator Harry Raymond's house was bugged, and his car was bombed while he was investigating government corruption in Los Angeles. The head of the LAPD's intelligence squad (which worked straight out of the mayor's office) was sentenced to two years to life at San Quentin Prison for the Raymond bombing. The backlash resulted in the resignation of the chief of police and twenty-three of his high-ranking henchmen.

Los Angeles district attorney Buron Fitts had been indicted in 1934 for bribery and perjury related to accusations that he took money to drop criminal charges against a wealthy real estate promoter, but he was acquitted two years later. In 1937, he was wounded by one of two shots fired by an unknown assassin through the windshield of his county-issued car. Fitts was struck in the left arm in the attack. During the 1940s, Clifford Clinton hosted a daily radio show during which he exposed public corruption in LA, focusing on Fitts, who he considered to be one of the most corrupt politicians in California.

In a report aired on November 20, 2004, on the CBS show *48 Hours*, true crime writer James Ellroy was quoted describing the state of criminal justice in Los Angeles in 1949. He said, "Reports recommending whether or not to file charges were on sale for $500 a pop. The detective bureau was a repository of drunks and cronies of high-ranking LAPD officers. At the time of Elizabeth Short's death, it was a very corrupt institution."

The Black Dahlia murder case was investigated in this quagmire of graft and corruption by a police department and prosecutor's office reeling from the scandals and revelations that had been going on for a decade.

Extra! Extra! Fresh Off the Wire!

Forensic science was in its infancy in 1947. The idea of linking science and technology to criminal investigation was a radical concept. The cops of the time never imagined the possibility of the forensic techniques that exist today. Yet, some investigators were hungry for any advantage they could find—wherever they could find it.

The SoundPhoto machine was a precursor to modern fax machines used by the press of that day to transmit news photographs. When Elizabeth Short's bisected corpse was found in Leimert Park, the police had no idea who she was. To speed up the identification, the *Los Angeles Herald-Express* offered the use of their SoundPhoto machine to transmit her fingerprints to the FBI in Washington, DC—in return for an exclusive on the story.

Arrest photo of Elizabeth Short taken by
the Santa Barbara Police Department. (Police photo)

The FBI had two sets of Elizabeth's prints on file—one from her employment at Camp Cooke and one from when she was arrested for underage drinking in Santa Barbara on September 23, 1943. Thanks to cooperation between the media and law enforcement utilizing the cutting-edge technology of the time, the body was identified the day after it was discovered.

Mr. Postal Inspector? Is there evidence in your sorter for me?

The most obvious lead in the case came from the correspondence addressed to the *Los Angeles Examiner* containing Elizabeth Short's personal effects.

On the afternoon of January 23, 1947, James Richardson, editor of the *Los Angeles Examiner*, received a phone call from an anonymous man congratulating him on the paper's coverage of the Short murder. The caller went on to say, "You seem to have run out of material. Maybe I can be of assistance." The call was followed by a special delivery envelope addressed to the paper, which was intercepted by a postal clerk on January 25, 1947.

Letter sent to the *Los Angeles Times* with
Elizabeth Short's personal effects. (*Times* photo)

In letters cut out of newspaper movie ads, the 8″ x 3 ½″ envelope was addressed to "Los Angeles Examiner and other Los Angeles Papers." It went on to say, "Here! Is Dahlia's Belongings, Letter to Follow." The postal clerk who intercepted the envelope that had come unsealed in transit contacted postal inspectors.

The envelope had been treated with gasoline, police theorized, for the purpose of eliminating fingerprints. The envelope was opened in the presence of the police, the postal inspectors, and members of the press. The twenty-three items inside were all personal property of murder victim Elizabeth Short.

The contents included:

1. Western Union Telegram regarding a missing trunk shipped via REA.
2. Railway Express Agency receipt, dated 6/1/46.
3. Part of sales slip printed in ink, Pacific Outdoor Advertising Company.
4. Business card, Pacific Outdoor Advertising Company.
5. Business card for A. D. Brix.
6. Business card for E. A. "Jack" Kleinan, House of Hollywood Realtor.
7. Typewritten Social Security card, signed "Elizabeth Short" in green ink.
8. Piece of notebook paper with Jimmy Harrigan's army base phone number.

9. A torn piece of notepaper with Carl Balsiger's phone number.
10. Notebook leaf with "Jimmy Bifulco" printed in pencil.
11. Scrap of paper with "Wayne Gregg" written in ink.
12. ID card "Elizabeth Short," in case of emergency, contact P. M. Short.
13. Abstract of record registry, City of Boston, "Elizabeth Short, daughter of…"
14. Card, Hollywood Wolves Association.
15. Business card for Brandt Orr, Dressen Realty Company, with personal note.
16. A Pacific Greyhound Lines parcel claim check, date stamped January 9.
17. Small snapshot of an aviator and a girl in the cockpit of a plane.
18. Small snapshot of a girl in a black fur jacket, black hat, with buildings in the background.
19. Photo of a man in an army uniform, standing near a tree, a frame house in the background.
20. Small snapshot of the victim and a man.
21. Small snapshot of an aviator in a flying suit and parachute, standing in front of a plane.
22. Snapshot of a woman dressed in a riding habit, standing beside a horse.
23. One black address and telephone book with "Mark Hansen" embossed in gold letters.

Two sets of fingerprints were taken from the outside of the envelope, but police feared those were left by postal workers. The fingerprints were sent by US Mail to the FBI, but they were unfortunately compromised en route. I have been unable to locate any detail on exactly how these prints were damaged. No prints were found on the contents of the envelope.

Let's Make a Deal

A series of letters then came to the press and law enforcement wherein the author claimed to be the Dahlia killer and offered to turn himself in. One of the pasted-up notes said, "I will give up in Dahlia killing if I get 10 years. Don't try to find me." Yet, despite an appointment set up for him to turn himself in, the author didn't show and claimed in a final note that he changed his mind because he felt he wouldn't get a square deal.

Say Goodbye to Hollywood

In a weird final twist to the correspondence saga, John Dillon (sometimes called Dollon), captain of the lifeguards at Venice Beach, found a note tucked in a shoe included in a pile of men's clothes discovered at the foot of Breeze Avenue on March 14, 1947. The note read:

> To whom it may concern: I have waited for the police to capture me for the Black Dahlia killing, but have not. I am too much of a coward to turn myself in, so this is the best way out for me. I couldn't help myself for that, or this. Sorry, Mary

The clothes included a herringbone tweed coat and slacks, a brown and white T-shirt, white jockey shorts, tan socks, and tan men's shoes estimated to be size eight. The clothes contained no laundry markings or identification to provide investigators with any clue about the identity of their owner. Authorities undertook a search for a body in the water, but the public record does not reflect any evidence that one was ever found and linked to the note.

Denise Diana Huddle

Not a Glass Slipper—and Definitely Not a Prince

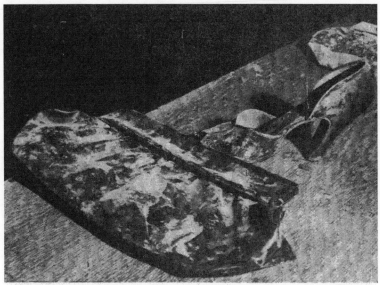

SHOE AND BAG IDENTIFIED—Bag carried by Elizabeth Short and a shoe she wore, shown with light dusting of ashes, were identified yesterday by Robert (Red) Manley, who brought her here from San Diego and left her at hotel six days before slaying.

Elizabeth Short's purse and shoe recovered from the dump. (*Times* photo)

On January 24, 1947 (the same day the envelope containing her personal effects was postmarked), Short's black handbag and black high-heeled shoe were recovered from the Los Angeles dump. A witness who operated a café at 1136 South Crenshaw Boulevard saw the purse and shoes on a garbage can, which was emptied by a garbage truck. Police tracked the garbage to the dump at 1819 East 25th Street and recovered the items, which were then identified by Robert "Red" Manley as belonging to the victim. Manley was the last person known to have seen Elizabeth Short alive.

The Crime Scene—Trampled by the Madding Crowd

Elizabeth Short's body discovered in Leimert Park. (*Daily News* photo)

On January 15, 1947, Betty Bersinger was walking with her young daughter to a shoe repair store when she discovered Elizabeth Short's mutilated body in a vacant lot between 39th Street and Coliseum Avenue in the undeveloped portion of the Leimert Park neighborhood in Los Angeles. Although multiple police officers and detectives arrived at the location, they failed to secure or preserve the crime scene.

The media descended on the vacant lot and tromped through the location undeterred, inflicting damage to the forensic environment that was too extensive to remediate. Modern experts contend that the gross mismanagement of the crime scene from the very start resulted in a level of contamination that rendered the scene and anything collected from it virtually useless from a forensic perspective.

The only potentially meaningful evidence at the crime scene was Elizabeth Short's mutilated body, an empty cement sack stained with spots of blood, a tire track, a bloody smear that could have been left by a shoe, and a one-inch spot of blood near the curb in the driveway.

Raiders of the Lost Evidence

As to the possibility of applying modern-day forensic science to the meager evidence collected that day—never mind. According to the detective in charge of the open case for the LAPD, all of the physical evidence collected in the investigation of the Black Dahlia murder has been lost or misplaced, and its current location is unknown to the LAPD. Either this is a lie of biblical proportions or some yahoo in the Los Angeles Police Department actually lost all of the physical evidence in the most sensational unsolved murder in the history of the state of California.

The discovery that critical evidence once held in the LAPD's custody was "missing" has just served to fuel more theories that the LAPD actively covered up the identity of the Black Dahlia killer. While government conspiracy theories are usually the province of the tin foil hat crowd, in the case of the known corrupt state of the city government of Los Angeles in general and the LAPD in particular during the time of the Short murder, this premise is not at all unreasonable.

CHAPTER 23

THE SUSPECTS

Mark Hansen—Rick Blaine Goes Hollywood (without the Heart of Gold)

The address book included in the envelope of Elizabeth Short's possessions was embossed with the name of her known associate, Mark Hansen. Hansen was a Danish immigrant who owned a number of movie theaters, mostly in the Los Angeles area. Additionally, he was the part owner of the Florentine Gardens nightclub at 5955 Hollywood Boulevard. Separated from his wife, Hansen lived in a house at 6024 Carlos Avenue, right behind the nightclub.

The Carlos house was a '40s down-market version of the Playboy Mansion. Single women (often burlesque dancers from floorshows at the Florentine Gardens) rotated through a revolving door while various (often shady) players on the LA nightclub scene floated in and out of the party house.

Mark Hansen asked Elizabeth to leave Carlos Avenue for the second and last time on November 13, 1946. While various witnesses stated that he was infatuated with Short, Hansen himself reported to police he had no romantic interest in her. This idea that Mark Hansen wasn't hot for Elizabeth Short seems like a supersized serving of malarkey to me. Why would a successful, separated man bring vulnerable young women off the street to stay in his home? Certainly Hansen didn't think the police would believe a bunch of Hollywood night crawlers were sitting around discussing abstract expressionism and reading Hemingway with Hansen's bevy of beauties? Regardless of the nature of Hansen's relationship with Short, it was apparently acrimonious at the end, as evidenced by him tossing her out of the house.

A witness wrote a letter to the district attorney's office on May 18, 1949, repeating information he claimed to have reported to the department immediately after the death of Elizabeth Short. The witness reported seeing a woman walking on Hollywood Boulevard in the direction of the Carlos Avenue house at around 10:30 a.m. on January 14, 1947 (the fifth day after Manley left Short at the Biltmore). The witness described the woman as a white American, about five-seven, 120 pounds, twenty to twenty-five years old, dark hair worn rather long, white or light-colored flower worn in hair on the right side, also some sort of pin or other jewelry. The woman was reportedly wearing a light-colored, about knee-length coat of a lightweight cloth, a black silk or other glossy material dress with a ruffled hem, light-colored hose, and high-heeled, open type, black shoes. The witness described the woman as "manifestly disturbed" and said "her manner suggested an angry mood."

Hansen admitted to receiving a phone call from Short in the week before her death, but he stated that he could not recall the exact date. The police alleged that Short called Hansen from the Biltmore Hotel on January 9, 1947, after Manley drove her back from San Diego. Ann Toth still lived with Mark Hansen, but she was out of town at the time of Short's call to Hansen at the Carlos Avenue house. Toth reported that Hansen told her of the phone call when she returned to his home and stated that Hansen knew that Short had been in San Diego, not the Bay Area where she had told Toth she was going for the holidays.

At the time of the murder, Mark Hansen was also associated with a physician, Dr. Patrick O'Reilly, who frequented the Florentine Gardens. O'Reilly was also a suspect in the slaying. The LA district attorney's file indicated that O'Reilly knew Short through Hansen. O'Reilly had a history of violent sexual crime, having been convicted of assault with a deadly weapon as a method of sexual gratification. On September 30, 1939, the forty-one-year-old Glendale osteopath had been convicted of sexually assaulting twenty-one-year-old Walene Jane McCarthy, a switchboard operator in his employ. In his closing arguments, the prosecutor at O'Reilly's trial branded O'Reilly "a sadist."

Mark Hansen was never charged in the death of Elizabeth Short. He died June 14, 1964, in Los Angeles, California.

Leslie Dillon & Jeff Connors—Leopold & Loeb or Beavis & Butt-Head?

Leslie Dillon was the alias of a man named Jack Sands who was a former Los Angeles bellhop. Dillon also claimed to have worked as a mortician's assistant at the Hahn Funeral Home in Oklahoma City in 1943. Dr. J. Paul De River was a psychiatrist who was either a civilian employee of or a consultant to the LAPD. Dillon was a former resident of Los Angeles, but was living in Miami, Florida, in October of 1948 when he contacted De River by letter about the Black Dahlia case.

Dillon stated that he knew who had killed Elizabeth Short, and the murderer's name was Jeff Connors. Initially, De River presumed that Connors was an alter ego for Dillon, but he later came to understand that Connors was, in fact, a real person.

After lengthy communications with De River, Dillon finally agreed to meet the psychiatrist in person in Las Vegas. Dillon returned to California with De River and other LAPD detectives who were traveling with them undercover. The entourage followed De River and Dillon to San Francisco where Dillon led them on a fruitless search for Jeff Connors. When Dillon revealed knowledge of the Short case that had not been made public, the police arrested him and took him back to Los Angeles.

Several witnesses placed Leslie Dillon in San Francisco at the time of the Short murder, but police were not entirely convinced of their credibility. Yet, the determination was made that the availability of multiple alibi witnesses would make prosecution of Leslie Dillon for the murder of Elizabeth Short unlikely to be successful. After six weeks of constant surveillance, Dillon was marked off the suspect list.

Dillon subsequently sued the LAPD for $100,000 for the alleged mistreatment he endured during his arrest and interrogation by the police. The outcome of the civil case is unclear, though multiple sources report that Dillon was paid some settlement amount by the city.

Through information gleaned from listening devices placed in Mark Hansen's home, LAPD detectives determined that "Jeff Connors" was actually an associate of Mark Hansen's named Artie Loy, who also used the alias Artie Laine (or Lane). Loy (Connors) was located in Gilroy, south of San Francisco, and arrested.

Loy gave a woman named Vicki Evans as an alibi, claiming she was his ex-wife and was with him while he was working at Columbia Studios the night before Short's body was discovered. But when questioned by the police, Evans reportedly replied, "I've never heard of the jerk." Evans's name had appeared earlier in the press when she was arrested on marijuana charges along with Hollywood star Robert Mitchum. Evans claimed she could not have been with Loy the night of the murder because she was in Miami visiting her father.

According to an article that appeared in the *Pasadena Independent* on January 13, 1949, Loy admitted to both knowing Elizabeth

Short and being in the Los Angeles area at the time of the murder. He even claimed to have seen her at a bar the night of January 14, 1947, just hours before her body was discovered in Leimert Park.

Police finally found Loy's real ex-wife and questioned her. She verified his alibi that he was working on the Columbia Studios lot between 2:00 and 11:00 p.m. the night before the murders. Loy was released for lack of evidence.

George Hodel—Bad, Bad George Hodel

Designed by Lloyd Wright in the Mayan revival style of the art deco period, the house at 5121 Franklin Avenue was built for John Sowden in 1926 in the Los Feliz neighborhood of Los Angeles—just off Hollywood Boulevard. Complete with a secret room, the exotic home is straight out of a noir mystery. In 1945, George Hodel purchased the house and moved into it. Dr. Hodel was married (legally and common law) to five different women with whom he had nine (possibly ten) children.

At the time of the murder, Dr. Hodel was one of the LAPD's top suspects. He had been a child music prodigy and a star medical student before starting his practice in Los Angeles, where he ran a venereal disease clinic. He was close friends with surrealist and Dada artist and photographer Man Ray and movie director John Huston, and was known for throwing lavish parties for Hollywood luminaries at his exotic Franklin Avenue home.

Several factors cast suspicion on Dr. Hodel in the years immediately following the murder. First, the police were of the opinion that Elizabeth Short's corpse had been bisected by virtue of a surgical procedure known as a hemicorporectomy. While Dr. Hodel was not a practicing surgeon, he had likely been trained in the procedure during medical school.

Second, there are reports that the Los Angeles district attorney's file contains notes indicating that a female witness reported that Hodel knew Elizabeth Short. However, the strength of this link is disputed by some researchers, and, to my knowledge, the witness has not been identified.

Death certificate of Ruth Spaulding. (George Hodel's secretary)

Dr. Hodel first came onto the radar of Los Angeles law enforcement when his secretary and clinic manager, Ruth Frances Spaulding, died under questionable circumstances on May 9, 1945. No charges were ever brought against Dr. Hodel, and Ruth Spaulding's death was ruled a suicide by overdose.

In October of 1949, Dr. Francis C. Ballard and his assistant, Charles Smith, were held over on charges of having performed an abortion on Tamar Hodel on September 11, 1949. The charges were associated with an investigation of George Hodel for sexual abuse of his fourteen-year-old daughter. In December of 1949, George Hodel went on trial for the sexual abuse charges, but he was acquitted by the jury. There are no subsequent articles in the press that I can find about the outcome of the abortion charges lodged against Ballard and Smith.

Jury Finds Dr. Hodel Not Guilty

Dr. George Hill Hodel, Hollywood physician, today was found innocent of a felony morals charge against a minor girl. A jury in Superior Court deliberated less than eight hours before reaching a verdict.

Article in *Los Angeles Evening Citizen News*, December 23, 1949.

Police installed listening devices in Hodel's house on Franklin Avenue and monitored the conversations in his home around the clock from February 15 to March 27, 1950. While the tapes themselves are missing, the original transcripts have survived. In one excerpt from the transcript, Hodel says:

"Supposin' I did kill the Black Dahlia. They couldn't prove it now. They can't talk to my secretary [Ruth Spaulding] anymore because she's dead."

In 1950, George Hodel moved to the Philippines, where he lived until he returned to the US in 1990. He died May 16, 1999.

George Hodel's son, Steve Hodel, became an LAPD homicide detective. Following George's death, Steve became convinced that his father murdered Elizabeth Short. After his retirement from the LAPD, Steve Hodel wrote a *New York Times* bestselling book, *Black Dahlia Avenger*, about his investigation into his father's role in the case.

In 2018, Steve Hodel released his third book on the Dahlia murder, *Black Dahlia Avenger III*. The afterward includes text and images of a newly discovered letter written by a police informant of the era claiming that someone named "G.H." was involved in police corruption and was being protected from the consequences of killing the Black Dahlia. The letter strikes me as rambling and ambiguous, and it never directly identifies George Hodel as "G.H." The writer of the letter has been dead for many years and is not available for comment.

Walter Bayley—*Dr. Jekyll and Mr. Hyde* Meets *The Lost Weekend*

Walter Bayley was a latecomer to the list of potential Dahlia killers. *Los Angeles Times* copy editor and writer Larry Harnisch made a curious discovery while working on a feature article for the *Times* on the fiftieth anniversary of the murder. In the course of his research for the piece, Harnisch came across the marriage record for Short's older sister Virginia's marriage to Adrian C. West. He was surprised to discover one of the witnesses on the marriage certificate was a Barbara Lindgren of 3959 South Norton Avenue, Los Angeles, California. This address is about a block from where Elizabeth Short's mutilated body was discovered.

Further research led Harnisch to the discovery that the house at 3959 South Norton Avenue was owned by one Ruth Bayley, the estranged wife of Walter Bayley, MD. Dr. Bayley was an esteemed gynecological surgeon who had begun an affair with his younger colleague, Dr. Alexandra von Partyka. When Ruth discovered the affair, she separated from Walter, and he moved out of the Norton Avenue house sometime in late 1946.

Walter Bayley died January 4, 1948, in the VA hospital in Los Angeles. His death certificate listed the cause of death as bronchopneumonia exacerbated by myocardial infarction and arteriosclerosis. Encephalomalacia is listed as an additional factor in his death.

Encephalomalacia is a degenerative brain disease that is essentially a softening of the brain tissue. Harnisch posits that the neurological disorder contributed to a shift toward violent and unpredictable behavior in Bayley. He also points to a profile done by retired FBI behavioral scientist John Douglas, which indicated that the dump site most likely had some significance to the perpetrator.

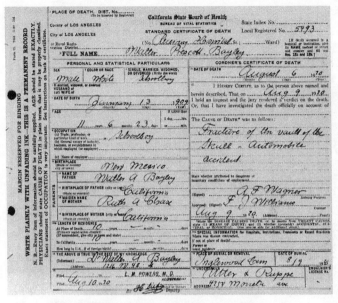

Death certificate of Walter Bayley's son. (Ancestry.com)

Additionally, Walter Bayley had a son who died when he was hit by a car at age eleven. The child's birthday was January 13—two days before the discovery of Elizabeth Short's body.

During my own cursory look at Walter Bayley, I discovered that he was involuntarily committed to the Stockton State Hospital for being "so far addicted to use of morphine as to be beyond self-control." The episode leading to his commitment was said to have been going on for about one year. He was committed November 18, 1912, and admitted to the hospital on November 21, 1912, at 4:45 p.m. He was discharged on January 16, 1914. This record indicates that Dr. W. A. Bayley, a prominent physician from a respected family, was involuntarily committed to a state psychiatric institution for just two days short of fourteen months for addiction to morphine.

60

No. *20037.* Name, *W. A. Bayley.*

COMMITTED—from *Los Angeles* County on *Nov. 18. 1912*
Petitioner, *A. J. Bayley* ; Judge, *Geo. H. Hutton.*
Examining Physician *Drs. W. L. Loomis & Lottie C. Park.*
Delivered by *A. J. Bayley* ; Assistant

ADMITTED—Date, *Nov. 21. 1912* ; hour, *4:45 P.M.* by *Harold Drown, Acty Supervr.*
Nativity, *America* . In U. S. — years; in California *32* years, Last from ✓
Sex, *Male* ; Age, *32* ; Color, *White* ; Civil state, *Married* ; Occupation, *Physician.*
Education, *Academic* ; Religion, *Protestant* ; No. Children, — ; No. Children now living, —

Birthplace of father ; Birthplace of mother,

Habits of parents as to liquors and drugs,

Peculiarities or chronic disease of relatives,

Insane, hysterical, or epileptic relatives,

Mental defects, peculiarities, and disposition previous to insanity,
Epileptic,

Physical defects, injuries, or sickness previous to insanity,

Habits as to liquor, tobacco, and drugs, or other vices,

Date and history of previous attacks. (If in a hospital for insane, state when and where.)

Present attack began, *about one year ago.*
History of onset and development, *Drug - habitue - morphine.*

Supposed cause; Predisposing, ✓ ; Exciting, ✓

Violent, ; Destructive,
Homicidal, ; Suicidal,
Incendiary, ; Habits,
Special delusions or hallucinations,

Facts indicating insanity, *So far addicted to use of morphine as to be beyond self control*

Sentence: *Term of detention not specified.*
Diagnosis: Commitment, *Morphine - habitue* ; Revised,
Post office address of friend or relative, *Relatives' names & address not stated. O. O. P. Feby 01—*
Telegraph address of friend or relative,
In case of death,
Financial statement, *Relatives able to pay $15.00 per mo.*
Discharged, *Jan. 16, 1914.* Why? *Recom. Dr. Hatch.*
Died, Cause,
Mental condition when discharged or died,

Admission record for Walter Bayley's commitment to
Stockton State Hospital. (Ancestry.com)

In Dr. Bayley's defense, he was never a suspect in the crime, was never charged with nor convicted of any criminal act, and died with an unblemished reputation, save for his marital infidelity. Beyond his daughter, Barbara, knowing Elizabeth Short's older sister Virginia, there is no evidence Walter Bayley had any direct contact with Elizabeth Short herself.

Yet, John Douglas's profile of the killer pointed to the dump site as a location of some significance to the murderer, and Bayley's family home was less than a block away—a home from which he had been exiled due to his infidelity. His daughter was acquainted with Elizabeth's sister, and he was a physician with surgical skills and addiction issues. Bayley ticks several boxes on the likely suspect list.

CHAPTER 24

INVESTIGATOR'S COMMENTS

The basic theory of traditional violent crime investigation involves identifying and locating potential suspects as individuals who, one, had some contact with the victim or were known to be in the vicinity of the victim in the period leading up to the incident in question, two, do not have a verifiable alibi for the time of the crime, and, three, could possibly have a motive and means to harm the victim. While substantially more sophisticated, modern investigative techniques still rely on these fundamental tenets. In the 1940s, these rules were pretty much all murder investigators had to go on.

Throw Mama from the Train

In the most challenging investigative scenario, the perpetrator commits a random act of violence against a complete stranger without any discernable motive. In this situation, the perpetrator has no previous connection to the victim and simply walks up and kills their unsuspecting target in a location without witnesses then escapes into the darkness, possibly even departing to another jurisdiction. Crimes in this category have always been particularly hard to solve, especially if they are isolated incidents or even if they are part of a pattern spanning a wide geographic area where the similarity of the crimes is obscured by distance and jurisdictional boundaries.

Investigative Quicksand

Crimes involving victims with unstable lifestyles are particularly challenging. A look at the previous section describing Elizabeth Short's movements over the preceding five years shows the profile of a victim who was almost completely devoid of any stable personal, romantic, social, employment, or even geographic relationships. While there has been much speculation about Elizabeth Short's lifestyle, there is no evidence in the public record linking her with actual prostitution. Yet, she was undoubtedly involved in a long series of short-term relationships that frequently involved staying overnight in hotels and apartments and houses with men she had just met—mostly in public venues.

This behavior is the cornerstone of a high-risk lifestyle. To make matters worse, Elizabeth Short frequently lied to her friends and relatives about where she was staying, if and where she was working, and with whom she was associating. This pattern of prevarication makes the overall investigation even more challenging because reports from family members and associates about the victim's activities are suspect from the start. This leaves even the most diligent and seasoned investigators throwing bowls of spaghetti against the wall, hoping to God that something will eventually stick.

Layer all of these challenges over a police department and city government riddled with corruption, where protection from prosecution was for sale like a blue-light special at Kmart, and it is no small wonder that the crime was never solved.

The Likely Suspects

The record seems to indicate that the police were very interested in Mark Hansen and his network of associates, including Leslie Dillon aka Jack Sands, Jeff Connors aka Artie Loy/Lane/Laine, and Dr. Patrick O'Reilly. Hansen ran a nightclub that featured burlesque dancers and frequently had young women staying in his home while he was separated from his wife. He certainly knew Elizabeth Short and had an ongoing, sometimes acrimonious, and possibly obsessive relationship with her. Hansen was also friends with Dr. Patrick O'Reilly, a physician with a history of violent crime who frequented the Florentine Gardens.

Dillon and Connors both had connections to Hansen. They also had connections to Miami, Florida, where Elizabeth Short had been just prior to her last sojourn in California. While I have seen no evidence that either man knew Elizabeth in Florida, *there are no coincidences in law enforcement* is one of the first adages taught to new detectives.

In modern investigations, police are trained to focus on individuals who come forth for no apparent reason to opine theories of the crime or otherwise "help" with the investigation. Dillon certainly fits the bill on that count because he fingered Connors in his letters to De River. Worse, during his communication with authorities, Dillon admitted to an interest in sadism.

Connors lied about Vicki Evans (who claimed to have been in Miami at the time of the murder) being his alibi. In the end, the only alibi witness Connors/Loy/Lane/Laine had was his actual ex-wife, who was eventually located by the police. Family members are generally considered weak alibi witnesses, especially in this case when the ex-wife only accounted for Connors's time between 2:00 and 11:00 p.m. the night before the body was discovered.

This cabal of Hansen, O'Reilly, Dillon, and Connors is the most logical suspect, in my opinion.

Weirdo or Wacko?

George Hodel was undoubtedly an unusual individual who lived a nontraditional lifestyle. His alleged comments overheard with the listening devices regarding the police not being able to prove he killed the Black Dahlia certainly do not point to innocence. However, while there are supposedly witnesses who claimed to link Hodel to Short, the links—at least in the public record—seem tenuous. At a minimum, they are not nearly as well established as the links between Short and Hansen.

It's not that I have trouble envisioning Hodel as a mutilation killer, I simply question the link between him and Elizabeth Short. If there was no link, I find it difficult to view this as a random act of violence against a stranger, most particularly because, as far as anyone has proven, it was a one-off.

The Mainlining Surgeon

I liked the idea of Walter Bayley even before I learned that he was a morphine addict so out of control that his family had him locked him up in a state hospital for over a year. Mostly, I liked the idea of Bayley because he was a physician specializing in surgery with the requisite skills to have performed the mutilation who also had ties to a house a block from the dump site. His dead son's birthday could have been a psychological trigger for the attack.

Yet, there is no known link between Bayley and Short beyond Bayley's daughter, Barbara Lindgren, signing as a witness on Elizabeth Short's sister Virginia Mae's marriage license. Barbara Lindgren is quoted by some sources as saying that she was simply a member of the church where Virginia was married and volunteered to stand up with her when a witness was needed. I have not seen any evidence that Lindgren and Virginia Short were bosom buds.

The Other Unknown Psycho

This one of my favorite options. Elizabeth Short was a busy girl when it came to dating...and moving around the country...and spending the night in different places with different men. One quick look at the timeline of living arrangements shows a lot of temporal gaps that would allow for meeting a lot of men who are not in the address book or who nobody else knew about. Some witnesses said Short reported being afraid of a soldier she lived with while working at Camp Cooke. Others said she talked about being afraid of someone during her final weeks staying with Dorothy and Elvira French, though she never named the person specifically. Some sources say Elizabeth identified this man as being of Italian descent, thus possibly pointing to the man named Sam Navarra who she dated in San Diego.

It is altogether possible that one of these unidentified acquaintances was the murderer.

I am particularly intrigued by the apparent suicide note left on Venice Beach taking responsibility for the murder. The credible notes to the press and law enforcement stopped after March 14, 1947. While I have no idea about what efforts were made to match any bodies washed up in the area to the writer of the note, and while I am more than willing to acknowledge the note and clothing could have been just one more false-confessional hoax related to the murder, I can't help but feel it's a viable lead.

INVESTIGATOR'S TIPS

While it is unclear if Elizabeth Short's social lifestyle played some role in her demise, it most certainly impeded the success of the investigation into her murder. In any case, she fell into a high-risk group of vulnerable women.

One great way to stay out of trouble is to avoid high-risk situations. Now that online dating is firmly entrenched in the American social experience, the question arises about how to do it and be safe. I have some suggestions on this topic.

What's Their Name?

Your first task is to be certain the person you are going out with is who they say they are. Short of asking for ID, there are some things you can do. Try to contact them at least once through a published number or email address (like a company directory or website). If they claim to have a professional license, check with the state licensing board (always public record) and try to match the address on the license to a business or home address you can tie back to the person you're communicating with.

Liar, Liar, Pants on Fire

The first rule of online relationships is to independently verify any information you receive if that information will influence a decision you are making. For example, if a person you meet mentions a recent divorce and you wouldn't go out with them if they were still legally married, then best you hop on over to the court and make sure that divorce happened and is final. In many jurisdictions, you can check at least a case index online, but you can always see the files in the courthouse where the divorce took place. While you're there, it's not a bad idea to check out other records to see how many times they've been sued.

Hi, Honey, I'm Home...

Second, in almost every state in the US, property tax records are public, and a very large percentage of them are searchable online. (There are a few exceptions where the records are private, most notably California.) If a person owns real property in their own name in a certain county, you can almost always look up the details in the property tax rolls.

The takeaway here is, while it may be interesting to check out your dating prospect's living situation, remember—they can look you up, too. So, if you are a homeowner and meet a person online, bear in mind that (assuming you don't live in one of those very few US jurisdictions where the rolls are private) your date can find out where you live if they know your name and how to use property tax rolls. If you are a homeowner, you should assume that anyone you've met who knows your legal name and the county you live in knows your address and the published value of your home.

Criminal Background Checks

Criminal background records are a murky, disorganized hodge-podge. Don't be fooled by TV shows where the cops yank a "rap sheet" out of the printer and have a complete story of every crooked thing the suspect has done since kindergarten. However, there are some basic things you can do.

First, most states have some type of criminal search you can run through their state police or state department of public safety. These searches are rarely free, but are generally moderately priced ($10–$25) and include a list of all state-level convictions that are reported to the database. In keeping with the principle of innocence until proven guilty, cases where the subject was not convicted will in many states be excluded from the public side of criminal databases.

The reliability of any criminal records search is limited by many factors, chief among them the amount of identifying data you include. Data resulting from a name-only search without a date of birth or Social Security number will likely include many folks who are not your subject and, in the case of common names, may be of little or no value. Of course, if your prospective honey-bunny committed six felonies in Maine, you're not going to see them if you are searching the Texas Department of Public Safety. I recommend checking every state where the subject has lived or worked in the past decade. It's not perfect, but it's a decent place to start.

Records of county and state court clerks, while geographically limited to a particular jurisdiction, are more comprehensive as to the details of offenses committed there and are not screened for guilty-only cases. Again, these are generally public records available at the county courthouse. Remember, they only cover crimes that occurred inside that clerk's jurisdiction, so I recommend checking every county in which the subject has lived in the past decade.

Also, you can check the national sex-offender database: United States Department of Justice National Sex Offender Public Website (nsopw.gov). Remember, you have to have the offender's legal name for this to work. If they give you an alias, the search is probably meaningless.

No professional investigator would consider relying on online services that sell "background" reports on people to the public. Even expensive reports that are sold to law enforcement and the legal community are nothing more than starting points for professional background checks. I'd say don't bother. These are probably a waste of your money.

The Meet-In-Person-Cute

So, where should you meet? I suggest a casual restaurant, preferably one where you are known. I made it a habit to connect with my best girlfriend and make sure that she was seeing me on Find My on her phone before I left on a date. I would let her know who I was meeting and where. (I often gave her my date's profile link from the dating site.) Then, I invited her to check on me through the location app later in the evening if she didn't see me home by the time she went to bed.

You're not sixteen anymore, bridling against parental restrictions. You are a grown-up adult out on your own dealing with people you have never met before who are not part of your social network. Make sure someone you trust knows where you are, who you are with, and when you plan to be home. Have a reasonable plan in place with that person in case you don't show up where you're supposed to be. That way, if you're in trouble, you know when the alarm is going to sound.

Just Say No to Requests for Money

There is no circumstance where you should consider that a request for money from a stranger online is legitimate, regardless of how long you have been communicating with them. The most frequent online dating scam is a bad actor who works to develop an online relationship with the mark then pleads some kind of hardship and asks for money. DON'T DO IT. Make up your mind about this before you start online dating—and don't deviate from the plan. As a PI, I can't tell you how many times I've heard this story from perfectly reasonable, smart, sophisticated businesspeople.

Trust Your Gut

Women are taught that we are hysterical, silly little fraidy-cats who jump at the sight of our own shadows, and as such, we should not trust our own judgment. This is pure hogwash.

If you're chatting with someone, meeting with someone, sleeping with someone…whatever you're doing…if you get the feeling that something is wrong, get yourself to safety. If that means stopping the chat, blocking the contact, leaving the restaurant, or grabbing your clothes and running down the street yelling for help, do it.

We are all equipped with natural warning systems. Ignoring these internal alarm bells makes no more sense than ignoring the smell of smoke or the sensation of heat. Get to safety. If you're wrong, nobody ever died of embarrassment. You'll get over that a lot sooner than you will being abducted by a psycho.

QUIZ

Test your knowledge about the Black Dahlia case.

The Black Dahlia Quiz | Criminals | 15 Questions (funtrivia.com)
https://www.funtrivia.com/trivia-quiz/People/The-Black-Dahlia-117821.html

SNARKY HUMOR

Cop: So, I'm writing you a ticket for driving alone in the car pool lane.

Me: You're going to feel really stupid when you look in my trunk.

REFERENCES & COOL SITES

The Black Dahlia in Hollywood
https://www.theblackdahliainhollywood.com/

Heaven Is HERE! The Murder of Elizabeth Short, the Black Dahlia; Los Angeles' Most Famous Unsolved Killing | LMHarnisch.com
lmharnisch.com

FBI Records: The Vault — Black Dahlia (Elizabeth Short)
https://vault.fbi.gov/Black%20Dahlia%20%28E%20Short%29%20/

Black Dahlia | FBI
https://www.fbi.gov/history/famous-cases/black-dahlia

Home | Steve Hodel
https://stevehodel.com/

The Delacorte Review » The Black Dahlia
https://delacortereview.org/2020/09/10/the-black-dahlia-the-long-strange-history-of-los-angeles-coldest-cold-case/

Black Dahlia murder solved? Shocking new details about aspiring actress Elizabeth Short's life and gruesome death | Fox News
https://www.foxnews.com/entertainment/black-dahlia-murder-solved-shocking-new-details-about-aspiring-actress-elizabeth-shorts-life-and-gruesome-death

Cold Case File: Black Dahlia | Forensic Science Society
https://forensicsciencesociety.com/thedrip/the-cold-case-black-dahlia

10 Shocking Facts About The Black Dahlia, Hollywood's Most Famous Unsolved Murder | Mental Floss
https://www.mentalfloss.com/article/572113/the-black-dahlia-murder-facts

BLACK DAHLIA MURDER | Retired LAPD detective reveals new evidence pointing to prime suspect — his father | The South Pasadenan | South Pasadena News

https://southpasadenan.com/black-dahlia-murder-retired-lapd-detective-reveals-new-evidence-pointing-to-prime-suspect-his-father/

Denise Diana Huddle

PART 6

WHO REALLY KIDNAPPED THE LINDBERGH BABY?

CHAPTER 25

WHAT HAPPENED?

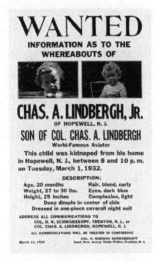

Information wanted poster regarding
the Lindbergh kidnapping. (FBI.gov)

At approximately 9:00 p.m. on Tuesday, March 1, 1932, twenty-month-old Charles Lindbergh Jr. was kidnapped from his nursery on the second story of the Hopewell, New Jersey home of his parents, Charles and Anne Morrow Lindbergh. Around 10:00 p.m., the baby's nurse found the child missing. Muddy footprints led from the crib to an open window, and a ransom note was left on the windowsill.

BACKGROUND

Charles Augustus Lindbergh Sr. revolutionized aviation and achieved worldwide renown when he made the first solo nonstop transatlantic flight from New York City to Paris on May 20–21, 1927. He married Anne Morrow on May 27, 1929, at the Morrow estate in Englewood, New Jersey. Their first child, Charles Augustus Lindbergh Jr., was born June 22, 1930.

THE KIDNAPPING

Around 10:00 p.m., when the baby's nurse, Betty Gow, found the child missing, she called for Mr. and Mrs. Lindbergh, who were at home. Charles Lindbergh searched the premises, and the police were summoned. Hopewell law enforcement contacted the New Jersey State Police under the command of Superintendent H. Norman Schwarzkopf (father of the commander of the coalition forces in Operation Desert Shield/Storm), launching the investigation into the crime of the century.

Definitely Not the Stairway to Heaven

Muddy footprints were found inside the nursery and on the ground near where a broken homemade ladder discovered on the property had been leaned against the house next to the nursery window.

Simulation of where the police believed the broken ladder was placed.
(New Jersey Dept. of State)

CHAPTER 26

THE RANSOM NOTES

Communication regarding payment of the ransom for the Lindbergh child was a long and complex affair. The night of the kidnapping, the first ransom note was found on the sill of the open nursery window.

March 1, 1932—Nursery Note Found on Windowsill of Lindbergh Home

Kidnapper demands $50,000 ($1,066,774 in 2022 money).

Dear Sir! Have 50.000$ redy 25.00$ in 20$ bills 15000$ in 10$ bills and 10000$ in 5$ bills. After 2-4 days we will inform you were to deliver the Mony. We warn you for making anyding public or for the polise the child is in gut care. Indication for all letters are signature and 3 holes.

March 4, 1932—Second Note Received
March 6, 1932, Postmarked March 4 in Brooklyn, NY

Kidnappers change demand to $70,000 and describe payment type.

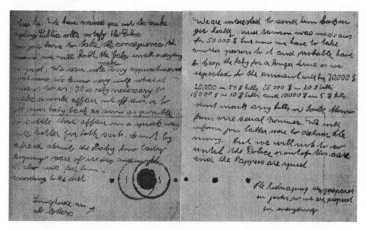

Dear Sir. We have warned you note to make anything Public also notify the Police now you have to take the consequences. That means we will hold the baby until everything is quite. We can note make any appointment just now. We know very well what it means to us. It is realy necessary to make a world affair out of this, or to get your baby back as soon as possible to settle those affair in a quick way will be better for both seds. Don't by afraid about the Baby. We ? keeping care of it day and night. We also will feed him according to the diet. We are interested to send him back in gut health. and ransom was made aus for 50000 $ but now we have to take another person to it and probable have to keep the baby for a longer time as we expected. So the amount will be 70000 $ 20.000 in 50$ bills 25.000 $ in 20$ bill 15.000 $ in 10$ bills and 10.000 in 5$ bills. don't mark any bills or take them from one serial nomer. We will inform you latter were to deliver the mony. but we will note do so until the Police is out of the case and the pappers are quiet. The kidnaping was prepared in years. so we are prepared for everyding.

March 6, 1932—Lindberghs Announce Go-Betweens in Press

Lindberghs authorize Slavy Spitale and Irving Bitz to act as their go-betweens.

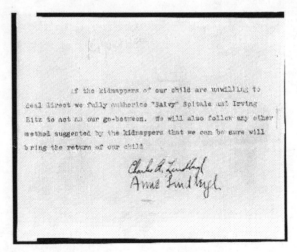

If the kidnappers of our child are unwilling to deal direct we fully authorize 'Salvy' Spitale and Irving Bitz to act as our go-between. We will also follow any other methods suggested by the kidnappers that we can be sure will bring the return of our child.

Charles Lindbergh

Anne Lindbergh

March 8, 1932—Third Note Received by Charles Lindbergh's Attorney

Kidnappers repeat $70,000 demand.

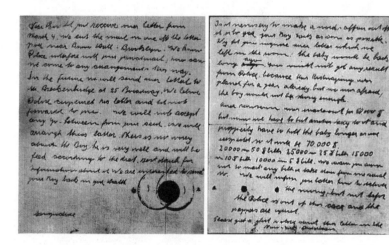

Dear Sir: Did you receive ouer letter from March 4. we sent the mail on one off the letter — near Bumn Hall - Brooklyn. We know Police interfere with your privatmail; how can we come to any arrangements this way. In the future we will send our letters to Mr. Breckenbridge at 25 Broadway. We believe polise captured one letter and did not forwarded to you. We will not accept any go-between from your sent. We will arrangh thees latter. There is no worry about the Boy. He is very well and will be feed according to the diet. Best dank for information about it We are interested to send your boy back in gut health. Is it necessery to make a world-affair out of it, or to get your boy back as soon as possible. Wy did you ignore oue letter which we left in the room! the baby would be back long ago. You would not get any result from Police becauce our kidnaping was pland for a year allredy. but we were afraid, the boy would not be strong enough. ouer ransom was made out for 50.000 $ but now we have to but another to it as propperly have to hold the baby longer as we expected so it will be 70.000 $ 20000 in 50$ bills 25000 in 25$ bills 15000$ in 10$ bills 10000 in 5$ bills. We warn you again not to mark any bills or take them for one seriel No. We will inform you latter how to deliver the mony, but not before the Police is out of this cace and the pappers are quite. Please grab a short notice about this letter in the New York American.

In a bizarre twist, Dr. John Condon, a complete stranger to the Lindberghs, volunteered $1,000 of his own money and stepped right up to help out, putting an ad in the local paper offering his services as a go-between with the kidnappers. Both the abductors and the Lindberghs accepted his offer. After this point, Condon was the only person in direct contact with the kidnappers.

March 8, 1932—Dr. John F. Condon's Letter to the Lindbergh Kidnapper Appears in the *Bronx Home News* (Condon signed newspaper communications with the code name "Jafsie.")

Dr. John F. Condon Makes Offer of $1,000 to Kidnapers for Return of Lindbergh Baby

I offer all I can scrape together so a loving mother may again have her child and Col. Lindbergh may know that the American people are grateful for the honor bestowed upon them by his pluck and daring. Let the kidnappers know that no testimony of mine, or information coming from me will be used against them. I offer $1,000 which I have saved from my salary as additional to the suggested ransom of $50,000 which is said to have been demanded of Col. Lindbergh. I stand ready at my own expense to go anywhere, alone, to give the kidnapper the extra money and promise never to utter his name to any person. If this is not agreeable, then I ask the kidnappers to go to any Catholic priest and return the child unharmed, with the knowledge that any priest must hold inviolate any statement which may be made by the kidnappers.

[Dr. John Condon]

March 9, 1932—Fourth Note Received by Dr. John F. Condon

Kidnappers agree to Dr. John F. Condon as intermediary and send letter for delivery to Lindbergh describing preliminary procedure for payment and exchange.

Mr. Dr. John Condon 2974 Decatur Ave. New York, NY

dear Sir: If you are willing to act as go-between in the Lind-bergh cace please follow stricly instruction. Handel incloced letter personaly to Mr. Lindbergh. It will explain everyding. don't tell anyone about it as soon we find out the Press or Police is notified everything are cansell and it will be a further delay. Affter you gett the money from Mr. Lindbergh put these 3 words in the New-York American.

Mony is redy

Affter notice we will give you further instruction. don't be affraid we are not out for your 1000 $ keep it. Only act stricly. Be at home every night between 6-12 by this time you wil l hear from us.

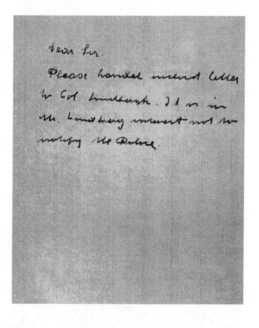

dear Sir. please handel incloced letter to Col. Lindbergh. It is in Mr. Lindbergh interest not to notify the Police.

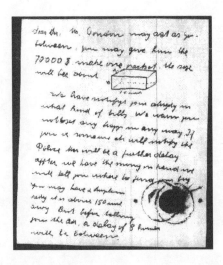

dear Sir, Mr. Condon may act as go-between. You may give him the 70000 $. make one packet the size will bee about [sketch of a box] we have notify your allredy in what kind of bills. We warn you not to set any trapp in any way. If you or someone els will notify the Police ther will be a further delay after we have the mony in hand we will tell you where to find yur boy You may have a airplain redy it is about 150 mil awy. But befor telling you the oDr. a delay of 8 houers will be between.

March 10, 1932—Lindberghs Authorize Condon to Act on Their Behalf

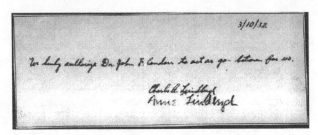

We hereby authorize Dr. John F. Condon to act as go-between for us.

Charles A. Lindbergh

Anne Lindbergh

March 12, 1932—Sixth Ransom Note Delivered to Dr. John Condon by Taxi Driver Joseph Perrone

Kidnapper instructs Dr. Condon in first steps to cemetery meeting with "John."

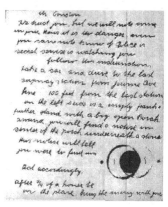

Mr. Condon

We trust you, but we will note come in your hous it is to danger. even you can note know if Police or secret servise is watching you follow this instruction.

Take a car and drive to the last supway station from Jerome Ave here. 100 feet from this last station on the left seide is a empty frankfurther stand with a big open Porch around, you will find a notise in senter of the porch underneath a stove.

this notise will tell you were to find us.

Denise Diana Huddle

act accordingly.

After 3/4 of a houer be on the place, bring the mony with you.

March 12, 1932—Note Found by Dr. John Condon at the Frankfurter Stand

Instructions directing Condon from frankfurter stand to cemetery meeting with "John."

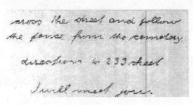

Cross the street and follow the fence from the cemetery direction to 233 Street. I will meet you.

Following these instructions, Dr. Condon met "John" in the Woodlawn Cemetery near 233 Street and Jerome Avenue on March 12, 1932. "John" agreed to furnish a token of the child's identity.

March 14 & 15, 1932—Dr. Condon's Message in Newspaper

Money is ready. No cops. No Secret Service. No press. I come alone, like last time. Jafsie.

March 16 & 17, 1932—Dr. Condon's Message in Newspaper

I accept. Money is ready. You know they won't let me deliver without getting the package. Please make it some sort of C.O.D. transaction. You know you can trust Jafsie.

March 16, 1932—Seventh Ransom Note and Sleeping Suit Received by Dr. Condon

Kidnapper refuses to have more in-person meetings, sends sleeping suit to prove they have the child, and gives instructions for next ad from Condon.

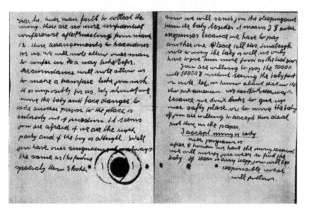

Dear Sir: Ouer man faill to collect the mony. There are no more confidential conference after we meeting from March 12. Those arrangemts to hazardous for us. We will note allow ouer man to confer in a way like before. Circumstance will note allow us to make a transfare like you wish. It is imposibly for us. wy shuld we move the baby and face danger. to take another person to the place is entirely out of question. It seems you are afraid if we are the right party and if the boy is allright. Well you have ouer singnature. It is always the same as the first one specialy them 3 holes.

Now we will send you the sleepingsuit from the baby besides it means 3 $ extra expenses because we have to pay another one. Please tell Mrs. Lindbergh note to worry the baby is well. we only have to give him more food as the diet says.

You are willing to pay the 70000 note 50000 $ without seeing the baby first or note. let us know about that in the New York-American. We can't do it other ways becauce we don't like to give up ouer safty plase or to move the baby. If you are willing to accept this deal put these in paper.

I accept mony is redy

ouer program is:

after 8 houers we have the mony received we will notify you where to find the baby If there is any trapp, you will be responsible what will follows.

March 18 & 19, 1932—Dr. Condon's Message in Newspaper

I accept. Money is ready. John, your package is delivered and is O.K. Direct me. Jafsie.

March 20 & 21, 1932—Dr. Condon's Message in Newspaper

Inform me how I can get important letter to you. Urgent. Jafsie.

March 21, 1932—Eighth Ransom Note Received by Dr. Condon

Kidnapper demands response in newspaper.

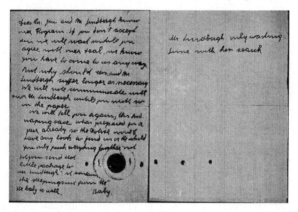

Dear Sir: You and Mr. Lindbergh know ouer Program. If you don't accept den we will wait until you agree with ouer deal. We know you have to come to us anyway But why should Mrs. and Mr. Lindbergh suffer longer as necessary we will note communicate with you or Mr. Lindbergh until you write so in the paper.

we will tell you again; this kidnapping cace whas prepared for a year already so the Police won't have any luck to find us or the child. You only puch everything farther out did you send that little package to Mr. Lindbergh? it contains the sleepingsuit from the baby. the baby is well.

Mr. Lindbergh only wasting time with his search.

March 22, 23, 24, & 25, 1932—Dr. Condon's Message in Newspaper

Thanks. That little package you sent me was immediately delivered and accepted as real article. See my position. Over fifty years in business and can I pay without seeing the goods? Common sense makes me trust you. Please understand my position. Jafsie.

March 26, 27, & 28, 1932—Dr. Condon's Message in Newspaper

Money is ready. Furnish simple code for us to use in paper. Jafsie.

March 30, 1932—Ninth Ransom Note Received by Dr. Condon

Kidnapper threatens to double amount of ransom demand if payment not made soon.

dear Sir: It is note necessary to furnish any code. You and Mr. Lindbergh know ouer Program very well. We will keep the child in ouer save plase until we have the money in hand, but if the deal is note closed until the 8 of April we will ask for 30000 more. also note 70000 - 100000.

How can Mr. Lindbergh follow so many false clues he knows we are the right party ouer singnature is still the same as in the ransom note. But if Mr. Lindbergh likes to fool around for another month, we can help it.

Once he has come to us anyway but if he keeps on waiting we will double ouer amount. There is absolute no fear aboud the child it is well.

March 31 & April 1, 1932—Dr. Condon's Message in Newspaper

I accept. Money is ready. Jafsie.

April 1, 1932—Tenth Ransom Note Delivered to Dr. Condon

Kidnapper sets ransom payment for Saturday, April 2, 1932.

Denise Diana Huddle

Dear Sir: have the money ready by Saturday evening. we will inform you where and how to deliver it. have the money in one bundle we want you to put it in a sertain place. Ther is no fear that somebody els will take it, we watch everything closely. Please tell us know if you are agree and ready for action by Saturday evening — if yes put in paper

"Yes everything O.K."

It is a very simple delivery but we find out very sun if there is any trapp. After 8 houers you gett the ad; from the boy, on the place you find two ladies. the are innocence.

If it is too late put it in the New York American for Saturday morning. Put it in New York Journal.

April 2, 3, & 4 1932—Dr. Condon's Message in Newspaper

Yes. Everything O.K. Jafsie.

April 2, 1932—Eleventh Ransom Note Delivered to Dr. Condon by Unknown Taxi Driver

Kidnapper gives Condon initial instructions to payment site.

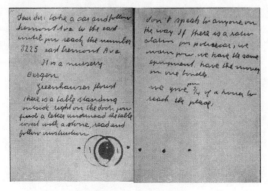

Dear Sir: take a car and follow Tremont Ave to the east until you reach the number 3225 east Tremont Ave.

It is a nursery. Bergen Greenhauses florist

there is a table standing outside right on the door, you find a letter undernead the table covert with a stone, read and follow instruction. Don't speak to anyone on the way. If there is a ratio alarm for polisecar, we warn you. we have the same eqipment. have the money in one bundle. We give you 3/4 of a houer to reach the plase

April 2, 1932—Twelfth Ransom Note Found at Bergen Greenhouse by Dr. Condon

Kidnapper gives Condon final directions to payment meet.

Cross the street and walk to the next corner and follow whittenmore Ave to the soud

Take the money with you. come alone and walk

I will meet you.

Denise Diana Huddle

April 2, 1932—Thirteenth Note Handed to Dr. Condon by "John" along with a Receipt for the Money.

Kidnapper gives Condon bogus location information for Lindbergh child.

The boy is on the Boad Nelly It is a small Boad 28 feet long Two persons are on the Boad. The are innosent. you will find the Boad between Horseneck Beach and gay Head near Elizabeth Island.

April 6, 7, & 8, 1932—Dr. Condon's Message in Newspaper

What is wrong? Have you crossed me? Please, better directions. Jafsie

April 10, 1932—*New York Daily News* Sunday Edition Summarized Jafsie Advertisements

Condon first entered the case on March 13, when an advertisement appeared in the Bronx Home News, which read as follows:

"Baby alive and well. Money is ready. Call and see us. Jafsie."

"Before that, on March 8, he had given an interview to a Home News reporter in which he offered $1,000 on his own account as a reward for the return of the baby and offered to act as intermediary between Col. Lindbergh and the kidnapers.

The interview is believed to have come to the attention of the Lindberghs who afterward got in touch with Condon.

Money is Ready.

On March 14 another advertisement appeared:

"Money is ready. No cops. No secret service. No press. I come alone like last time. Please call. Jafsie."

The next day the same advertisement appeared and on March 16 a more definite note appeared in the advertisement:

"I accept. Money is ready. You know they won't let me deliver without getting the package. Please make it some sort of C. O. D. transaction. You know you can trust Jafsie."

That ad was repeated on March 17 and on the next day appeared:

"I accept. Money is ready. John, your package is delivered and O.K. Direct me. Jafsie."

This appeared again on March 19. The next day the following appeared:

"Inform me how I can get important letter to you. Urgent. Jafsie."

This appeared again on March 21. The next day a longer ad was published.

"Thanks. That little package you sent me was immediately delivered and accepted as real article. See my position. Over 50 years in business and can I pay without seeing goods? Common sense makes me trust you. Please understand my position. Jafsie."

This was repeated on March 23, 24 and 25. On March 26, the ad said:

"Money is ready. Furnish simple code for use in paper. Jafsie."

Repeated Ad for 2 Days.

This was repeated for the next two days and then two days passed without an ad. On March 31 the ad reappeared:

"I accept. Money is ready. Jafsie."

This was repeated the next day. On April 2 the ad advised:

"Yes. Everything O. K. Jafsie."

This was repeated for two days, and there was no ad on April 5.

On April 6, 7 and 8 the ad showed that plans had gone wrong, saying:

"What is wrong? Have you crossed me? Please better directions. Jafsie."

That was the last of the Jafsie ads.

CHAPTER 27

THE BODY IS DISCOVERED

According to an account in the May 13, 1932 edition of the *New York Daily News*, on May 12, 1932, William Allen, a forty-year-old laborer, left his three companions, Orville Wilson, Livingston Titus, and Orville Kraft, with their two tree-filled trucks and ventured into a copse of trees on the grounds of the St. Michael's Orphanage in Hopewell, New Jersey.

As he ducked beneath a branch, he saw a small human skull protruding from the ground. He uncovered the baby's corpse, and called for his companions. Leaving one member of the group at the grave site, the other three men raced into town and contacted the police, who sped to the scene.

Police took two articles of clothing from the corpse and delivered them to the home of the Lindberghs. Betty Gow, the baby's nurse, identified the clothing as that in which she had dressed Charles Lindbergh Jr. the night of the kidnapping. She later identified the corpse at the Trenton morgue based on "distinguishing marks." Betty Gow's identification was later confirmed by the Lindberghs' physician, Dr. Philip Van Inglen, who had delivered the baby and had examined him just two weeks prior to the abduction.

THE INVESTIGATION

Feds Send Reinforcements to Stormin' Norman's Dad

From the time of the kidnapping, the FBI's role in the investigation was merely that of assisting the New Jersey authorities, primarily the New Jersey State Police headed by H. Norman Schwarzkopf Sr. At the time, kidnapping was not a federal offense. But because of Charles Lindbergh's prominent role in the country, the federal government went beyond its obligations to place all of its law enforcement resources at the disposal of Superintendent Schwarzkopf.

On May 26, 1932, Superintendent Schwarzkopf announced a $25,000 reward (roughly $500,000 in today's money) for information leading to the apprehension and conviction of the kidnapper.

The Talking Pine Trees

This is my favorite part of the Lindbergh kidnapping investigation. I'm a major science nerd, and I love nothing more than hearing about nit-picking wonks pencil whipping bad guys into prison using just their brains and cunning. Unlike the scary talking trees in *The Wizard of Oz*, the trees in this story spoke only to Arthur Koehler, and they told the secrets of murder. Koehler was a wood technologist at the US Forest Products Laboratory in Madison, Wisconsin, and he is my kind of hero.

When Koehler saw pictures in the media of the ladder used in the Lindbergh kidnapping, he wrote a letter to Charles Lindbergh offering his assistance in analyzing any clues he could find in the wood used in the ladder, but he received no response.

Yet, ten weeks after the kidnapping, in May 1932, the New Jersey State Police sent wood samples from the ladder to the US Forest Products Laboratory, and Koehler was assigned to evaluate them, so he ended up on the case after all. Immediately upon seeing it under the microscope, Koehler knew the first sample was North Carolina pine, which grows in not only in North Carolina, but in states from Texas across the Gulf Coast and up the eastern seaboard to New Jersey. He also saw pieces of Douglas fir, which grows west of the Rockies, and birch and Ponderosa pine, which were regularly shipped to the East Coast from western forests.

Subsequently, Superintendent Schwarzkopf asked the Forest Service to send a wood expert to New Jersey to assist in the investigation, and Arthur Koehler was selected for the assignment. There, Mr. Koehler had the opportunity to study the ladder in its entirety.

His first determination was that it was constructed by a slovenly and inept carpenter. The workmanship was shoddy and amateurish, and the construction had been done with poorly maintained tools. The top section of the ladder rails had been dressed with a hand plane that was dull and nicked, leaving distinctive tool marks that could tie the plane to the ladder—in the event the plane was ever located.

The Douglas fir rails had wire nail holes indicating that the lumber had been used before it was fashioned into the ladder, probably in a temporary application. However, the pine rails in the top section of the ladder had square nail holes made by old-fashioned cut nails, suggesting a more permanent prior use. The absence of any rust around these nail holes indicated that the lumber had previously been used in an interior application. More importantly, the spacing of the nail holes was irregular, and Koehler discerned that it would be possible to positively identify the structure from which the pine rails were taken if the nails were still present in the original location.

Since North Carolina pine was cheap and common, Koehler reasoned that it was unlikely to have been shipped from far away. When he left New Jersey, Koehler had the ladder shipped to his lab in Madison for further study. Working from tool marks he found on the pine rails, Koehler used his almost-encyclopedic knowledge of milling equipment to determine the precise specifications of the planer at the mill that had dressed the North Carolina pine that was eventually used to form the rails of the ladder.

After speaking with planer manufacturers, Koehler determined that the type he was looking for was not manufactured on the East Coast. He then took the Southern Lumberman's Directory and wrote to every pine mill from New York to Alabama, inquiring if they utilized a planer fitting the specifications he had discerned. Only twenty-five mills answered that they had planers that matched his description.

Koehler then asked all of those mills to send samples he could compare to the tool marks he had found on the Lindbergh ladder. From that work, he determined that the lumber used in the pine rails of the kidnapping ladder was originally milled in McCormick, South Carolina, at a facility owned by the Dorn family. After visiting the mill and reviewing their records, he determined that the lumber had been milled at the Dorn location sometime after September 1929.

Dorn's Mill, McCormick, South Carolina.
(Photo courtesy of SC Dept. of Archives and History,
Columbia, SC. National Register file.)

Koehler narrowed down a list of all Dorn shipments of North Carolina pine made after September 1929 to shipments made to locations north of the Potomac River. After an amazing and extremely complex example of critical thinking layered on top of incredible investigative instincts, Koehler discerned that, of all the lumber shipped from the Dorn mill between September 1929 and March 1932, the lumber used to make the pine rails of the top section of the Lindbergh ladder had come out of a 1929 shipment from Dorn to the National Lumber and Millwork Company in the Bronx, New York.

Koehler and his stalwart partner in the lumber investigation, Inspector Lewis Bornmann from the New Jersey State Police, visited the National Lumber and Millwork Company. Although all of the lumber from the 1929 Dorn shipment that National had received had been sold long before, the manager remembered that a storage bin had been constructed sometime around 1929 from lumber of that type of wood for use in their yard. When Koehler removed a piece of lumber from the bin and compared the tool marks to those on the ladder, he determined that it was an exact match. Koehler could therefore prove scientifically that the lumber used in the ladder found on the Lindbergh estate had been acquired from the 1929 shipment the National Lumber and Millwork Company in the Bronx had received from the Dorn mill in McCormick, South Carolina.

Comparison of milling marks in ladder rail #13 with lumber
from National Lumber and Millwork Co., New York.
(New Jersey Dept. of State)

After examining the bin, while Koehler and Bornmann were visiting with the manager at National, they had their badges hanging over the pockets of their shirts. In a strange twist of fate, during our hero's visit to the lumberyard, two men came into the store to buy plywood. While the customers were waiting for the cashier to get change from the safe, they spotted the badges and left without their plywood. The manager thought this was suspicious and ran out to the parking lot to get their license number. He recognized one of the men as his former employee, Bruno Richard Hauptmann.

Tracing the Ransom—Show Me the Money!

Widespread public fear of the banking system raged after the run on the banks that marked the beginning of the Great Depression. According to TheGreatDepressionCauses.com, 9,000 of the 25,000 banks in the US at the beginning of the Depression had failed by 1933. Faith in the US economy and its currency was about as strong as belief in the Easter Bunny.

In 1933, during the fourth year of the Depression, Americans were hoarding gold at an unprecedented rate. Because the Federal Reserve Act of 1913 required the US Treasury to maintain a 40 percent gold reserve backing all US currency printed by the Bureau of Engraving and Printing, hoarding of gold by citizens limited the ability of the government to issue currency and thus hamstrung the monetary policy decisions of the Federal Reserve. In short, Franklin Roosevelt feared he could not drag the US out of the economic swamp of the Great Depression as long as Americans were hoarding gold.

So, he dusted off some powers granted to the president during World War I and issued Executive Order 6102 making it illegal for individual citizens to hold physical gold or gold certificates.

Executive Order 6102 recalling gold coin, bullion, and certificates. (Federal Register)

Recall Notice on Ransom Cash

The announcement on April 5, 1933, of Executive Order 6102 was a major turning point in the Lindbergh case. The order required all persons to deliver on or before May 1, 1933, all but a small amount of gold coins, gold bullion, and gold certificates owned by them to the Federal Reserve in exchange for $20.67 (equivalent to $413 in 2022) per troy ounce. This was significant because $40,000 of the $50,000 ransom was paid in gold certificates. This mass recall of gold certificates made any gold certificate from the ransom money stand out like a shark at a guppy convention when it hit the banking system.

Follow the Money

On May 23, 1932, the FBI in New York City informed banks in the greater New York area that they were actively involved in the case and asked all financial institutions to keep a lookout for the ransom money. In early 1934, pamphlets with the serial numbers of all ransom bills were distributed to anyone handling currency in banks, clearinghouses, grocery stores in certain communities, insurance companies, gas stations, airports, department stores, post offices, and telegraph companies. The FBI's New York City bureau requested all banks and branches exercise an extremely close watch for the bills. Key cards with condensed information about the bills were also distributed, and bank officials and individual employees were personally contacted to keep interest alive.

Listing of Lindbergh kidnapping serial numbers. (New Jersey Dept. of State)

Mystery on West 149th Street

On May 2, 1933, 296 $10 gold certificates and one $20 gold certificate from the Lindbergh ransom were identified by the Federal Reserve Bank of New York having been received with deposit tickets dated May 1, 1933, for the account of J. J. Faulkner, 537 West 149th Street. After extensive investigation, the depositor was never located.

Turning Up the Heat

In August and September of 1934, a total of sixteen gold certificates from the Lindbergh ransom were discovered, most from the Yorkville and Harlem areas of New York City. Three-man teams composed of members of the New Jersey State Police, the New York City Police Department, and the FBI personally visited all banks in Greater New York and Westchester County. The intense law enforcement involvement and the resulting bank attention to the matter resulted in banks discovering the certificates closer to the times at which they were passed.

And We Have a BINGO!

At about 1:20 p.m. on September 18, 1934, the assistant manager of the Corn Exchange Bank and Trust Company at 125th Street and Park Avenue called the New York City bureau of the FBI and reported that a $10 gold certificate had been discovered just minutes before by a teller in the bank. The bank determined that they had received the certificate in a deposit from a gas station located at 127th Street and Lexington Avenue.

Investigators learned that on September 15, 1934, an alert attendant had received the bill in payment for five gallons of gasoline. The driver fit the description of the individual who had passed other bills in recent weeks (all of whom reportedly looked very similar to the sketch of "Cemetery John" provided by police artists working with John Condon). The gas station attendant was suspicious of the gold certificate, and, fearing it might not be honored by the bank, recorded on it the license number of the vehicle driven by the man who paid with the note. The license number was registered to Bruno Richard Hauptmann of 1279 East 222nd Street, Bronx, New York.

The Feds Are Gonna Getcha—One Way or the Other

Hauptmann's house was placed under surveillance throughout the night of September 18, 1934. At 9:00 a.m., September 19, a man matching the description of Cemetery John emerged from the house and got into his Buick, which was parked nearby. He was taken into custody by a trio of officers from the NJSP, NYPD, and the FBI. Police found a $20 gold certificate from the ransom money in his wallet at the time of his arrest. The kidnapper was in custody 932 days after Charles Lindbergh Jr. was taken from his crib in Hopewell, New Jersey.

CHAPTER 28

THE EVIDENCE AGAINST HAUPTMANN

Once Hauptmann was in custody, the evidence against him piled up like trash during a garbage strike.

Ill-Gotten Gains

During a search of Hauptmann's home, police found a pair of shoes they later linked to a purchase made with one of the ransom bills previously recovered by the FBI. Hauptmann admitted to making several other purchases with the ransom money.

Comparison of artist's sketch of "Cemetery John" and
police photo of Hauptmann. (FBI.gov)

Double Indemnity

On September 19, the taxi driver, Joseph Perrone, positively identified Hauptmann as the individual from whom he had received the ransom note Perrone then delivered to Dr. Condon. Shortly thereafter, Dr. Condon himself identified Hauptmann as "Cemetery John" with whom he had met and to whom he paid the ransom.

Caught with the Cash

Gas can with ransom money found in Hauptmann's garage. (FBI.gov)

A search of Hauptmann's home revealed $13,000 in ransom notes and certificates hidden in a gas can in Hauptmann's garage.

When Hauptmann was first questioned, he rattled off several of his previous places of employment, including the National Lumber and Millwork Company. Once Hauptmann was in custody, Koehler was summoned to Hauptmann's home to search for clues that might tie Hauptmann to the ladder.

Denise Diana Huddle

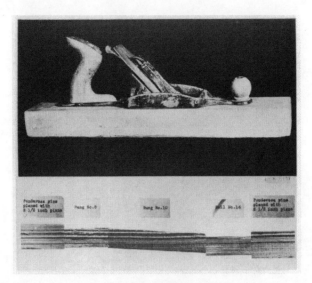

Nicked wood plane belonging to Hauptmann.
(New Jersey Dept. of State)

In the garage, Koehler found the nicked plane that was used on the top rails of the ladder.

Hauptmann attic, Bronx. Space from which ladder rail
#16 was shown to have been removed.
(Trial evidence, www.HistoricTrialTranscripts.com)

Inside of the attic, he discovered that boards had been cut out of the floor. The remaining boards matched exactly the North Carolina pine from the 1929 Dorn shipment.

Hauptmann attic, Bronx. Nail holes in ladder rail #16
matched to nails in Hauptmann ceiling joists.
(Trial evidence, www.HistoricTrialTranscripts.com)

Where the attic floorboards had been removed, Koehler found four nails protruding from the ceiling joist, and he was able to fit the rail from the Lindbergh ladder over those four nails. The holes matched the nail shape and spacing pattern exactly. The tree rings and wood grain from the remaining boards in the attic floor matched the ends of the boards used in the ladder.

Koehler was one of the most important witnesses at the trial of Bruno Richard Hauptmann, and the evidence he gave was critical in the prosecution securing a guilty verdict and a sentence of death for the kidnapper. Talk about revenge of the nerds! Bravo, Mr. Koehler!!

Arthur Koehler told the entire story of his investigation in great detail in the April 25, 1935 edition of the *Saturday Evening Post*. You can read it at https://s3.amazonaws.com/files.saturdayevening-post.com/uploads/reprints/Ladder_story/index.html. It's a fun read.

The Handwriting on the Wall

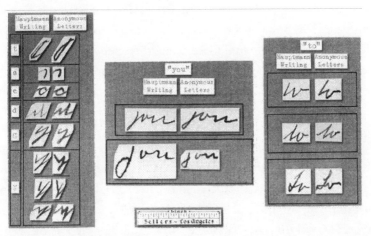

Handwriting analysis of Hauptmann and ransom notes conducted by FBI. (FBI.gov)

Hauptmann's handwriting was matched by the FBI crime lab to the distinctive writing in all of the ransom notes.

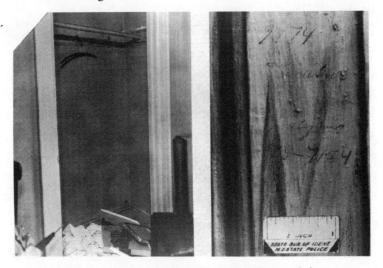

Closet in Hauptmann house with Condon's address and phone number written on the wall. (New Jersey Dept. of State)

Carpenters scribble measurements on lumber all the time. Lumberyards often give away flattened pencils that won't roll just for this purpose. Hauptmann, however inept, was a carpenter, and true to form, he wrote Dr. John F. Condon's address and telephone number in pencil on the wood inside of a closet in his home.

The Train to Conviction Leaves the Station

On September 26, 1934, Hauptmann was indicted in the Supreme Court, Bronx County, New York, on charges of extortion. On October 8, Hauptmann was indicted in Hunterdon County, New Jersey, for murder. Two days later, the governor of New York honored the requisition of the governor of New Jersey for the surrender of Bruno Richard Hauptmann, and Hauptmann was transferred to the Hunterdon County Jail in Flemington, New Jersey, on October 19, 1934.

THE LINDBERGH KIDNAPPING AND THE LAW

Bruno Hauptmann was never tried for kidnapping. Since kidnapping was not a federal crime and was only a misdemeanor in New Jersey, prosecutors were desperate to file charges that would lead to the death penalty for Hauptmann, yet there was insufficient evidence to prove premeditation in the murder of the child.

Clothes Make the Crime

However, in a brilliant stroke of legal insight, the prosecution realized that the value of the expensive clothes the child was wearing at the time of the abduction exceeded the minimum amount for felony burglary in New Jersey. So, the New Jersey prosecutors charged

Hauptmann under the felony murder doctrine for a death resulting during the course of a burglary. Hauptmann was convicted and executed for a death that resulted during the felony theft of the baby's expensive clothes.

As a result of the abduction and murder of Charles Augustus Lindbergh Jr., the United States Congress passed what is called the Lindbergh Law (18 U.S.C. §§ 1201–1202) making kidnapping a federal crime when the abductee is taken across state lines. The law was later amended to give juries the opportunity to recommend the death penalty if they see fit.

Despite numerous unsuccessful appeals, Hauptmann was destined for execution. At 8:44 p.m. on April 3, 1936, in the New Jersey State Prison, 2,000 volts of electricity were sent through Bruno Richard Hauptmann's body, resulting in his death.

CHAPTER 29

DID HAUPTMANN ACT ALONE?

While there is little doubt that Bruno Richard Hauptmann was deeply involved in the kidnapping of the Lindbergh baby, the question of whether or not Hauptmann acted alone has persisted for over ninety years. Several issues in the events surrounding the kidnapping have never been fully resolved.

Suspicious Minds Want to Know

The first question is how it was that the kidnapper knew the Lindberghs would be in Hopewell that night.

Since Lucky Lindy landed in Paris on May 21, 1927, he had become one of the most famous men in the world. Lindbergh was an introvert who did not thrive in the limelight. Yet, after his transatlantic flight, he became a worldwide sensation overnight. His life became one long string of parades, public appearances, photoshoots, and press interviews. Lindbergh found the new lifestyle exhausting. Emotionally and psychologically drained, he and his wife, Anne, were building their Hopewell home on the 390-acre estate as a haven to escape from the manic public life that had been thrust upon them.

The house was not quite finished in March of 1932. The

Lindberghs had been staying at Anne's parents' estate in Engle-wood while their new home was under construction. Desperate for solace from their public life, the couple had taken to slip-ping away over the weekends and spending Friday to Monday in Hopewell, occupying the finished parts of the house before return-ing on Monday to Englewood. They took only the baby, Charles Jr., their dog, Wahgoosh, and a skeleton staff with them—usually the baby's nurse, Betty Gow, and butler/handyman Olley Whately and his wife.

However, that particular weekend, the Lindberghs' son was sick with a cold, and the couple decided that it would be best to stay in Hopewell so that the child could breathe clean, fresh country air and not endure the stress of the trip back to Englewood until he recovered. It was not like surveillance on the house from the public road was easy, as the property was buried inside of a 390-acre estate, a half mile from the road. In short, the kidnapper had to know they were there.

So, the first issue that points to Hauptmann having an accom-plice is that someone had to tell Hauptmann that the Lindberghs were not in Englewood where they were supposed to be.

The second mystery about the kidnapping is how Hauptmann knew which window to use to access the nursery. From pictures of various angles of the house, my estimate is that the home had over thirty windows, maybe closer to forty. There was no evidence at the scene that the ladder had been placed at any other window. How did the kidnapper know which window to choose?

The third conundrum is that the Lindberghs were at home, awake, and downstairs when the baby was taken. Betty Gow and the Whatelys were also in the house. So was Wahgoosh, their dog. Family members reported that Wahgoosh regularly barked at strangers, but he didn't bark at all that night. All five of the human occupants of the house claimed they didn't hear a thing. How did a stranger put a ladder up against a house, open a window, climb inside, and kidnap a baby without a single one of the adults in the house hearing a thing? And why didn't a sick baby cry when a stranger picked him up and carried him down a ladder? And how did a single person plan to climb down a ladder carrying a twenty-month-old baby in the first place?

Fourth, only $13,000 was found when the ransom money was discovered in the gas can in Hauptmann's garage. Even counting the notes that had been caught by banks and found in his wallet, I can't come up with more than $16,330 in ransom money recovered. Where was the rest of the money?

I can't help but notice that $50,000 divided three ways would be $16,666.67. It's not hard to imagine another $337 of Hauptmann's one-third share of the ransom money slipping through the banking system without being detected. If that's the case, then where did the other two-thirds of the money go?

The Butler Didn't Do It...but Maybe the Nanny Did

During her testimony at Hauptmann's trial, Betty Gow admitted to telling her boyfriend, Henry "Red" Johnson, that the Lindberghs were not returning to Englewood on Monday. Johnson worked on a yacht owned by the partner of Anne Morrow Lindbergh's father. Gow said she might have told "other people," as well.

Gow also admitted to being acquainted with Violet Sharp, a maid working at the Morrow estate in Englewood where the Lindberghs were living while their new home at Hopewell was being finished. Violet knew that the Lindberghs were staying at Hopewell outside of their regular routine.

Not Too Sharp

Violet Sharp's identification card.
(US Department of Labor; Jaquo.com)

When questioned by the police, Violet Sharp reported that the night of the kidnapping she had been on a blind date with another couple, seeing a movie. Yet, she could not remember the name of her date, the names of the other couple, or the name of the movie. When questioned again, she subsequently changed her story to say she and her date and the other couple were at a speakeasy, not at a movie. After the body was found, the police questioned her a third time, and she changed her story again before she became ill and collapsed during the interview. When the police arrived to continue the interview the next day, Violet had committed suicide by eating silver polish containing cyanide.

Denise Diana Huddle

CHAPTER 30

THE DARKER SIDE OF CHARLES LINDBERGH

Charles Lindbergh was undoubtedly a great pilot and a visionary in many ways. But he was also a lying, four-timing adulterer. When it came to his family relationships, he was one twisted sister. In his opening salvo, he married the wealthy heiress, Anne Morrow, on May 27, 1929. Their first child, Charles Augustus Lindbergh Jr., was born June 22, 1930, just three months shy of shotgun territory. After the death of Charles Augustus, Lindbergh went on to father five more children by Anne Morrow Lindbergh.

Careu Kent Is No Superman

In Lindbergh's post-transatlantic flight career, he traveled all over the world and spent a substantial amount of time in Germany. In 1957, he began a relationship with a woman in Munich twenty-four years his junior named Brigitte Hesshaimer. The clandestine relationship apparently continued until his death and produced three children who knew Lindbergh only as Mr. Careu Kent. Apparently, he never saw fit to tell them he was their father. The kids only discovered their true biological identities when the middle child found over a hundred love letters from Lindbergh to her mother. Their relationship was subsequently verified by DNA testing.

All in the Family

As if that wasn't bad enough, simultaneously, Lindbergh was conducting another clandestine adulterous relationship with Brigitte's sister, Marietta, with whom he had two more children. (Check it out—Brigitte's and Marietta's children are both first cousins and paternal half siblings.)

Mixing Business with Pleasure

And because the third time's a charm, Lindbergh was also probably shacked up with his personal secretary and German translator, a woman known only as Valeska with whom he is said to have had another two children.

In the last days of his life, Lindbergh reportedly wrote letters to all three of his mistresses from his hospital bed. In all the missives, he requested that they each maintain the secrecy of his relationship with them after his death. That lasted until Brigitte died and her middle daughter convinced her siblings to undergo DNA testing then go public.

So, let's count 'em up: six with Anne, three with Brigitte, two with her sister, Marietta, and two more with translator and secretary, Valeska, for a grand total of…(drum roll, please) thirteen kids by four women—all at the same time.

Lindbergh and the Nazis

On October 18, 1938, while attending as the guest of honor a dinner party at the American embassy in Berlin, Lindbergh was awarded the Service Cross of the German Eagle by Hermann Goering on behalf of Adolf Hitler. Even under intense public pressure after America entered the War, Lindbergh refused to return the medal.

In the years leading up to America's entry into WWII, Charles Lindbergh became heavily involved in the America First movement, which sought to keep the US out of the conflict. America First was widely known to espouse antisemitic views in the context of what was often construed as a pro-Hitler bent. By 1941, Lindbergh had become the chief spokesman for America First.

On September 11, 1941, Lindbergh gave a speech at the Des Moines Coliseum, and what he said that day followed him for the rest of his life. Lindbergh blamed three groups for trying to push America into the war: the British, the Jews, and the Roosevelt administration.

In the course of his speech, he made two comments about American citizens of the Jewish faith that evoke heated responses even to this day. In regard to Jewish Americans and their role in the politics of the potential US involvement in the war, Lindbergh said, "Their [the American Jews'] greatest danger to this country lies in their large ownership and influence in our motion pictures, our press, our radio, and our government." He went on to say, "We cannot allow the natural passions and prejudices of other peoples to lead our country to destruction." So, to hear Lindbergh tell it, Jews in America were a dangerous, other people.

In his diaries, he wrote: "We must limit to a reasonable amount the Jewish influence…Whenever the Jewish percentage of total population becomes too high, a reaction seems to invariably occur. It is too bad because a few Jews of the right type are, I believe, an asset to any country."

Yikes, Charlie.

Bad News for the Rainbow Coalition

But it just gets better. Like many racist wackos of the era, Lindbergh became obsessed with immortality and eugenics—so much so that he teamed up with Nobel Prize–winning French-born scientist and famed eugenics proponent, Dr. Alexis Carrel. Lindbergh and his mentor, Carrel, worked together for over a decade and eventually built a mechanical heart that became a technological precursor to the heart-lung or bypass machine.

In an insightful piece that appeared in the *Windsor Star* on October 6, 1941, the Canadian paper compared quotes from Carrel and Lindbergh on various topics to illustrate Carrel's influence over Lindbergh's thinking. On the subject of race, the *Star* quoted Carrel as saying, "The most highly civilized races, the Scandinavian, for example, are white. The lower races generally inhabit countries where the light is violent and the temperature equal and warm. The northern French are far superior to the Mediterranean French."

The *Star* then showed a statement by Lindbergh quoted from a 1939 *Reader's Digest* article as an example of the similarity of Lindbergh's views to those of his pal, Dr. Carrel. "It [aviation] is a tool specifically adapted for Western hands, a scientific art which others copy in a mediocre fashion, another barrier between the teeming millions of Asia and the Grecian inheritance of Europe—one of those priceless possessions which permit the White race to live at all in a pressing sea of Yellow, Black and Brown."

Not only did he think white people were superior, he was unabashed in his advocacy for eugenics, intraracial marriage, and "proper breeding." The March 11, 2022 edition of the *Milwaukee Independent* quotes Lindbergh as saying in 1938, "Now it is perfectly obvious that a high type of people will not result from indiscriminate marriage, or from the mixing together of all classes and races. We will not create better children by mating white with Negro, or by throwing America and Europe open to the Asiatic. On the contrary,

Denise Diana Huddle

we must choose with the utmost care. We must surround ourselves with people who add quality of mind and strength of body to our community, with people whose sons and daughters [blood] we are willing to have mixed [mix] with the blood of our children…"

These quotes raise the question whether Lindbergh was scattering his lily-white "superman seed" around Germany through his three mistresses as a result of his eugenic ideas about populating the world with the "right" kind of people. They also raise another issue—was Lindbergh troubled enough by his first-born son's minor health issues to have participated in the child's kidnapping?

What the Smart Guys Think

Rutgers historian, Dr. Lloyd C. Gardner, discusses these issues in the 2012 afterward to his 2004 book, *The Case That Never Dies: The Lindbergh Kidnapping*. In the afterward, Gardner describes the child's medical and physiological imperfections. "…he [Charles Jr.] appears to have been afflicted with a rickets-like condition that affected the development of strong bones. He required mega doses of vitamin D and daily exposure to a sunlamp kept cribside. He also had hammertoes on his left foot, a too-large cranium, and unfused skull bones."

Gardner also finds it curious that Lindbergh was scheduled for a speaking engagement at a dinner in New York City the night of the kidnapping, but for the first time in his celebrity speaking career, he no-showed the appearance. Dr. Gardner wondered out loud during an interview on the PBS show *Nova* if Lindbergh skipped the appearance, instead coming back to Hopewell from the city to facilitate the crime and make certain the kidnappers were not detected.

All things considered, a decade after he first wrote his book, Dr. Gardner finally came to the conclusion that Lindbergh was part of the plot.

In a report in the July 31, 1993 edition of the *South Florida Sun Sentinel*, reporter Lynn Girard described the findings of criminal defense attorney Gregory Ahlgren and veteran criminal investigator Stephen Monier published in their book *Crime of the Century: The Lindbergh Kidnapping Hoax*. Ahlgren and Monier point out that, in a modern child-murder investigation, the parents would be the first suspects and would be subjected to the most in-depth scrutiny. Yet, the Lindberghs were never even questioned.

The authors describe a horrifying event that took place two months before the actual kidnapping where Lindbergh played a "practical joke" on the household by hiding poor little Charles Jr. in a closet and then announcing that the baby had been kidnapped. His wife and their staff panicked and furiously searched the house and grounds for twenty terror-filled minutes before Lindbergh got his son out of the closet and laughed as he passed the child to his mother.

Lindbergh's attachment to the child is described by many sources as weak. He reportedly referred to Charles Jr. as "it." In any case, Lindbergh seemed anxious to get rid of the child's body once it was discovered. William Allen discovered the baby's remains on May 12, 1932. After a brief autopsy determined the cause of death to have been a massive fracture of the skull that occurred approximately two to three months before the body was discovered, Lindbergh insisted that the child's remains immediately be cremated and the ashes scattered. According to Ahlgren and Monier, the baby's corpse was cremated May 13, 1932, at Trenton, New Jersey.

CHAPTER 31

INVESTIGATOR'S COMMENTS

There is no doubt in my mind that Bruno Hauptmann was involved in the kidnapping of the Lindbergh baby. The wood evidence alone would convince me. Add on evidence from the eagle-eyed gas station attendant who wrote Hauptmann's license plate number on a bill from the ransom money, a can full of the ransom bills in his garage, and Condon's number written on his closet wall, and there's an airtight case against Hauptmann. As to the question of an accomplice, I believe there was one.

The Missing Loot

The fact so little of the ransom money was ever recovered is a leading factor in this conclusion. That the amount recovered is so close to a one-third share of the total ransom is even more striking.

Hauptmann Wasn't Vishnu

In various accounts of the incident, the broken ladder was found different distances from the house, but it seems most likely it was found about sixty yards from the marks in the mud below the nursery window. The house was at least half a mile from the road. How could one man alone have carried that ladder all the way from wher-ever he left his vehicle? More importantly, how did he carry it that sixty-some-odd yards away from the house alone while carrying a baby? The job simply required more than two hands.

An Inside Job

I'm convinced that Bruno Hauptmann had no independent way of knowing that the Lindberghs would be staying in Hopewell on Tuesday. He had no way of knowing which of the house's scores of windows led to the nursery. The pool of people who should have had that knowledge is very small.

Furthermore, I do not believe that a strange man could slap a ladder against the exterior wall of the Hopewell house, open the window, walk across the second-floor nursery, pick up a sick baby, and haul him out the window without anyone of the five adults in the house hearing something. The premise is absurd.

Why in the world would Violet Sharp tell the police such a ridiculous story about her whereabouts the night of the kidnapping, change her tale twice, and then kill herself by eating silver polish before facing another round of questioning? To me, that strongly implies a consciousness of guilt.

Dr. John Condon

Condon was accepted as a man who appreciated Lindbergh's heroism and just wanted to help out. In today's law enforcement environ-ment, Condon would be considered a prime suspect simply because of this behavior. In the time of the kidnapping, the New Jersey State Police and the FBI were ultimately convinced that Condon was just a Good Samaritan trying to assist the Lindberghs. I'm not sure I buy that, but I see no evidence in the record to support my instinct.

Lying Lindy

Lindbergh was a pathological liar of epic proportions. He had not one, but three mistresses simultaneously while his wife, Anne, was home raising their five surviving children. Nowhere has any even semireliable source implied that Anne and Charles Lindbergh had an open relationship. While some sources report Anne may have suspected that Charles was being unfaithful, I haven't found anyone who reported she had ever agreed to the polyamorous arrangement. No other way to say it—Lindbergh was cheating on his wife for decades of their marriage.

Lindbergh visited his German mistresses regularly and spent time with his children there, but he insisted all three women introduce him to the children by a pseudonym. He co-opted their mothers into silence while he lied to the children every time he saw them about the most fundamental part of their existence—their biological origins.

Combine this inherent character defect with his ideas about eugenics and weeding out the weaklings, and it's not hard to imagine him participating in a plot to remove the child from his household. The "practical joke" about the baby being kidnapped several weeks before the child was actually taken is way too coincidental for my taste.

My conclusion: Hauptmann was the actual kidnapper, but he had help from inside the Lindbergh/Morrow households. Whether that help came from a servant, like Violet Sharp, or Lindbergh himself…we'll never know.

INVESTIGATOR'S TIPS

Hard to imagine, but most burglars enter the dwelling through an unlocked door or window—on the front of the house. Get free checklists from the National Crime Prevention Council for staying safe at home (https://www.ncpc.org/wp-content/uploads/2017/11/homechk2.pdf) or in an apartment (https://www.ncpc.org/wp-content/uploads/2017/11/aptchk.pdf).

QUIZ

Test your knowledge about the Lindbergh kidnapping.

The Lindbergh Kidnapping Case Quiz | People | 10 Questions
https://www.funtrivia.com/trivia-quiz/People/The-Lindbergh-Kidnapping-Case-249505.html

SNARKY HUMOR

Denise Diana Huddle

REFERENCES & COOL SITES

CrimeArchives: Bruno Hauptmann | Ransom Notes and Related Communications
http://www.crimearchives.net/1935_hauptmann/html/ransom.html

Lindbergh Ransom Note | NIST
https://www.nist.gov/image/167-n-9945010jpg

Kidnapping - Impact Of The Lindbergh Kidnapping - Law, Hauptmann, Death, and Murder - JRank Articles
https://law.jrank.org/pages/1553/Kidnapping-Impact-Lindbergh-kidnapping.html

Kidnapping - Crime of the Century: The Tragic Kidnapping of Charles Lindbergh Jr.
http://60631721.weebly.com/kidnapping.html#Offers%20of%20Help

Lindbergh Baby Kidnapping/Ransom notes
https://www.historictrialtranscripts.com/lindbergh-kidnapping-ransom-notes

New Jersey Department of State
https://www.nj.gov/state/archives/slcsp001.html

The State of New Jersey v. Bruno Richard Hauptmann
https://famous-trials.com/hauptmann/1393-hauptmannappeal

Kidnapped Lindbergh Baby Found Dead | HISTORY
https://www.history.com/this-day-in-history/body-of-lindbergh-baby-found

Body Found | CRIME OF THE CENTURY
https://crimeofthecentury.weebly.com/body-found.html

Lindbergh biography details his anti-Semitism | San Diego Jewish World
https://www.sdjewishworld.com/2020/02/15/
lindbergh-biography-details-his-anti-semitism/

Review: From high-flying hero to eugenics advocate | PMC
https://www.ncbi.nlm.nih.gov/pmc/articles/PMC2621292/

Who Killed Lindbergh's Baby? | NOVA | PBS
https://www.pbs.org/wgbh/nova/video/who-killed-lindberghs-baby/

Lindbergh Kidnapping | The Saturday Evening Post
https://www.saturdayeveningpost.com/2013/02/lindbergh-kidnapping/

Lindbergh's Double Life | Charles Lindbergh House and Museum | MNHS
https://www.mnhs.org/lindbergh/learn/family/double-life

Lindbergh Accuses Jews of Pushing U.S. to War
https://www.jewishvirtuallibrary.org/
lindbergh-accuses-jews-of-pushing-u-s-to-war

Charles Lindbergh: Des Moines Speech – Clippings and Commentary
https://www.historiography-project.org/1941/09/11/
charles-lindbergh-des-moines-s/

Lindbergh Case - Persons of Interest/Suspects
https://sites.google.com/site/lindberghbabycase/
persons-of-interest-suspects?pli=1

How Charles Lindbergh's Nazi Associations Ruined Him
https://allthatsinteresting.com/charles-lindbergh-antisemitism

Secret families of Charles Lindbergh | The Irish Times
https://www.irishtimes.com/news/
secret-families-of-charles-lindbergh-1.449275

CRIME: On Sour land Mountain (Cont'd) | TIME
https://content.time.com/time/subscriber/article/0,33009,743377-1,00.html

Charles Lindbergh Search
http://www.charleslindbergh.com/search.asp

The Lindbergh "Kidnapping" - A Hoax? | LindberghKidnapping-Hoax.com
http://www.lindberghkidnappinghoax.com/ransom.html

The Great Depression Causes, Effects, Facts, Unemployment
https://thegreatdepressioncauses.com/

PART 7

WHO MURDERED LIZZIE BORDEN'S PARENTS?

CHAPTER 32

The house at 92 2nd Street in Fall River, Massachusetts. (Public domain)

Lizzie Borden took an ax
and gave her mother twenty whacks;
After seeing what she'd done
She gave her father twenty-one.

America has always loved a good dysfunctional family story. The destructive passion plays of screwed-up families are the tabloid equivalent of radio's somebody-done-somebody-wrong songs. We're particularly fascinated by the bizarre and violent doings of seemingly "nice" families comprised of upper-middle-class Protestant white folks doing each other in by gruesome means—and all for nothing more than a better position at the clan's ample financial trough. So, it's not surprising that, by February of 1894, children were chanting what has come to be called the Lizzie Borden Doggerel.

While the number of whacks has evolved over time from twenty to forty, the rhyme remains part of our culture 130 years after the Borden murders in Fall River, Massachusetts. The facts that Lizzie Borden was acquitted of any involvement in the deaths of her father and stepmother, the murder weapon was never conclusively identified, and the number of whacks was wrong have done nothing to erase the verse from modern culture and just serve as further evidence that reading about rich blue bloods bashing each other's brains in makes us all feel better about the unhinged aspects of our own weird little worlds.

February 4, 1894 article from the *St. Louis Globe-Democrat* describing first known report of the Lizzie Borden Doggerel. (Newspapers.com)

The origin of the doggerel has long been a topic of conjecture. However, the earliest known record of its existence is from a February 1894 newspaper story concerning a woman reporting that her child was chanting the rhyme.

The rapid and widespread integration of the verse into the American vernacular shows how, even 130 years ago, the American public

Denise Diana Huddle

was enthralled with the possibility of a proper, nineteenth-century white Christian woman hatchet murdering her wealthy parents.

The Borden murders took place against a backdrop of the women's suffrage movement. Twenty years after Susan B. Anthony was first arrested and tried for voting in New York, Lizzie Borden's attorneys were appealing to the patriarchal ideals of her all-male jury to convince them that a woman of her station could not possibly have committed such heinous acts. And it worked—Lizzie skated on the charges.

WHAT HAPPENED?

Crime scene photos of Abby Borden (Wikimedia Commons) and Andrew Borden (Wikipedia).

On August 4, 1892, at 92 2nd Street in Fall River, Massachusetts, Andrew Borden (age sixty-nine) and his second wife, Abby Durfee Gray Borden (age sixty-four), were found dead of multiple wounds inflicted by a sharp-edged hacking instrument judged to be some type of axe or hatchet. Abby Borden was found upstairs lying face-down on the floor of a guest bedroom of the family home, the victim of nineteen blows to the head. Downstairs, Andrew Borden was discovered in the sitting room, slumped on a divan, the victim of eleven similar blows to his face and head.

BACKGROUND

Andrew Borden was descended from old Fall River money. However, his branch of the family had lost their original wealth, and Andrew grew up in poverty. Though he began his career as a carpenter, eventually he became a furniture dealer and a casket maker. By the time of his death, he was a successful businessman with a varied portfolio of interests. He owned multiple rental properties and served on the boards of several banks, and his net worth was estimated at $300,000, roughly equivalent to $9.6 million in 2022 money.

Despite their substantial wealth, all Horatio Alger characters well remember their youths in poverty and understand on a visceral level the tenuous nature of financial fortune. Andrew Borden had grown up watching his own family struggle with money while his cousins enjoyed the finer things in life. Unlike those who inherit vast estates, those who earn their own recall with great clarity all the effort and risk it took for them to amass their fortunes from the ground up.

While Andrew Borden squeezed his dollars until the eagles screamed, his spinster daughters' resentment festered like a boil. Sick and tired of using a basement privy in a house without electricity, Lizzie and Emma longed for the glamorous life of flush toilets and incandescent lights found in the mansions of Fall River's most exclusive neighborhood, The Hill.

The Mabelle F. Swift.

Mr. Charles W. Anthony's new sloop yacht Mabelle F. Swift returned from a 10-days' trip yesterday, with a thoroughly satisfied party of amateur sailors. They were Messrs Simeon Borden, James F. Jackson, H. B. Durfee, W. F. Winslow and R. W. Bassett. Mr. Anthony accompanied them the first day and left them at Westport Harbor. The yachtsmen are loud in their praise of their craft and have nothing but pleasant things to say of Capt. Harriman and the steward—the most excellent steward. They cruised along the coast to Buzzards Bay, through Vineyard Sound to Nantucket and back, stopping whenever the inclination overtook them. The sloop, they say, is commodious, finely fitted, able and very fast. From their experience in her, they judge that she can stand almost anything in the way of hard weather, and she appears fast enough to beat about anything of her size. During the trip no one suffered from cold. On the contrary it was hot, even on the water, but they lived with much more comfort than they could have had had they been ashore last week.

Clipping from August 3, 1892, about Lizzie's paternal cousin Simeon Borden. (*Fall River Daily Evening News*)

On the day before the murders, the *Fall River Daily Evening News* reported on a luxurious yacht returning to Fall River's harbor. Among the yachtsmen listed in the article was Andrew Borden's cousin, Simeon Borden. One can only imagine how it galled Lizzie to read about how the gleaming sloop was sailed into the harbor by one of her cousins while she was stuck on dumpy 2nd Street using chamber pots and whale oil lamps because her cheapskate father refused to fund the more elegant lifestyle she felt she deserved.

The Terrible Trifecta of Family Tragedy

Stingy as he may have been, Andrew Borden had faced his share of challenges. After having grown up poor, he married Sarah Anthony Morse on Christmas Day of 1845. Sarah was the mother of his three daughters: Emma Lenora, Alice Esther, and Lizzie Andrew Borden. Emma was born March 1, 1851, Alice followed on May 3, 1856, and Lizzie came along July 19, 1860.

The Bordens' middle daughter, Alice Esther, died March 10, 1858, at the age of one year, ten months, leaving Emma and Lizzie as Andrew and Sarah's only surviving children.

The loss of a child is one of the most traumatic events the human psyche can face. As if that wasn't bad enough, Andrew's wife, Sarah Anthony Morse Borden, died on March 26, 1863, of "uterine congestion and spinal disease." In modern medicine, uterine congestion syndrome is a condition associated with dilation of the veins in the uterus and pelvic region. It is unclear what this meant in Victorian times. Modern uterine congestion syndrome is not directly associated with spinal disease, and Sarah Borden's death record doesn't state if the two issues were related in her case. Regardless of the exact cause of her death, within a span of five years, Andrew Borden lost his baby daughter and his wife, then faced the prospect of raising his surviving children—Emma, aged twelve, and Lizzie, aged three—by himself in Victorian-era New England.

Andrew toughed it out and somehow made it on his own until he married Abby Durfee Gray on June 6, 1865, a little over two years after his first wife died.

Trouble in Bougie-land

Despite Abby Borden having helped raise Andrew's two motherless daughters, there was persistent discord in the Borden household. As if the chronic stress between Andrew Borden's pronounced frugality and the champagne dreams of his social-climbing daughters wasn't enough, a more recent greed-fest had played out at 92 2nd Street. Specifically, Lizzie and Emma had been upset with their father and stepmother over their father's beneficial gifts to their stepmother's family. The girls had their bloomers in a bunch over what they viewed as Abby and her family snarfing up resources that would otherwise be available to them—if not in the present, at least in the future when their father shuffled off this mortal coil.

In particular, when Abby's sister hit hard financial times and was facing the social devastation of a physical eviction, Andrew Borden intervened and purchased the real estate where his sister-in-law was living and put it in Abby's name. While doing so made plenty of sense—it undoubtedly smoothed out relations in his marriage, helped out his sister-in-law, and prevented the public humiliation of having one of his relatives thrown out on the street—Lizzie and Emma were in a snit about what they perceived of as the unfairness of this act, in that the interloping Gray family got something they didn't.

In response to their complaints, Andrew gave them a property of equal value that they could rent out for income. But the spa-queen sisters soon tired of the travails of being landlords, and in response to their renewed dissatisfaction, Andrew purchased the property back from them for $5,000 (the equivalent of roughly $160,000 in 2022 money). Despite this largesse, the tension in the household persisted through the time of the murders. It seemed nothing Andrew Borden did would satisfy the avaricious desires of his status-grubbing daughters.

THE PLAYERS

The Borden family, their maid, and their visitor.
(www.crimearchives.net, Denise Huddle image)

In so far as the Borden murders were basically a locked room mystery, it's important to establish exactly who was living at the house and who was known to be present there on the day the crimes took place. In the summer of 1892, the residents of the house were: Andrew J. Borden, Abby Gray Borden, Andrew's spinster daughters, Lizzie and Emma Borden, and Bridget (Maggie) Sullivan, the family's housekeeper.

On the day of the murders, August 4, the following people were in the Borden house at some point before the bodies were discovered: Andrew J. Borden, Abby Gray Borden, Lizzie Borden, Bridget (Maggie) Sullivan, and John Morse.

Bridget Sullivan was a twenty-six-year-old Irish immigrant working in the Bordens' home and living in their attic bedroom. John Morse was Sarah Anthony Morse Borden's brother, making him Andrew Borden's brother-in-law by his first wife and Emma and Lizzie's maternal uncle.

Emma Lenora Borden had gone to Fairhaven, Massachusetts, in late July to visit the Brownell family and have some clothes made. She remained there through the time of the murders and was never considered a suspect.

John Morse provided a verified alibi that, at the time of the murders, he was either with the relatives he was visiting or en route on a horse trolley with six priests. The relatives verified the visit. The horse cart conductor didn't remember Morse, but he did remember the priests. Morse's alibi was ultimately judged reliable, and he was eventually cleared as a suspect.

Just to recap: Emma was out of town staying with friends. Scratch her from the suspect list. Morse was alibied by a bunch of relatives and a trolley conductor. Scratch him, too. Andrew and Abby didn't bludgeon themselves to death, so a murder/suicide is off the table. That leaves either Bridget, Lizzie, Bridget and Lizzie, or an intruder on the suspect list.

CHAPTER 33

THE TIMELINE

August 2, 1892—The Puke-athon

Abby Borden and Bridget Sullivan were suffering from severe nausea and vomiting. Abby went across the street to her physician, Dr. Seabury Bowen, and reported that she believed she had been poisoned. Dr. Bowen dismissed her concerns and wrote her illness off to food poisoning.

Prior to the introduction of modern electrical refrigeration, many people suffered from what was called "summer sickness." Absent refrigeration, food spoiled much more quickly in the summer than in the winter, so food poisoning was a common summer ailment. Yet, despite having lived in that area for her entire life, Abby Borden was convinced her nausea was the result of someone having poisoned her, a possible indicator that life behind closed doors at the Borden household was a lot more Bates Motel and a lot less Brady Bunch than outward appearances led the public to believe.

August 3, 1892—*The Man Who Came to Dinner* Meets Cassandra of Troy

John V. Morse arrived at the Borden home unannounced, in town on business from nearby South Dartmouth, and the Bordens invited him to spend the night in their spare room.

Meanwhile, Lizzie Borden visited her sister Emma's friend, Alice Russell, who later recounted that Lizzie talked about burglary attempts on the Borden home and threats against Andrew Borden, attempts and threats no one else seemed aware of. Lizzie went on to tell Alice of her foreboding sense that something bad was going to happen.

Without the benefit of a crystal ball or a single tarot card, Lizzie foresaw a terrible fate befalling her father the very night before the poor guy got hatchet murdered. Yet she apparently felt no need to warn dear old Dad about this ominous feeling, instead telling only her sister's friend about it.

August 4, 1892—D-Day: The Murders

At 9:00 a.m., John Morse left the Borden house after breakfast to visit relatives in Fall River. Twenty minutes later, Andrew Borden took off for work, leaving Lizzie, Abby, and Bridget alone in the house.

Around 9:30 a.m., Abby Borden sent Bridget outside to wash windows and then went upstairs to clean the guest room where John Morse had spent the night. Abby Borden was killed sometime between 9:30 and 10:00 a.m. Her time of death was determined by the authorities based on blood coagulation. During the period after Abby sent Bridget outside to wash the windows and prior to Andrew Borden's return from work, Lizzie was the only person known to have been alone inside the house with Abby Borden. Lizzie's whereabouts during this time are unclear, except to say she was somewhere on the Borden property.

At 10:45 a.m., Andrew Borden returned to the house and was unable to get his key to open the front door, which was locked from the inside. Bridget opened the door for him and reported hearing the sound of Lizzie laughing coming from the top of the front stairs. After unlocking the door for her boss, Bridget Sullivan returned to the attic to rest.

Here is Bridget Sullivan's later testimony about the locked door and Lizzie's laughter:

Q. Will you describe what you heard which attracted your attention?

A. Well, I heard like a person at the door was trying to unlock the door and push it but could not, so I went to the front door and unlocked it.

Q. Did you hear the ringing of any bell?

A. No, sir, I don't remember to hear any bell.

Q. When you got to the front door what did you find the condition of the locks there?

A. I went to open it, caught it by the knob, the spring lock, as usual, and it was locked. I unbolted it and it was locked with a key.

Q. So that there were three locks?

A. Yes, sir.

Q. What did you do with reference to the lock with the key?

A. I unlocked it. As I unlocked it I said, "Oh pshaw," and Miss Lizzie laughed upstairs. Her father was out there on the doorstep. She was upstairs.

Q. Upstairs; could you tell whereabouts upstairs she was when she laughed?

A. Well, she must be either in the entry or in the top of the stairs, I can't tell which.

Q. Was there any talk passed between you and Mr. Borden as he came to the door?

A. No, sir; not a word.

Uneasy Lies the Head That Wears the Crown

Lizzie reported greeting her father and helping him off with his boots so he could take a nap on the divan in the sitting room. Andrew asked Lizzie where Abby was, and Lizzie responded that Abby had received a note requesting her presence at the home of a sick friend and that she had gone to tend to them as requested.

By 11:00 a.m., Andrew Borden was killed in the downstairs sitting room. Shortly after 11:00 a.m., Lizzie called out for Bridget that she had found her father dead, reportedly saying, "Maggie, come down! Come down quick; Father's dead; somebody came in and killed him."

Bridget Sullivan was alibied for the time of Abby's murder by the neighbor who saw her outside washing the windows. Assuming that both murders were committed by the same perpetrator, the fact that Bridget was alone in her attic room at the time of Andrew Borden's murder was not an issue, especially when Lizzie herself verified that Bridget had returned to the attic immediately after Andrew's arrival. That left Lizzie as the only person known to have been alive in the house unaccounted for at the time of Andrew's murder.

Alibis and Big Fat Lies

Yet, if Bridget was washing the outside of the windows (which we know she was because a neighbor verified seeing her), how did she not see anything that was going on in the house for the period from 9:30 to 10:45 a.m.? How could she have not heard the screams? Just because Bridget was seen outside at the time of Abby's murder in no way meant that she didn't see who did it or, at the very least, know way more about it than she let on.

CHAPTER 34

THE AUTOPSIES & INQUEST

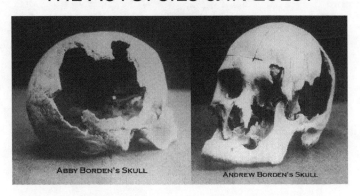

Images of skulls shown at the trial. (Fall River Historical Society)

The coroner's inquest into the murders took place on August 9, 1892, in the courtroom over the police headquarters in Fall River. Lizzie Borden requested the assistance of counsel, but her attorney was not allowed inside the courtroom on the grounds of privacy restrictions surrounding the conduct of inquests. At the inquest, Lizzie's testimony was inconsistent, particularly regarding her whereabouts in and around the Borden home on the morning of the murders.

Shortly after the murders, the victims' stomachs had been shipped to Harvard for examination. No trace or indication of poison was found in either stomach. The bodies of Andrew and Abby Borden were autopsied at Oak Grove Cemetery by W. A.

Dolan, medical examiner, assisted by Dr. F. W. Draper. Andrew's autopsy began at 11:15 a.m. followed by Abby's, which began at 12:35 p.m. on August 11, 1892, one week after death. The skulls were saved as evidence.

Pants on Fire—Lizzie's Inquest Testimony about the Events of August 4, 1892

Lizzie's conflicting and often rambling testimony began with a description of the scene when she came down from her room around 8:45 a.m. Breakfast was over and Morse was not present. She spoke to Andrew and Abby on her way to the basement privy. Abby was dusting in the dining room and reported having finished cleaning the upstairs bedroom that Morse had used with the exception of some small pillowcases that needed to be put on pillows. When Lizzie returned from the basement privy, she assumed Abby had gone out. Maggie (her nickname for Bridget Sullivan) went out to wash windows, and Andrew went out "after 9:00." Lizzie ironed handkerchiefs—or she was preparing to iron handkerchiefs.

Q. What was the next thing that happened after you got down?

A. Maggie went out of doors to wash the windows and Father came out into the kitchen and said he did not know whether he would go down to the post office or not. And then I sprinkled some handkerchiefs to iron.

Q. Tell us again what time you came downstairs.

A. It was a little before nine, I should say. About quarter. I don't know sure.

Q. Did your father go downtown?

A. He went down later.

Q. What time did he start away?

A. I don't know.

Q. What were you doing when he started away?

A. I was in the dining room, I think. Yes, I had just commenced, I think, to iron.

And later:

Q. When your father went away, you were ironing then?

A. I had not commenced, but I was getting the little ironing board and the flannel.

When Andrew Borden arrived home, she was in her room.

Q. Where were you when the bell rang?

A. I think in my room upstairs.

Q. Then you were upstairs when your father came home?

A. I don't know sure, but I think so.

Or on the stairs.

Q. Did you come down before your father was let in?

A. I was on the stairs coming down when she let him in.

Q. Then you were upstairs when your father came to the house on his return?

A. I think I was.

Or in the kitchen, or maybe it was the dining room…

Q. Are you sure you were in the kitchen when your father returned?

A. I am not sure whether I was there [in the kitchen] or in the dining room.

Q. You were not upstairs when he came home?

A. I was not upstairs when he came home, no sir.

Then, after Andrew got home, she went to the barn to get a fishing sinker. Maybe he had been home for fifteen or twenty minutes when she came in and found him dead.

Q. How long was your father in the house before you found him killed?

A. I don't know exactly because I went out to the barn. I don't know what time he came home. I don't think he had been home more than fifteen or twenty minutes. I am not sure.

Or maybe she was in the barn for fifteen or twenty minutes.

A. ...Then I went into the kitchen and from there to the barn.

Q. Whereabouts in the barn did you go?

A. Upstairs.

Q. To the second story of the barn?

A. Yes sir.

Q. How long did you remain there?

A. I don't know. Fifteen or twenty minutes.

Q. What doing?

A. Trying to find lead for a sinker.

Or maybe she was ironing and stopped to go to the barn.

Q. Can you give me any information how it happened at that particular time you should go into the chamber of the barn to find a sinker to go to Marion with to fish the next Monday?

A. I was going to finish my ironing. My flats were not hot. I said to myself, "I will go and try and find that sinker. Perhaps by the time I get back, the flats will be hot." That is the only reason.

The story about the mysterious, missing note allegedly summoning Abby to tend to a sick friend was as garbled as the rest of Lizzie's testimony.

Q. Then why did you not suppose she had gone?

A. I supposed she had gone.

Q. Did you hear her come back?

A. I did not hear her go or come back, but I supposed she went.

Q. When you found your father dead, you supposed your mother had gone?

A. I did not know. I said to the people who came in, "I don't know whether Mrs. Borden is out or in. I wish you would see if she is in her room."

And:

Q. Did you make any search for your mother?

A. No sir.

Q. Why not?

A. I thought she was out of the house. I thought she had gone out. I called Maggie to go to Dr. Bowen's. When they came in, I said, "I don't know where Mrs. Borden is." I thought she had gone out.

And:

Q. Do you know of any employment that would occupy your mother for the two hours between nine and eleven in the front room?

A. Not unless she was sewing.

And:

Q. Never mind about yesterday. Tell me all the talk you had with your mother when she came down in the morning.

A. She asked me how I felt. I said I felt better but did not want any breakfast. She said what kind of meat did I want for dinner. I said I did not want any. She said she was going out; somebody was sick, and she would get the dinner, get the meat, order the meat. And I think she said something about the weather being hotter, or something; and I don't remember that she said anything else.

The note was never recovered, and the sick friend was never identified.

Victorian Drunk Dialing

Lizzie's only possible defense for the babbling nonsensical inquest testimony regarding her actions and whereabouts the morning of the murders is that Dr. Bowen had prescribed her morphine the day before to help her deal with the shock of the deaths of her parents. While being under the influence of morphine could certainly make you seem confused, being stoned on opiates is also likely to make it harder to fabricate a false alibi explaining how you didn't notice an intruder hatchet murdering your parents over a ninety-minute period while you were alone with them in a 3,411-square-foot house divided into four levels without any hallways.

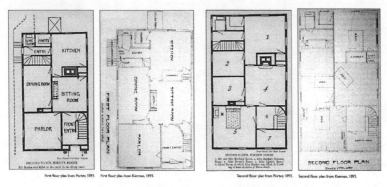

Floor plans of 92 2nd Street. (Porter 1893)

Two days after her rambling performance at the inquest, Lizzie Borden was arrested for the murder of her father and step-mother. The next day after that, she entered a plea of not guilty. On August 22, 1892, Judge Josiah Blaisdell ordered Lizzie to face a grand jury. She was indicted in November 1892. As an interesting side note, her indictment was attested to by the assistant clerk of the Bristol County Superior Court—none other than her yacht-sailing cousin, Simeon Borden.

INDICTMENT.

COMMONWEALTH
vs.
LIZZIE ANDREW BORDEN.

MURDER.

Commonwealth of Massachusetts.

BRISTOL SS. At the Superior Court begun and holden at Taunton within and for said County of Bristol, on the first Monday of November, in the year of our Lord one thousand eight hundred and ninety-two.

The Jurors for the said Commonwealth, on their oath present,—That Lizzie Andrew Borden of Fall River in the County of Bristol, at Fall River in the County of Bristol, on the fourth day of August in the year eighteen hundred and ninety-two, in and upon one Andrew Jackson Borden, feloniously, wilfully and of her malice aforethought, an assault did make, and with a certain weapon, to wit, a sharp cutting instrument, the name and a more particular description of which is to the Jurors unknown, him, the said Andrew Jackson Borden feloniously, wilfully and of her malice aforethought, did strike, cut, beat and bruise, in and upon the head of him, the said Andrew Jackson Borden, giving to him, the said Andrew Jackson Borden, by the said striking, cutting, beating and bruising, in and upon the head of him, the said Andrew Jackson Borden, divers, to wit, ten mortal wounds, of which said mortal wounds the said Andrew Jackson Borden then and there instantly died.

And so the Jurors aforesaid, upon their oath aforesaid, do say, that the said Lizzie Andrew Borden, the said Andrew Jackson Borden, in manner and form aforesaid, then and there feloniously, wilfully and of her malice aforethought did kill and murder; against the peace of said Commonwealth and contrary to the form of the statute in such case made and provided.

A true bill.

HENRY A. BODMAN,

HOSEA M. KNOWLTON,   Foreman of the Grand Jury.

District Attorney.

Bristol ss. On this second day of December, in the year eighteen hundred and ninety-two, this indictment was returned and presented to said Superior Court by the Grand Jury, ordered to be filed, and filed; and it was further ordered by the Court that notice be given to said Lizzie Andrew Borden that said indictment will be entered forthwith upon the docket of the Superior Court in said County.

Attest:—

SIMEON BORDEN, Jr.,
Asst. Clerk.

A true copy.
Attest: *Simeon Borden* Clerk.

Indictment of Lizzie Andrew Borden for murder. (Superior Court of Bristol County/Famous-Trials.com)

CHAPTER 35

THE TRIAL

Lizzie Borden's trial began June 5, 1893, in the courthouse in New Bedford, Massachusetts.

Twelve WASPy Men

Lizzie Borden was tried before a jury of twelve white men, none of whom were from Fall River. This is the panel before which defense counsel played out their "good girl" defense strategy.

Jurors in Lizzie Borden's trial. (Fall River Historical Society)

According to the transcript, a three-judge panel comprised of Hon. Albert Mason, chief justice, and Hon. Caleb Blodgett and

Hon. Justin Dewey, associate justices, presided over the trial. The government was represented by Hon. Hosea M. Knowlton, district attorney for the Southern District, and Hon. William H. Moody, district attorney for the Eastern District. The state asked for the death penalty.

Newspaper sketches of prosecutors Knowlton (*Fall River Daily Globe*) and Moody (*Fall River Daily Herald*).

Move Over, Marcia Clark

While, at first blush, it's hard to imagine how the state could bungle this prosecution, the district attorneys faced three major hurdles in their path to conviction.

First was the general lack of any physical evidence connecting Lizzie to the murders. Several axes and hatchets were found in the home, one of which had a broken handle. Yet, while the blades could have made the wounds found on the corpses of Mr. and Mrs. Borden, no human blood was conclusively identified on any of the tools. The hatchet with the broken handle was a product of the Underhill Edge Tool Company of Nashua, New Hampshire, and is currently in the Fall River Historical Museum. It is considered by many to be the murder weapon, but there was no conclusive evidence to support this assumption.

Denise Diana Huddle

Second, they had no eyewitnesses to the crime, primarily because Bridget Sullivan stuck to her "hear no evil/see no evil" story.

The third major problem the prosecution had to overcome was the lack of any blood anywhere on Lizzie's person or clothing as observed by any of the neighbors or law enforcement officers responding to the scene after Lizzie supposedly alerted Bridget that Andrew Borden was dead.

Houdini Did It

When it came down to it, the prosecution's case was entirely circumstantial. By estimates made at the time based on coagulation of the decedents' blood, Abby died approximately ninety minutes before Andrew. If that was in fact the case, and if both husband and wife were murdered by the same perpetrator, where did the killer secret him or herself between the killings in a house devoid of hallways or closets without being detected by either Bridget or Lizzie? How did the killer hatchet murder two adults without either woman hearing anything in a house that small?

Newspaper sketches of defense attorneys Jennings, Robinson, and Adams. (*Fall River Daily Herald*)

Money, Money, Money!

Money may not buy happiness, but it definitely hires damn good lawyers. Lizzie Borden marshaled the ample resources of her inheritance to employ the Victorian version of O. J. Simpson's "Dream Team." In addition to local counsel, Andrew Jennings, Lizzie employed M. O. Adams of Boston (a former assistant district attorney for Suffolk County) and George D. Robinson (the former governor of Massachusetts).

The defense strategy focused primarily on the Victorian idea that a proper, upper-class Protestant Yankee woman who taught Sunday school could not possibly commit such a violent crime. That position, coupled with the successful exclusion of two potentially damning pieces of evidence, capped off with the state's totally circumstantial case, was enough to earn an acquittal.

What the Jury Doesn't Know Can't Hurt You

Critical to the defense's ultimate victory was their success in suppressing two key pieces of evidence. First, the defense was able to exclude Lizzie Borden's rambling and contradictory testimony regarding her whereabouts the morning of the murders given at the inquest. On the grounds that she asked for counsel before testifying and was denied it, the judges ruled that the transcript of her testimony could not be presented at trial.

Miss Lizzie in the Library with Prussic Acid

The second huge win for Team Lizzie came when the testimony of Eli Bence was not allowed. Mr. Bence was the clerk at D. R. Smith's apothecary on Columbia Street at the corner of South Main in Fall River. Had he been allowed to testify, he would have sworn that Lizzie Borden came into the store the day before the murders and attempted to purchase ten cents' worth of prussic acid, also known as hydrogen cyanide. Prussic acid is a colorless, extremely poisonous and flammable liquid that boils slightly above room temperature.

Eli Bence: pharmacist/clerk who refused Lizzie's request for prussic acid. (Photo source unknown)

Prussic acid is best known as the primary ingredient in Zyklon B. So deadly, it was the gas favored by the Nazis for mass murder during World War II.

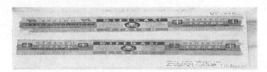

Zyclon label from Dachau concentration camp. (Wikipedia)

Some medical practitioners of the Victorian era prescribed highly diluted prussic acid for various aliments. (One such avant garde genius noted that this treatment, while useful, should not be substituted for bloodletting.) No matter how ridiculous the idea of a therapeutic purpose for cyanide may have been, any prescription required the hydrogen cyanide to be highly diluted. Even as early as 1825, an article in *The Lancet* went into great detail about its lethality in humans and reported that hydrogen cyanide in its pure form was one of the most poisonous substances ever known.

Yet, Lizzie told Bence she needed the acid to repair a seal skin cape. This is about as rational as walking into a nuclear power plant and asking for a couple of ounces of plutonium because you need to unclog your drain. Aside from acting as a precursor in chemical manufacturing, the only purpose for pure hydrogen cyanide is to kill mammals. Mr. Bence refused to sell Lizzie the acid without a doctor's prescription.

After several witnesses were questioned outside the presence of the jury regarding the legitimate uses of prussic acid, the judges elected to exclude Mr. Bence's testimony and that of the two store customers who would attest that Lizzie was in the store at the time Mr. Bence stated.

Paging Dr. Scarpetta—Please Report to the DA's Office in Fall River

The prosecutors in the Lizzie Borden case needed a CSI team like people in hell need a fire extinguisher. But, alas, Sir Edward Henry's system for fingerprint analysis was still four years away, and Edmond Locard didn't formulate his principle of trace evidence for another fourteen years. The Bordens were killed in the Dark Ages of forensic science. Given these limitations, the state was unable to produce any physical evidence linking Lizzie Borden to the murder of her father and stepmother. The murder weapon was never even conclusively identified.

"Out, Damned Spot" Meets "Burn, Baby, Burn"

The most striking physical evidence presented by the defense was the absence of any blood on Lizzie Borden's clothes or person. Given that Andrew Borden's blood was still dripping when the doctor and police arrived on the scene, he could not have been dead for very long. Couple that with the timeline provided by Bridget Sullivan's testimony that Andrew Borden arrived home shortly after she heard the church bells ring at 11:00 a.m., there was little or no time for Lizzie to have killed Andrew then changed her clothes before crying out for Bridget that her father was dead.

Emma and Lizzie's friend, Alice Russell, reported finding Lizzie burning a dress in the kitchen fire in the 2nd Street house on August 7, 1892, immediately following the funeral for her father and stepmother. Lizzie claimed she was burning the dress because it had paint on it. Even if the dress was soaked in blood, it went up in smoke long before the trial.

The Victorian Code Talkers

A search of the house did not yield any bloody dress. When a pail of bloody towels was found in the basement, Lizzie directed the police to Dr. Bowen, who told them "it was all right." The assumption is that these were menstrual towels. With the oooh ick attitude of a newlywed man sent on an emergency midnight tampon run, the men on both sides of the case apparently decided that the bloody rags were something they didn't want to discuss because the subject of the towels never came up again.

Was not talking about "lady business" more important than analyzing what might have been the one piece of physical evidence in the case? With all of the talking in code that went on regarding this topic, there is no telling who meant what.

If Lizzie was not menstruating, then the bucket of bloody towels would have likely been the key piece of evidence in the entire investigation. Would Dr. Bowen have known Lizzie was menstruating at the time the search turned up the towels? Could the towels have belonged to Bridget? If so, how would Dr. Bowen have been in a position to speak to Bridget's menstrual cycle?

Patriarchal ideas about the fundamentally yucky and unspeakable nature of female bodily functions may have caused all parties involved to ignore what was potentially the most critical evidence in the whole case.

The Family Will Receive Guests at the Home for a Meal and Evidence Destruction

Much has been made about Alice Russell's testimony regarding Lizzie burning the dress. It was this testimony that cinched the grand jury indictment of Lizzie Borden for the murders. However, it was apparently not enough to convince the jury of her guilt beyond a reasonable doubt.

While the jury was probably right that the link between the act of burning a dress and the act of hatchet murdering the Bordens was not strong enough on its own to justify putting a defendant to death, the idea that Lizzie ran right home from her parents' funeral and started torching damaged clothes from her closet tests credulity. What had she supposedly been painting when she stained the dress? Why not give the dress to charity or cut it up for rags—or use it for menstrual towels? And why bother with it at all immediately following the funeral, never mind while guests were still in the house? Granted, every person grieves in their own way. But, at the very least, this behavior makes it plain Lizzie wasn't terribly broken up about Andrew's and Abby's passing.

THE ACQUITTAL

Courtroom sketch of Lizzie Borden hearing the verdict. (*Fall River Daily Herald*)

After her disastrous inquest testimony landed Lizzie on trial for her life, she quickly got hip to the benefits of the Fifth Amendment and opted not to testify on her own behalf. Since she never spoke again about her whereabouts on the morning of the murders, we have no way of knowing what went on in the house beyond saying that Lizzie did not have a consistent story.

When the final arguments concluded and the jurors departed to deliberate, it is reported that they were unanimous on their first vote—all in favor of acquittal. However, since the trial had been such a lengthy and highly publicized affair, they opted to complete their forms and wait an hour and a half before notifying the court they had reached a verdict.

CHAPTER 36

THE AFTERMATH

Maplecroft at 306 French Street in Fall River. (Public domain)

Luck Is What She Made It

Funny how it worked out… The fact that Abby died before Andrew kept Abby (and her heirs at law) from inheriting her widow's share of Andrew's estate. With her stepmother literally out of the way, as Andrew's only surviving children, Lizzie and Emma inherited his entire estate of approximately $300,000. Cha-ching.

Movin' On Up

Just like the Jeffersons, it took Lizzie and Emma a whole lot of tryin' just to get up that hill. But no sooner had the verdict freed Lizzie of the threat of the death penalty or life in prison than the Victorian version of Patty and Selma Bouvier pooled their newly inherited resources and skedaddled to a big house in Fall River's most exclusive neighborhood (The Hill), where they assumed the lifestyle they had always longed for.

Brahmin Mean Girls

Yet, despite her lavish inheritance, Lizzie was ostracized from polite society. Even her church pals who had been her most ardent supporters during the trial refused to share a pew with her on Sundays. It seemed that Lizzie's so-called friends were more interested in defending the archetype of proper upper-middle-class church ladies than supporting Lizzie as an individual. Once she was acquitted, they dropped her like a hot flat iron.

Lizzie and the Five-Fingered Discount

In 1897, a warrant for Lizzie's arrest was issued in Providence, Rhode Island. She was accused of stealing two paintings on porcelain from the TildenThurber Company, but the warrant was never served, and nothing ever became of the charges.

The Sister Act Closes

Lizzie and Emma lived together in their mansion called Maplecroft from 1893 to 1905, when Emma moved away suddenly. The sisters never spoke again.

Denise Diana Huddle

Lizzie and Nance O'Neil

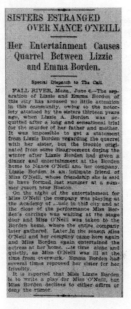

June 7, 1905 newspaper article about Lizzie and Emma
Borden's falling out. (*San Francisco Call*)

The precise details of the schism between Lizzie and Emma were never known. However, the press reported that the split was related to Lizzie's relationship with a well-known actress of the era, Nance O'Neil (sometimes O'Neill, née Gertrude Lampson). Elisa Rolle reports in her book *Queer Places* that Lizzie met Nance through a mutual friend, Riccia Allen, at a summer resort near Lynn, Massachusetts, in 1904. In an article describing Emma's decision to move to Fairhaven, the local Fall River newspaper, the *Evening Herald*, described Lizzie's relationship with Nance saying, "The two were mutually attracted and became constant companions."

> Miss Emma Borden has gone to Fair-
> haven to live, and it is also true that
> Miss Lizzie still lives at the residence
> on French street which she purchased
> some years ago.
>   The incident which probably gave
> rise to many of the stories that are
> current had its beginning in a summer
> resort last year near Lynn. Miss Liz-
> zie was spending the warm months
> there and in the course of time one
> of the friendships she formed was
> with Miss Nance O'Neil, the well
> known actress. The two were mutu-
> ally attracted and became constant
> companions.

Fall River Evening Herald reporting on Lizzie and Nance.

Rumors of a romantic relationship between Lizzie and Nance O'Neil were just that—rumors. No public declaration was made by either party of a romantic involvement. If there was something going on between the women, it's no small wonder that Lizzie kept it on the q.t. Lesbian couples on The Hill in Victorian Fall River were about as welcome as sausage at a vegan buffet.

Aside from avoiding sexual innuendo, Lizzie and Nance were hardly shy about the more platonic aspects of their relationship. Elisa Rolle goes on to describe in her book that Nance became involved in several lawsuits while she was residing in Boston, and that Lizzie assisted with the payment of her legal fees. Rolle also posits that Lizzie helped O'Neil with the down payment on a farm O'Neil acquired in Tyngsboro, Massachusetts.

The Party's Over

According to Rolle, by 1906, the Tyngsboro property was fore-closed by the bank, and O'Neil's relationship with Lizzie Borden had ended. Whatever the nature of their relationship may have been, from that point on, Nance, at least publicly, headed down the straight and narrow. In 1916, O'Neil married Alfred Hickman, a British film actor who costarred with her in a 1917 movie, *The Fall of the Romanovs.*

LIZZIE BORDEN MAY MARRY.

It Is Said She Will Wed a School
Teacher Soon.

FALL RIVER, Mass., Dec. 12.—For a number of days there has been circulated a rumor that Lizzie A. Borden, who was tried and acquitted of the murder of her father and stepmother, Mr. and Mrs. Andrew J. Borden, is to be married to Orrin A. Gardner of Swansea, an adjoining town. Miss Borden's friends decline to make any statement regarding the marriage, but a dressmaker who admits making new cloth-

MISS LIZZIE BORDEN.

ing for Miss Borden says that they are not for a wedding trip and not bridal in character and makeup. Mr. Gardner, whose name has been connected with Miss Borden, is 30 years of age and a school teacher in Liverton. He is at present building a new house at Swansea and his neighbors there are convinced he intends matrimony.

Article describing the possible marriage between Lizzie and
Orrin Gardner. (*Marshall Evening Messenger*)

Lizzie never married, though rumors of impending nuptials had circulated in December of 1896 prior to her relationship with Nance O'Neil.

Lizzie and Emma—Together Again Forever

LISBETH BORDEN, FAMED GIRL, DIES

Fall River, Mass., June 2.—(AP).— Miss Lisbeht A. Borden, who was acquitted of the murder of her father and mother in 1893 after one of the most celebrated murder trials in New England, died at her home here last night.

Obituary for Lizzie Borden. (*Yonkers Herald*)

Lizzie remained at Maplecroft until her death in 1927 from pneumonia, judged to have been a complication from gall bladder surgery a year earlier. Emma fell down the stairs in her home the same day and died nine days later from nephritis.

Lizzie and Emma are both buried in the Oak Grove cemetery with Abby, Andrew, and Alice.

Denise Diana Huddle

CHAPTER 37

INVESTIGATOR'S COMMENTS

As noted above, the suspect pool is pretty shallow—Bridget, Lizzie, Bridget and Lizzie, or an intruder. Lizzie and Bridget were the only occupants of the Borden household known to have been present on the property at the time of the murders. Bridget had an alibi for Abby's murder, having been seen by a neighbor outside the house washing windows. However, questions have circulated for over a century about how the murders took place without Bridget hearing or seeing something suspicious through the windows.

I wonder the same thing. There were no hallways in the house and only one tiny closet. Between forty-five and ninety minutes elapsed between the time Abby was killed and the time Andrew died. Where could a killer hide for that long in a 3,411-square-foot house divided into four levels of 853 square feet per level—and hide well enough that neither Lizzie nor Bridget discovered them in all that time?

Moreover, the question of motive arises. Who was the primary target? Assuming it was Abby, then why didn't the intruder just run away after killing her? If Andrew was the actual target, why kill Abby? Why not just wait outside the house until Andrew showed up and kill him? If the killer entered the home to kill Andrew only to be discovered by Abby and then killed her to prevent apprehension, then why didn't Abby sound an alarm that Bridget or Lizzie could have heard? What could possibly have been the motive for an intruder to kill both Abby and Andrew?

The Dynamic Duo

In a fictionalized version of the events surrounding the murders, the author Ed McBain imagined that Lizzie and Bridget were lovers. When Abby caught them in bed and became enraged, Lizzie killed her. Then when Andrew returned and discovered the murder, Lizzie killed him as well and had Bridget dispose of the murder weapon while Lizzie burned her bloody clothes and disposed of the rags she used to clean up in the bucket reserved for menstrual towels.

However interesting this tale may be, it was just that—a fictionalized version of what might have happened. There is no hard evidence available to date to support this theory. The salacious nature of Lizzie as a murdering lesbian makes the whole story even more intriguing. While both Lizzie and Emma were spinsters, there is no conclusive evidence of either of them engaging in lesbian relationships.

Fiction or not, McBain's scenario has a certain resonance to it. Lizzie, the malcontented social climber, is further put upon by having to hide her illicit lesbian relationship with Bridget. She's never liked Abby much to start with, but now Abby and her relatives are starting to nibble around the edges of Andrew's financial pie, leaving smaller slices remaining for Lizzie and Emma when Andrew eventually makes his way to the Great Beyond.

Since Bridget didn't stand to inherit, the only reason for her to help Lizzie would have been a deep personal relationship, promises of a share of the inherited money, or both. In any case, Lizzie and Bridget being in on it together resolves the question of how Bridget could have gone through the entire morning looking through the windows without noticing a hatchet murderer wandering through the house with a bloody axe. Furthermore, the tag-team nature of the killing in this scenario would have relieved Lizzie of the necessity of hiding her murderous behavior from the only possible witness.

Shortly after the trial, Bridget returned to Ireland. Where she got the money for the trip is unknown. After a stay in her home country, she returned to the United States, this time going to Butte and Anaconda, Montana, where she had family and a friend named Minnie Green. Rumors circulated that one of Lizzie's attorneys made a payoff to Bridget and instructed her to leave the country immediately following the acquittal. However, there is no evidence of either a payoff or instructions by the attorney or anyone else to leave the US. After taking up residence in Montana, Bridget married John Sullivan and remained married to him until his death.

So what really happened? Did Lizzie act alone? Did she kill her father and stepmother in a rage or did she do it for money? Was Bridget her unindicted coconspirator? Or did an intruder sneak into the house and kill the Bordens for a reason no one has even considered? Legally, there is only one answer to that question. Lizzie Borden was found not guilty of the murders that took place at 92 2nd Street in Fall River, Massachusetts, on August 4, 1892.

While I agree with the jury that I can't say beyond a reasonable doubt that Lizzie killed her parents, I can't find a way to make an intruder theory work in my mind. In the end, I think Ed McBain was onto something. In my opinion, the most likely scenario is that Lizzie did it and Bridget turned a blind eye and helped her cover it up.

INVESTIGATOR'S TIPS

Since we've been talking about the possibility of an intruder having entered the Bordens' home, here are some quick things you can do to make your house safer:

- Lock all your doors and windows. Nope...not kidding. One in three burglars enter the home through an unlocked opening.

  * Use dead bolt locks with at least a 1″ throw into strike plates installed with 3″ screws.
  * Supplement window latches with add-on locks or by wedging dowels in the tracks, or both.
  * Put pin locks on sliding glass doors or brace them with dowels in the tracks.

- Don't post pics of you scaling Machu Pichu on Facebook until after you get home. And don't let your friends accidentally do this to you, either, like *Here's a pic of me and Denise at the beach in Florida* when your name is tagged with the photo. (And don't fool yourself into thinking those "privacy" features on social media sites are going to save you.)

- Concentrate extra effort on your front door and windows. That's where over half of all burglars enter homes. Have these areas well lit and not obscured by shrubs or foliage. Make sure the door is solid core and at least 1 ⅜″ thick with a strong dead bolt lock. Lock reinforcers (metal jackets that wrap around the door by the lock) and security strike plates help prevent kick and pry-ins. Add secondary locks and braces to the windows.

- Make sure your house looks occupied. Don't let mail pile up or leave packages on the stoop. If you use a timer to turn on lights, have it set at random times.

Denise Diana Huddle

- Security is like a chain—it is only as strong as its weakest link. Mounting a $200 Medeco dead bolt in a hollow-core door next to an open window is a silly way to spend your money.
- Walk around your house pretending you've locked yourself out. Look for the easiest way you could get in with the least amount of damage. The burglar is going to see that, too.
- If you have to leave a key outside, put it in a lockbox (like Realtors use).

QUIZ

Take this quiz to test your knowledge about the case of Lizzie Borden.

Lizzie Borden Quiz | Lizzie Borden | 25 Questions
https://www.funtrivia.com/trivia-quiz/People/Lizzie-Borden-90265.html

SNARKY HUMOR

I love this meme I found at Cheezburger.com.

LIZZIE BORDEN AGE 2

REFERENCES & COOL SITES

The Trial of Lizzie Borden: Selected Photos
https://famous-trials.com/lizzieborden/1446-photos

Inquest Testimony of Lizzie Borden | Famous-Trials.com
https://famous-trials.com/lizzieborden/1444-inquest

Autopsies | Lizzie Andrew Borden Virtual Museum and Library
https://lizzieandrewborden.com/evidence/autopsies.htm

Lizzie Borden
https://www.historictrialtranscripts.com/lizzie-borden-trial-transcripts

Lizzie's Will & Probate Accounting | Tattered Fabric: Fall River's
Lizzie Borden
https://phayemuss.wordpress.com/source-documents/

Lizzie Borden Timeline | Lizzie Andrew Borden Virtual Museum
and Library
https://lizzieandrewborden.com/chronologies/lizziebordentimeline.htm

The Trial of Lizzie Borden: A Chronology
http://law2.umkc.edu/faculty/projects/ftrials/LizzieBorden/
bordenchrono.html

Lizzie Borden's parents found dead | HISTORY
https://www.history.com/this-day-in-history/
borden-parents-found-dead

The Trial of Lizzie Borden: An Account
https://famous-trials.com/lizzieborden/1437-home

The Trial of Lizzie Borden | YouTube
https://www.youtube.com/watch?v=DJWEaA7bgKw&t=2687s

Myth Busting Lizzie Borden: Facts on the Lie of an Enigmatic Woman | YouTube
https://www.youtube.com/watch?v=TxgN0reggBA&t=386s

Lizzie Borden Case | Mental Health, Personality, & Psychopathy | YouTube
https://www.youtube.com/watch?v=j7UgEAnYz58

Author Talk with Cara Robertson | YouTube
https://www.youtube.com/watch?v=jDQlfuVGx7M

Cara Robertson – The Trial of Lizzie Borden - History Author Show | YouTube
https://www.youtube.com/watch?v=JVrSXNCjRMQ

NHC Virtual Book Talk: "The Trial of Lizzie Borden" | YouTube
https://www.youtube.com/watch?v=iBSkm11B0Vo&t=723s

CrimeArchives: Lizzie Borden | Trial testimony: Bridget Sullivan, June 9, 1893
http://www.crimearchives.net/1893_borden/html/1893-06-09_borden_trial_testimony_sullivan.html#

The Strange Story of Bridget Sullivan, by Sally Campbell – The Hatchet: A Journal of Lizzie Borden & Victorian America
https://lizzieandrewborden.com/HatchetOnline/the-strange-story-of-bridget-sullivan-by-sally-campbell.html

Lizzie Andrew Borden (July 19, 1860-June 1, 1927) | Lives Our Ancestors Left Behind
https://livesleftbehind.wordpress.com/2016/08/25/lizzie-andrew-borden-july-19-1860-june-1-1927/

Crime Scene Photographs | Lizzie Andrew Borden Virtual Museum and Library
https://lizzieandrewborden.com/evidence/crimescenephotographs.htm

The Borden Trial: Biographies of Key Figures
https://famous-trials.com/lizzieborden/1436-biographies

Case Personalities – Page 7 – Lizzie Borden : Warps & Wefts
https://lizziebordenwarpsandwefts.com/category/case-personalities/page/7/

queerplaces - Lizzie Borden | ElisaRolle.com
http://www.elisarolle.com/queerplaces/klmno/Lizzie%20Borden.html

Denise Diana Huddle

ENJOYED *ANTHRAX TO ZODIAC*?
YOU CAN MAKE A DIFFERENCE!

Please leave your honest review of the book. As much as I'd love to, I don't have the financial capacity like New York publishers to run national ad campaigns for my books.

But I have something much, much more powerful! Committed and loyal readers.

If you enjoyed the book, I'd be so grateful if you could spend five minutes leaving a review on the book's Amazon page.

Thank you very much.

Denise

ACKNOWLEDGMENTS

I would like to thank the following people who have been of help to me in this project.

First, I'd like to thank Thomas Umstattd Jr. and James L. Rubart for their help and inspiration. I am a die-hard fan of the *Novel Marketing* podcast and an alumni of their Book Launch Blueprint course (among others). James Rubart was instrumental in encouraging me to write this book. Thomas Umstattd lent his marketing expertise and suggested that I record it as an audiobook and release the chapters as podcasts. They both have patiently answered countless questions as I worked through the project during the past year. As an indie author, I'd be lost without the training I've gotten from Thomas and James and from the information they so generously share for free through authormedia.com and the *Novel Marketing* podcast. Their courses are fantastic.

I'd also like to thank award-winning author Mike Marano of Get of My Lawn Personal Instruction. Mike is an excellent teacher and life-long aficionado of true crime and suspense. I wrote most of this book while taking his true crime and suspense course, and there's no way it would be the book it is without that class and Mike's expert instruction. (Anything in the book that you don't like...blame that on me.) My friend and bestselling author, Mariah Stone, invited me to take the course with her and participated enthusiastically in workshopping various of these chapters during the class. As always, her input was insightful and important to the book. I'm lucky to have her and her husband, Michael, as my friends. Patrick Sullivan was our classmate, and he was a faithful and dedicated participant in our critique group. I appreciate his help, as well.

A special thanks from the bottom of my heart goes out to my intrepid beta readers: Kevin and Annie Barker, Becky Brown, Michelle Garza, Deena Guptil, Kim Hine, Maria Zontou, and Phillip Zozzaro. These generous folks gave hours and hours of their valuable time to me for free. They read and commented on chapter after chapter of this book out of the goodness of their hearts. Each and every comment they made had an impact on the book, and I can not say how thankful I am to these lovely people who were total strangers to me and volunteered for this task. They supported me all along, and I now am honored to consider them friends.

Beth Attwood did the copy editing and proofreading. I could not ask for a better professional to fine-tune my work. I am so fortunate to have her. Any remaining errors are mine.

Please visit my website at denisedianahuddle.com to learn more about me and my books and to get lots of free goodies.

Made in the USA
Middletown, DE
15 June 2024

55849115R10229